Applying Wittgenstein

Continuum Studies in British Philosophy

Series Editor: James Fieser, University of Tennessee at Martin, USA

Continuum Studies in British Philosophy is a major monograph series from Continuum. The series features first-class scholarly research monographs across the field of British philosophy. Each work makes a major contribution to the field of philosophical research.

Applying Wittgenstein

Rupert Read

Edited by
Laura Cook

continuum

Continuum International Publishing Group
The Tower Building, 11 York Road, London SE1 7NX
80 Maiden Lane, Suite 704, New York NY 10038

www.continuumbooks.com

British Library Cataloguing-in-Publication Data
A catalogue record for this book is available from the British Library.

ISBN-10: HB: 0-8264-9450-1
ISBN-13: HB: 978-0-8264-9450-4

Library of Congress Cataloging-in-Publication Data
A catalog record for this book is available from the Library of Congress.

Typeset by Kenneth Burnley, Wirral, Cheshire
Printed and bound in Great Britain by Biddles Ltd, King's Lynn, Norfolk

Contents

Permissions

The author wishes to thank the following for permission to use copyright material:

Jerry Goodenough for material from *UEA Papers in Philosophy*, Vol. 16. Read, R. (2005), "Just in Time: Notes for the Meeting of Wittgenstein and Zen".

Cambridge University Press for permission to reproduce material included in: Read, R. (2002), "Is 'What is Time?' a Good Question to Ask?", *Philosophy* 78, 24–43, and Read, R. (2003), "Time to Stop Trying to Provide an Account of Time", *Philosophy* 77, 193–209.

Blackwell for permission to reproduce material from Read, R. (2003), "Against 'Time-slices'", *Philosophical Investigations* 26:1, 24–43.

Johns Hopkins University Press, for permission to reproduce extracts from the following material: Read, R. (2003), "Literature as Philosophy as Psychopathology", *Philosophy, Psychology, Psychiatry* 10:2, 115–24 and Read, R. (2003), "On Delusions of Sense: A Response to Coetzee and Sass", *Philosophy, Psychology, Psychiatry* 10:2, 135–42.

Routledge for material from "Wittgenstein and Faulkner's Benjy: Reflections on and of Derangement", in Gibson, J. and Huemer, W. (eds) (2004), *The Literary Wittgenstein*.

Taylor and Francis for Read, R. (2001), "What does 'Signify' Signify?" *Philosophical Psychology* 14:4, 499–514, and Read, R. (2001), "On Approaching Schizophrenia through Wittgenstein", *Philosophical Psychology* 14:4, 449–75.

Faber and Faber for permission to use extracts from 'The Anecdote of the Jar', Fabliau of Florida' and 'Thirteen Ways of Looking at a Blackbird' from *The Collected Poems of Wallace Stevens*.

The publishers have made every effort to contact copyright holders. However, they would welcome correspondence from any copyright holders they have been unable to trace.

To the memory of a great applier of Wittgenstein,
James Guetti: 1937–2007

Acknowledgements

The author would like to thank the friends, colleagues and students who have helped bring this project to fruition: most especially of course, Laura Cook! Suggestions from participants at the UEA Wittgenstein Workshop have greatly shaped the material in this book, as have comments on earlier versions of various papers. In particular, Rupert would like to thank Phil Hutchinson, Alice Crary, Louis Sass, Jon Cook, J. M. Coetzee, Michael Dummett, Wes Sharrock, Nadine Cipa and Angus Ross.

And, of course, and above and beyond: Juliette.

The editor would like to thank the following people for the suggestions, conversations and encouragement which have kept this project moving, particularly Mark Gregory, Ian Whittley and Jerry Goodenough. Laura also owes a debt of gratitude to the author for his unstinting support and patience during this project. Finally, this project would have been impossible without Lucy Cook, best friend and mentor, whose advice, encouragement and support has helped quiet my self-criticism.

Both of us would like to thank the staff at Continuum for their great forbearance and assistance in the course of this project: most especially, Sarah Douglas.

We dedicate this book to the memory of James Guetti, a dear friend and mentor whose influence upon the material in this book is immeasurable. Guetti's faithful and yet creative application of Wittgenstein has inspired the way in which we have come, in this manuscript, to conceive the role of the critic afresh. In an era when the crude marshalling of 'theory' has often proved the order of the day, this deeply impressive attunement and subtlety has had a great impact upon the philosophical development of both the author and editor of this book. Guetti cautioned against the theorization of literature, which tends to render many of the better aspects of (literary, and other) texts inaudible. Perhaps his most important legacy is to be found in his ability to show his readers how to *listen* to literature, without silencing it with Theory. As such, it is hoped that this book will contribute to the lasting legacy of his work.

Abbreviations

PI   Wittgenstein, L. (2001), *Philosophical Investigations.* Trans. G. E. M. Anscombe, Blackwell.

T-LP   Wittgenstein, L. (1921), *Tractatus Logico-Philosophicus.* Trans. Ogden, 1981, Routledge.

D1   Dummett, M. (2000), "Is Time a Continuum of Instants?" *Philosophy* 75, 497–515.

D2   Dummett, M. (2003), "How Should We Conceive of Time?" *Philosophy* 78, 387–96.

D3   Dummett, M. (2003), "A Brief Concluding Comment", *Philosophy* 78, 409–10.

A Note on Quotations

Within the limits of the constraints imposed upon us by Continuum's house style, we try to follow Wittgenstein's practice (as also explicated by Baker "Quotation-Marks in Philosophical Investigations Part One" (2002), *Language and Communication* 22: 37, 68). Briefly and roughly: we use double quotes for 'actual' quotes (whether real or imagined), while using single quotation marks for non-actual quotes, including 'scare quotes'.

Foreword

Laura Cook

The readiness with which Wittgenstein's work has been appropriated by literary critics often belies both the subtlety of Wittgenstein's own work, and that to which it is applied. In his well-known essay, "Is There a Text in this Class?"[1] Stanley Fish draws upon the 'Wittgensteinian' term 'form of life' in order to support his notion of the interpretative community as generating the meaning of a particular text. At base, this is a reformulation of what he tacitly takes to be the Wittgensteinian maxim of 'meaning as use'. However, what Fish tacitly reads as a Wittgensteinian maxim or thesis is instead better regarded as a non-assertoric practical 'reminder' of the sort that would prove useful to the philosopher who, in his theorization, has ceased to use words in a way that we would normally consider to be meaningful. (Ironically, but not unusually, Fish is not 'pragmatic' or 'pragmatistic' *enough* in his appreciation/application of the working of language. Like virtually everyone else, he remains a theorist – and remains *de facto* mesmerized by the allegedly 'central' case of *assertion*.) In reminding us of the relevance of context as 'determinative' of meaning, Wittgenstein is *not* offering a theory to be applied in all contexts, for (to begin with) there is a great difference between everyday utterance or the 'language game' in play in a particular interpretative community, and the type of language employed in literary texts. Indeed, when we try to interpret texts via employing a theory, we are often struck by the way in which our interpretation necessarily leaves a 'residue' which our theorization has left untouched. We have a suspicion that there are aspects of the text which have been rendered inaudible, leaving our interpretation seeming somehow provisional and arbitrary. Whilst this type of interpretation may sometimes prove useful or interesting, it ultimately subsumes the literature which it seeks to elucidate into a pre-existing theoretical framework, thus overlooking the potency that the literature has in its own right. *If we can state the meaning of a poem or piece of prose in propositional terms, then the literary work itself is rendered redundant.*

The work of Fish provides us with a picture of Wittgenstein which is allied with the accounts of his work given by commentators such as Strawson and Malcolm.

Such 'doctrinal' readings[2] are furthest from the sentiment of this book, since these commentators hold Wittgenstein as advancing theories of language use. However, whilst *seemingly* closer to the resolute reading offered here, it is the e*lucidatory* reading of Wittgenstein which forms the prime target of our criticism. Read and I would argue that this account, advanced by commentators such as P. M. S Hacker, in fact presents a more insidious threat to the reception of Wittgenstein's work than the 'doctrinal' account. Hacker *et al.* regard Wittgenstein as departing from a metaphysical account of relationship between language and world in the *T-LP*, to a non-theoretical description of language use in the later work *PI*. It is at this point, in the later work, that elucidatory commentators regard Wittgenstein's philosophy as having a 'therapeutic' aim, for the meaning of words is regarded as fixed by the way in which they are used, and in furnishing us with descriptions of everyday language, Wittgenstein is held to be facilitating a 'cure' for our temptation to search for explanations. However, resolute readers of Wittgenstein contend that it is possible to speak of therapeutic endeavour in relation not only to the *Tractatus* (*contra* the standard account) but also the entirety of Wittgenstein's *corpus*, arguing that this point has hitherto not been taken seriously – i.e. that the 'elucidatory' readers do not in the end take seriously Wittgenstein's therapeutic intent and resolution[3] in his *later* work. We (Read and I) follow Diamond *et al.* in diagnosing 'elucidatory' commentators as tending to assume that language can be surveyed from an external point of view. In the standard accounts we also find the 'Ordinary' tacitly and very dubiously treated as a form of supra-evidence with which to settle philosophical arguments (as in the case of Fish, and, more obviously, in many of those purporting to follow both Austin and Wittgenstein[4]). Thus, albeit covertly, 'elucidatory' readers find themselves committing Wittgenstein to the very same position on language to which he is committed by his doctrinal readers.

In opposition to the 'standard' interpretations, Diamond and Conant have newly proposed a 'resolute', 'therapeutic' reading of Wittgenstein, which has become increasingly influential. This approach takes nonsense seriously as a term of criticism: nonsense is not a special or hidden kind of sense, and there is no content to what nonsense is trying to say, if it could only succeed in breaking the 'linguistic rules' it allegedly violates. Rather, nonsense is a 'resolute' failure to mean, and nothing more. The unwitting (or witting) purveyor of nonsense is failing to choose which way to use her words, 'hovering', such that the words 'flicker'. The resolute reading sees *continuity* in Wittgenstein's thought, with the *Tractatus* regarded as anticipating the later work in a profound way that has been overlooked by the 'standard' readings – principally, in being already fully committed to such an 'austere' conception of nonsense, and thus being identified as *itself* a therapeutic work, irreducible to propositional expression, of whatever kind.[5]

Except at its opening, in the opening sections of Part 1, the present book is *not* (except on occasion, in passing) an exegetical work. Read *assumes* throughout the broad viability and indeed correctness of the resolute approach to Wittgenstein's entire post-1918 corpus.[6]

And thus, in advancing a 'resolute' reading, we regard Wittgenstein as possessing *no 'positive' vision of philosophy* (or of language) at all, 'only' a 'negative' account of the temptations to illusion and nonsense to which we are all subject. We must therefore consider the sentence-forms Wittgenstein uses as (at moments when we want to lean on them) deliberately *coming apart from his philosophical aim.*[7] When Wittgenstein succeeds, we shall not imagine 'everyday language', 'forms of life', or 'the use of language' as technical terms, or as entities *at all.* The challenge, presented to us by Wittgenstein, is for us to attempt to philosophize, to *think,* without putting forward any 'position' *at all.* It should be evident then, that it is congruent with the aims of this book that a textual re-examination of Wittgenstein's work should occupy a relatively small space, since *to apply Wittgenstein is not to muse in the abstract over how his terms 'work'.* In fact, one might suggest that Wittgenstein scholarship tends to foster an 'attachment' to his words, in which phrases like 'form of life' come to be reified, and treated as quasi-technical terms. Instead, the more controversial claim offered here is that to practise 'therapy', to truly *apply* Wittgenstein, does not necessarily even mean using (any of) the 'terminology' offered in his corpus.[8] For when Wittgenstein invites us to see what some words are being used to do, he is *not relying on an implicit theory, nor even putting forth a 'view'.*[9]

Thus, this work seeks to 'apply' Wittgenstein in a way that does *not* depend upon a covert theorization of phrases such as 'meaning as use', or the employment of phrases such as 'form of life' as technical terms. Rather this application of Wittgenstein evidences a serious attempt to 'do' philosophy without reliance on theory, or any purveyance of controversial theses.[10] Thus, the structure of this monograph, albeit possessing a certain linearity, might be said also to comprise a series of *circles,* which overlap, mutually inform each other, and yet resist the temptation to offer a theoretical underpinning. In this sense, the structure of this book perhaps parallels Wittgenstein's own method in his *Philosophical Investigations,* which similarly *resists* and undermines the generation of a philosophical thesis or system.

With these considerations in mind, we are in a position to say that the method according to which Read applies Wittgenstein is roughly thus: a 'New Wittgensteinian'[11] perspective is brought to bear upon a particular issue or problematic of 'interpretation', such as how we are rightly to 'understand' the prose of Faulkner, or how we are to read (and question) Dummett's philosophy of time. In doing so, the aim is to *perspicuously present* the phenomenon examined (literature; mental experience (normal and pathological); time 'itself'), so that we are disabused of our *desire* to theorize. This, in turn, is related back to, and is shown to inform the Wittgensteinian conception/method(s) of philosophy, including the way that commentators have failed to resist the temptation to theorize Wittgenstein's own work. Thus, the structure of the monograph facilitates a genuine dialogue between philosophy and the perhaps seemingly disparate subject areas that Wittgenstein's method is here applied to, where the conception of philosophy is enriched in acknowledging its own intrinsically rhetorical and 'literary' nature.

In the first Part, on language, the author[12] begins by applying Wittgenstein's remarks on *meaning* to language, examining the consequences our conception of philosophy has for the ways in which we talk about meaning. We should not imagine would-be Wittgensteinian phrases such as "Meaning is use" nor even thought-provoking sentences like "[T]he given . . . is forms of life" as inform-ing us of anything, nor even in the end as instructing us to do something (though that imagined understanding of them is certainly a lot better than the first). To understand Wittgenstein aright is to understand him (negatively) as inviting us to engage in a process of *overcoming*. Wittgenstein's *own* terms and phrases, let alone more troubling 'Wittgensteinian' 'slogans' such as "meaning is/as use", need to be 'worked through'; for most philosophical questions – and the positions which we take up in response to those questions – are based in and on an unsatisfactory relationship between us and our words, a kind of linguistic confusion in which we want to say things that (we ourselves uncomfortably acknowledge) don't make any sense. We must throw away the sentences about 'forms of life', and' even about 'use', and about 'language-games', that Wittgenstein leads us into; they really are, at the end, entirely empty. Without such overcoming, the struggle that is Wittgenstein's philoso-phy is unfulfilled.

Of course, it is undoubtedly difficult to disabuse ourselves of the temptation to talk of language without recourse to theory. In order to assuage this dif-ficulty, Part 1 offers a reminder in the form of a distinction between pre-sumption and 'assumption' in our 'philosophical' talk about the supposed 'underpinnings' of language. The term 'presumptive' is intended to bring into prominence that there are 'assumptions', which must be made in the course of language-use, which are so fundamental that the very word "assumption" itself starts to risk misleading us, with its connotations of 'Whatever one can assume, one can also not assume.' In speaking of '*necessary* presupposition' – of presumption – we must try to see "(meaningful) consequences" as indissol-uble from, and presumptive for, further linguistic behaviour/action. So: what could actually be meaning, what has the consequences of meaning, cannot be inner items or experiences.[13] An important distinction is thus to be drawn between *meaning* (and its interleaved consequences, without which it is not meaning at all) on the one hand and 'grammatical' effects on the other. Inner processes have *effects* – including "grammatical effects", effects upon one which result from systematic aspects of the language, such as we are much subject to in the operation of good poetry, and these effects can be much more than mere individual psychological associations. But it is meaning in its ordinary sense - it is actual use - which has consequences, which is *consequen-tial.*

To return to the example of Stanley Fish, we can now see the way in which this 'reminder' may prove salutary; for Fish treats literary works as if they could be held to *mean* in a consequential way, i.e. in the same way in which everyday language works. *Contra* Fish, we might argue that the effect (and affect) of much poetry and literature is instead the result of grammatical effects, rather than (of) working language. To use Guetti's expression: in poetry we see language 'idling', 'thematizing' its own connotative nature. Again, the distinction between consequentially meaningful language and the poetic is *not* to be regarded as a rigid boundary. Rather, these are therapeutic moves. It is important to note that in drawing attention to the differences between working and idling language, we are not offering a definition of these terms; rather such terms are used in a comparable fashion to the way in which Wittgenstein uses terms such as 'form of life', i.e. 'provisionally', *transitionally*. What Part 1 attempts to show, in the form of a *reminder*, is that an appreciation of these differences should alert us to the dangers in assuming that the way we are wont to treat language-in-use is in fact appropriate for literary language. We are reminded that the philosopher's (scientistic) tendency to *assimilate*, and in particular to assimilate all cases of language to everyday assertoric language, is tenacious and widespread, even in domains (e.g. in the work of Fish or of Derrida) where one might least expect it.

The appreciation of the connotative nature of literary language, which the discussion in Part 1 attempts to foster, is explored further in Part 2. The recognition of grammatical effects as differing from the consequentially *meaningful* can aid us in our reading of poetry; at the least, by removing the temptation to read poetry in certain bad, reductionist, paraphrasal ways. For relinquishing the attempt to assimilate the literary into everyday terms enables us to *hear* the elements of the text that have been rendered inaudible by our attempts at translation. A close-textual analysis of Wallace Stevens' 'Thirteen Ways of Looking at a Blackbird' shows that the 'ways of looking', the apparently *visual* aspect invited by the poem, are undercut at each instance. We do not see the 'blackbird' in Steven's poem, rather the word "blackbird" tends to veer towards mention more than towards use, and the language of the poem as a whole is "*idling*" as a car engine idles: it is not working language. It can make a beautiful noise; and a complex noise that prompts us to notice and comprehend much about it and about the world and about words and noises – but that is not the same as taking us from A to B. Stevens' employment of figurative language frustrates our attempt to find a context in our everyday way of speaking (*à la* Fish) in which its terms can be considered meaningful. Despite initial appearances, the poem neither shows us, nor even necessarily points towards, any blackbird, real *or imaginary*. If we wish to maintain that the poem is 'meaningful', then we must recognize that we are operating with a radically different / peculiarly non-standard conception of meaning. (That is fine, if that is what one wants to do; but it is liable to be unhelpful and confusing to others.) Thus the analysis of the poem offered by Read herein, and Stevens' poem itself, provide a reminder of the *many meanings of meaning*. In this way, the analysis of Stevens' poem parallels Wittgenstein's own method. The 'action' of Stevens' poetry, as its invitations to the reader dissolve upon that reader, makes more strikingly perspicuous what has eluded many readers of Wittgenstein: much the same method, of inviting the reader to adopt a perspective or an idea, and then seeing whether it really does/yields what we want from it, or whether it instead collapses upon us. 'Thirteen Ways of Looking at a Blackbird' and Steven's other great poems do philosophical work *of their own*; this is poetry as philosophy, but poetry that *remains* poetry, all the same. To see Stevens as Wittgensteinian is therefore also to start to see Wittgenstein as Stevensian, i.e. to see that Wittgenstein's words are themselves evanescent, and that his way of writing has a critically important literary aspect. What we can finally draw from the analysis of Stevens is a 'philosophy' that is cognizant of its own literary nature; able to recognize when the words it employs are doing work, or whether and when language is in fact 'idling'.

As Read's analysis of Stevens shows, the blurring of grammatical effect and meaningful language is disorientating, resulting in the sensation of strangeness which permeates not only Stevens' work, but much modernist literature in general. As Louis Sass has pointed out, modernist literature foregrounds the sensation of failing to mean, which is at basis the motivation behind the impulse to philosophize. Sass' project in *Madness and Modernism* is to offer a new description of schizophrenia, through a comparison with philosophical scepticism and modernist literature. The schizophrenic parallels the sceptic in experiencing the relationship between words and world as problematic. This perceived gap between what we *can* say about the world and what we *wish* to say about the world is registered in philosophical scepticism. Solipsism, as the 'epiphany' or telos of scepticism, is demonstrative of a desire to speak beyond the 'limits' of language – as if we could set ourselves apart from, and above, any worldly context. The solipsist is confused by language, and finds it 'inadequate' to his purposes; thus he feels himself under pressure to change it.

In order to examine the confluence between certain pathological states and scepticism, Part 2 then turns to examine one of the great writings on severe mental affliction: William Faulker's *The Sound and the Fury*. The three first-person narratives in this novel each possess what we might term a 'strong grammar', a mode of hanging together that resists and rejects interpretation *even as it sometimes seems to offer interpretations*. Here, drawing on his published exchanges on the nature of madness with the literary psychologist Louis Sass and the Nobel Prize-winning writer J. M. Coetzee, the author expounds a literary critic – James Guetti – putting Wittgenstein to work and in doing so, brings literature, philosophy and what is now referred to as 'the philosophy of psychopathology' into mutually informative dialogue. In this section, the reader is presented with a way of seeing Faulkner *as* Wittgensteinian, a way which yields a distinctive and novel set of doubts concerning whether severe mental illnesses (e.g. 'hard cases' of schizophrenia) can be usefully said to be understood/understandable (at all). Sass' attempt to render schizophrenia intelligible as a species of lived-scepticism is shown to be problematic. Bearing in mind the 'reminder' given in Part 1 (i.e. of the differences between grammatical effects, and that which can be considered as consequentially meaningful) it is argued that scepticism itself is not an inhabitable, meaningful position – and thus by extension cannot be straightforwardly used as an allegory for schizophrenic or any other abnormal or pathological (mode of) experience. Read's analysis of Benjy's narrative, in Faulkner's *The Sound and The Fury*, is a reminder of what is missed/passed over when we translate a narrative governed by grammatical effects into everyday, 'sensible' terms. Benjy's narrative is characterized by its apparently alien 'experience' of time, which we might, roughly following Sass, locate as the result of something like lived sceptical doubts concerning the past.[14] However, whilst this characterization may prove useful, ultimately any reflective conceptualization we attempt to give of time is necessarily transitional, and we must be reminded of the fact that what we are inclined to say about time, by way of conceptualization is ultimately one picture among others, necessarily failing to 'capture' the experience of living-in-time. Faulkner registers this in his evocation of Shakespeare's 'Life is a tale told by an idiot'; for the literary presentation of time provided by *The Sound and the Fury* resists neat conceptualization.

Following on from the literary depiction of what we might call the 'psychopathological' experience of time, comes Part 3 of the book. Here, the author turns to examine *philosophical* accounts of time, finding a strong link between (e.g.) solipsism of the present moment as depicted in philosophy, and such 'psychopathological' states as are depicted in Faulkner's presentation. For Read, philosophic accounts of time tend towards the psychopathological, and signify nothing meaningful . . .

Based on their lengthy published exchange in the pages of *Philosophy*, the author offers an extended critique of Michael Dummett's philosophy of time. Dummett's work is regarded as a deep but prime example of the way in which philosophers' attempts to theorize time results in nonsense. Whilst Dummett appears to be putting forth a plausible post-Anti-Realist theory of time, actually, his account is profoundly vulnerable to Wittgensteinian objections, which ultimately, by throwing light on the true nature of lived time, indicate the surprising degree of complicity between philosophical theory and lived problems of time, problems that are insoluble by philosophical theorizing. Continuing his critical engagement with Analytic philosophy of time, the author next examines the self-undermining nature of the popular 'time-slice' conception of time, arguing that there is *nothing that it could mean* to isolate time (e.g. moments) in this fashion. Rather he shows that taking the philosophy of Wittgenstein seriously is to acknowledge that epistemological and metaphysical questions concerning 'time' are not intellectual problems in need of a solution. In fact, such 'solutions' to scepticism, in this case our sense of 'boggling' at the present – or at time itself – are actually more likely to be *exacerbated* as a result of our attempts to theorize and 'make sense' of them. However, this is not therefore to *dismiss* these moods as somehow extraneous to the business of philosophy. Rather, such moods (upon which we dwell in our co-authored 'Conclusion' to the present work), as intrinsic potentialities of the human condition, need to be recognized perhaps *as the only* true business of philosophy: our most serious philosophizing must *involve us* in an engagement, perhaps even, at times, in a virtual immersion in these types of mood. So, it seems that Sass' interpretation of schizophrenic utterance, 'translations' of Benjy's narrative into sense (and indeed, all paraphrases of literary works!) somehow miss the mark, failing to capture the strange and disconcerting power they exert upon us. What the analyses in the preceding Parts show is that attempts to master time philosophically, to offer a final interpretation of a text, or more broadly, to conceptualize our everyday experience, are prone to collapse. For once we begin to seek a theoretical underpinning on which to base our experiences, we begin to feel a sense of *loss*: that there is something which remains inexpressible, lost to us in theory and language, which we are nevertheless attempting to address or approximate. (The challenge is therefore to do justice to this sense, without the standard recourse to 'ineffabilism'.[15]) This realization has not (until the advent of 'the New Wittgenstein') been made by many commentators of Wittgenstein, nor indeed by the Western philosophical tradition in general. By contrast, it appears to be recognized in Eastern philosophy, particularly in Zen and Ch'an Buddhism. In his Afterword to this book, which considers further prospects for applying Wittgenstein, Read also briefly alludes to a suggestion of his that there is room for a re-reading of key texts in the Western philosophical tradition, along the same lines that have been attempted with regard to Wittgenstein in this monograph. That is to say: one can as it were re-read many of the great texts of the Western canon (notably Berkeley, Hume, Kant, Nietzsche, Marx, Frege) as to some extent 'anticipating' Wittgensteinian 'therapeutic' philosophy; and such re-reading focuses on 'literary' aspects of the texts in question, and suggests a greater affinity with some non-Western philosophy than is standardly observed.

Thus the application of Wittgenstein ends where it first began, since *Applying Wittgenstein* is a circling, a constant returning to the truly 'therapeutic' conception of philosophy which can be achieved by bringing seemingly disparate subject areas – and philosophers – into dialogue. In the Preface to *PI*, Wittgenstein suggests that *of necessity* his philosophical thinking goes "criss-cross in every direction". Wittgenstein's seemingly 'non-linear' mode of philosophizing – his apparent oscillation between aesthetics, philosophy of maths, philosophy of language, philosophy of mind, and metaphilosophy – is usually regarded as a defect in his writing. However, in terms of the confluence between philosophy and literature that Read hopes to establish in this book, it is *a strength*, an unavoidable reflection of and on the nature of philosophical work.[16]

Introduction

On *Applying* Wittgenstein

Rupert Read

This book is an exercise in applying Wittgenstein. As such, it aims at two main audiences. First and foremost, it aims to be a research monograph, accomplishing the tasks laid out in my editor's Foreword, and constantly alluding to and engaging with philosophical etc. texts and ideas (Wittgenstein's and others) that are not even explicitly present in my own text, knowledge of which will enrich a reader's appreciation of my book; but it aims also to be a book most of which can be read with understanding and appreciation by intelligent laypeople with only a relatively basic acquaintance with philosophy and with Wittgenstein's writing. This is as it should be: first, because Wittgenstein wrote in such a way as to be accessible without a technical apparatus, without a jargon; and second, and crucially, because this book seeks to apply Wittgenstein to some matters of widespread interest not just within but also beyond the academic world.

Books which succeed in reaching both the audiences I have in mind are exceedingly rare. This book may well fail, for instance by falling between two stools. But I cannot henceforth ignore the question of audience, and merely do the best I can, letting the cards fall as they may, because this book is intended, as all true (Wittgensteinian) philosophy ought to be, as a set of exercises in *therapy*. The point of philosophy, after Wittgenstein, is to help one's audience to cease to be tortured by various intellectual delusions. (And one's 'audience' includes oneself; as others have said before me, *Philosophical Investigations* is a philosophical self-help book, and was, too, for its author.) But an author has very little control over who picks up or uses their book; only over how well they fashion it for the audience they envisage (in this respect, if perhaps in no other, the *Tractatus Logico-Philosophicus* was an unsuccessful book, a flawed book) and over what they choose to write about.

So, the reader might ask: why choose to write about *this*? Why apply Wittgenstein? Or, to put the question more bluntly: why should we care about what Wittgenstein said? After all, in the end all he was was one odd, posh, very rich (at least, until he gave it all away) and privileged man who issued a wealth of strange and fertile pronouncements. What does it matter what he said? Isn't it more important whether anything that he said can be interpreted as something true and important?

This attitude is partly right and partly wrong. It is wrong chiefly in that it misses something that might be important in *how* Wittgenstein writes. Namely:

that the importance of his writing may not lie, or at least may mostly not lie, in the truth (or falsity) or even in the importance of *what* he wrote, but of *how* he wrote.[1] I reject, that is, the attitude, almost ubiquitous until relatively recently in analytic philosophy and even in Wittgenstein scholarship, that holds that it does no harm to 'translate' or 'paraphrase' Wittgenstein's idiom into 'plain prose'. This attitude tends to hold sway even among many of those who explicitly claim to reject it.[2]

I suggest that it is worth caring about 'what' Wittgenstein said because it is worth caring about the profoundly challenging and deeply therapeutic *way* in which he thought and wrote. We are presented with a form of 'philosophy' that genuinely resists paraphrase; that forces the reader who understands him to think for themselves; that reorients the entire axis of our philosophical investigations.

But I said above that the attitude represented above was also partly right. How so? Thus: in the end, it is only of real importance what Wittgenstein's philosophy presents if that philosophy actually *is* deeply thought-provoking, therapeutic, revolutionary, etc. In other words: beyond the confines of a stifling narrow scholarship or a very particular corner of cultural history, it *doesn't really much matter* what exactly this particular man thought or wrote, when or why. The analytic philosophers who read Wittgenstein are *right* at least not to allow themselves to become trapped in trying to figure out what exactly Wittgenstein meant with some set of words or other, or even how this exemplifies what Wittgenstein called "our method" in philosophy, or his style. These things are of almost negligible importance – unless it is actually the case that Wittgenstein's ideas, his way of thinking, his methods, his styles of writing, were and are of real value. *Important.*

Those of us who take ourselves to be followers of Wittgenstein had better do so primarily for this reason. Not because we might want to believe that the man was a god who got nothing wrong; nor because we perhaps believe that his thought is intrinsically fascinating to follow and hermeneuticize; but because we believe that much of what and how he said and wrote was of lasting importance, utterly independent of the fact that it was *he* who said it. In the end, it matters relatively little, then, whether Wittgenstein is being accurately interpreted by his followers. Instead, we, as it were, make a bet that it is worth trying to interpret him accurately, *because* we have evidence that our belief that his was a great and innovative mind is justified. That evidence presumably consists mostly in actual experience, our own (and others'), of finding Wittgenstein's ideas illuminating, idol-shattering. Of finding his way of approaching philosophical questions novel and valuable, his styles of writing his way through them liberating. We try to understand 'what' Wittgenstein was saying, because it helps us understand the philosophical history of philosophy better (philosophy, unlike science, being a 'subject' in which the past is never completely dead), because it helps us to do *philosophy* better, because we think his contribution to our philosophy now one of value.

In the final analysis, compelling proof that we have got Wittgenstein wrong, in relation to some matter where we are confident that the philosophy we have identified as 'Wittgenstein's' is right, should certainly not result in us giving up our philosophical ideas or practice, but in us recognizing that Wittgenstein was *not* infallible. (That said, I believe that Wittgenstein erred but rarely, that he was prone to exaggerate his own failings and mistakes, and that close attention to his texts, close following of their and his philosophic ways, and preservation of his styles of writing against what I smilingly term 'the heresy of paraphrase', are generally most conducive to philosophical insight.) The proof of the philosophy is in the eating: that is, in the working of we Wittgensteinian philosophers.

Thus it follows that exegesis has to come to an end somewhere.[3] Sooner or later, it is important simply to do philosophy, after Wittgenstein.

There are perhaps limits, however, as to how much 'metaphysics' or 'epistemology' or other alleged 'core areas' of philosophy one will want to do, after Wittgenstein. One reason for this is that there is an important sense in which Wittgenstein efficaciously 'deconstructed' the notion that there are any such things as metaphysical or epistemological questions, issues or problems. A notunrelated reason is that Wittgenstein of course therapeutically covered and explored these 'areas' a lot himself, in his voluminous writings. Of course, there is always more to be done: watching out for Wittgenstein's own blind spots; updating his thinking to deal with contemporary theories and threats that he gave little or no attention to or could not have anticipated; and so on. But, due to Wittgenstein's thought that the impulse to metaphysics is the impulse to mire oneself in nonsense, it is in any case not, of course, the Wittgensteinian way to think that these 'core areas' have any *privileging*. Wittgenstein thought, in my view rightly, that (as Rhees might have it) philosophy was/is one: the variegated problems and the methods to heal them in philosophy of law and philosophy of logic are not so very different; philosophy of maths can be illuminated by philosophy of mind and vice versa; aesthetical problems are (best) intertwined with problems encountered in reflection on maths and mind . . . Logic does not discriminate. (It is just such 'criss-cross' philosophy that I am to practise in the present work, which can appear to move in a linear fashion, but which actually moves seamlessly and 'circularly' back and forth between its various 'topics'.)

To sum up, then: in my view, much of the most important and challenging work to be done in philosophy today is not the exegesis of Wittgenstein; at the very least, as explained above, not for its own sake. It is of great import to establish and teach why Wittgenstein wrote what and how he did – *if* his writings are of lasting importance. In order to establish that, *we have to go beyond those writings*. They have to function as a pointer. If one scrutinizes the pointer forever, one is completely missing the point . . .

The true test of Wittgenstein's philosophy, the test of its vitality, of its reach, of its being more than a set of observations which are of use in the areas where he made them, is to apply his methods where he did *not* much apply them. Only this can test whether there really is a kind of unity to philosophy; and only this can make philosophy after Wittgenstein something that we *practise* rather than recite; the valuable activity of a growing cultural force, not the esoteric preoccupation of a clique.

Exegesis must come to an end somewhere, because it can only be a means to an end: that of doing philosophy. It is utterly to miss the point, to fixate on Wittgenstein's 'views' on such and such; he had none, *qua* philosopher. But it is missing the point too to fixate on how and why Wittgenstein chose to diagnose and lay to rest a certain set of confusions; what matters is whether Wittgenstein's chosen methods work. And what matters is whether we can learn how *to go on.* (One does not know how to play chess if one can only repeat sequences of moves that one has seen before.) This is what I seek to do in this book, building on others who have gone before me. For instance, in Part 2 of the book, arch-appliers of Wittgenstein such as my teachers and colleagues James Guetti and Louis Sass – and building of course on Wittgenstein's own remarks in these areas; but chiefly seeking to go my own way in applying or taking the *kind* of thing that Wittgenstein did to pastures new. I try to do what must be done, sooner or later, if Wittgenstein is to live. (There is no doctrine to apply. And his ('our') method is always methods – whatever is appropriate for the area, the case, the occasion – and the audience . . .) Here – tending to emphasize somewhat different aspects[4] to those covered by my editor, above, in her more detailed Part-by-Part 'introduction' to this work – is an almost linear thumbnail sketch, which I hope you will later throw away, of the progress of this book, as an applying of Wittgenstein:

Beginning, laying a kind of foundation, I 'apply' Wittgensteinian method in Part 1 to an 'area' about which he thought and wrote a *lot*: language, and most importantly *everyday* language. In doing so, I seek to further our recollection of how this works, by considering some ordinary cases, and by *looking* at how language necessarily proceeds, dialogically – and novelly.

Then, in greater depth, I consider a kind of flipside of such everyday language, which Wittgenstein himself considered far less: literature. Language whose order of novelty is different, language which acts very differently – or, better, which doesn't in the ordinary sense *act* at all, i.e. language via which *nothing* is carried out. Language in *this* condition is a kind of minor theme in Wittgenstein's symphonic later work; it is there as a necessary 'complement' to the cases (assertoric, performative, etc.) that take most of our attention in philosophy. In Part 2 of this book, I major on this minor theme. I think about how literature works (on one) via its idling, thinking about this *via cases* such as the poetry of Wallace Stevens. In the course of doing so, I explore not just the literary as a 'complement' to the everyday, but the pathological as a 'complement' to the normal. Literature considered, after Wittgenstein, as sometimes presenting a kind of philosophy of psychopathology.

Shakespeare's Macbeth commented bitterly that life was a tale told by an idiot. William Faulkner authored such a tale, and filled it with sound and fury, signifying a great deal – on a particular interpretation of the word "signify". In the closing segment of Part 1, I argue that that interpretation, common in

'Continental Philosophy' and 'Literary Theory', tends to be unhelpfully ambiguous between 'meaningful consequences' and 'grammatical effects'. A word signifies by meaning in the sense of what it is used to do/say, etc.; and in the sense of what it connotes, what associations it is (meant to?) stimulate, etc.[5] These two senses are related, even complementary: *but they had better not be confused.* In the former sense, I submit that 'The sound and the fury' signifies nothing; that, in that very particular sense, Macbeth turns out to be right.

Philosophers tend to tell a different kind of tale about life – or at least, about time. Drawing on Wittgenstein's scattered but (I suggest) deeply important remarks about time, I suggest that their tales mostly signify nothing: that they fail to decide what they want to mean by their words, such that their words do not amount to a sense. (Sadly, they also mostly lack any potentially redeeming literary merit, either.) Part 3 of this book applies Wittgensteinian thinking to the thinking of time, attempting to return our thinking about time to the way we '*do*' time, every day[6] in a way that does not quietistically repress anything. Such a 'return' does not neatly dissolve away or settle all problems. The book's Conclusion, co-written with my editor, draws together some of the ways in which a pathological way of living time is not merely a failure of rationality, or a cognitive deficit. Rather, there is no way of rationally forcing a healthy relationship with time. Philosophical problems, we suggest, following Cavell, are in the end problems of *mood.* Time is not something that one can get intellectually right in a way that is decisive. What one returns to, when one returns reflectively to being in time, is a life that is larger even than the methods of therapy can settle. And thus we ally Wittgenstein with Heidegger, in the endeavour to apply philosophy to real problems of life, in a way that does not simply and pointlessly order those problems to leave, or to be quiet.

Lastly, in the 'Afterword', I look briefly at further prospects for the application of Wittgenstein. I consider briefly what has thus far been achieved by myself and others, in this domain, and consider what more awaits doing: in for instance the 'social sciences', the 'human sciences', in bringing Wittgenstein into conversation with Chomsky and Zen Buddhism, in politics and other world-changing activities, and more.

There are interesting respects and 'domains', I believe, in which thinking Wittgenstein returns us to ourselves as we already are/were, but yet does not leave everything *normatively* as it is. This book is in the end a first concerted *resolute* stab at *some* of those respects, and *some* of those domains – most focally, literature, madness and time.[7]

Part 1

Language

1.1 Towards a Working *Through* of 'Meaning as Use'

"Meaning", Wittgenstein says, "is not a process which accompanies a word. For no process could have the consequences of meaning" (*PI*, II. xi.). He is most interested here, of course, in ruling out the notion that meaning is a 'mental process', a matter of the allegedly mysteriously and ineluctably 'inward' lives of language-users. But even if one were inclined to accept such an exclusion, the breadth of the claim that urges it might seem puzzling. 'Processes' in general surely have results, effects, even products; why should these be held distinct from the kind of 'consequences' that *meaning* has? What makes the action of meaningful expression – as opposed to that of 'processes' – *distinctively* consequential?[1]

Part of the difficulty of this question stems from what can seem to be the infrequency and inconclusiveness of Wittgenstein's explicit attentions to it:

> Why can't my right hand give my left hand money? – My right hand can put a deed of gift into my left hand. My right hand can write a deed of gift and my left hand a receipt – But the further practical consequences would not be those of a gift. When the left hand has taken the money from the right, etc., we shall ask: "Well, and what of it?" And the same could be asked if a person had given himself a private definition of a word; I mean, if he has said the word to himself and at the same time has directed his attention to a sensation. (*PI* 268)

But even if the force of "Well, and what of it" is evident, and one understands that such a question might often effectively expose the meaninglessness not only of 'private ostensive definitions' but also of other varieties of pseudo-linguistic behaviour, it may not be entirely clear why it should do so. The criterion of 'consequences' is not articulated but presupposed here; and because these consequences are said to be "further" and "practical" it might be inferred here both that they occur only after the fact of a meaningful expression and even that their "practicality" is somehow 'un-linguistic', so that the proof of language's meaning might have to be sought, somehow, 'outside language'. The first inference, I shall try to show, is true in a way but apt to be misleading, especially if it were taken to imply the second – for, appealing though it is, nothing is ultimately more contrary to Wittgenstein's thinking than an appeal to any such 'outside', any such notion of non-linguistic activity as disjoint from linguistic activity (see *PI* 7, 23).

But therefore it may seem puzzling that no more explicit treatment of these consequences – preventative of this misunderstanding – is apparently offered in Wittgenstein's later work. Yet this, I shall argue, is because of the magnitude or, perhaps better, the 'depth' of his conception of them.

1.2 Presumption versus Assumption

In short, for the reason that such consequences are fundamentally "*presump-tive*" both to Wittgenstein's descriptions of meaningful linguistic practice and to that practice itself, any general account of them has quite literally gone without saying.[2] But when one wants to articulate it – as one may want to in doing philosophy – what one is wanting to do is to elicit a justification for or (better) an elucidation of perhaps the most famous sentence in his work, "For a large class of cases – though not for all – in which we employ the word 'meaning' it can be defined thus: the meaning of a word is its use in the language" (*PI* 43).[3]

What do I mean, though, by "presumptive"? This term (which I have explained and utilized in detail elsewhere[4]) is intended to bring into prominence that there are 'assumptions', which *must* be made in the course of language-use, which are so fundamental that the very word "assumption" itself starts to risk misleading one, with its connotations of "Whatever one can assume, one can also not assume." I am speaking rather of 'necessary presup-position' – of *presumption*. I am suggesting that one try to see "(meaningful) consequences" as indissoluble from, and presumptive for, further linguistic behaviour/action.[5]

PI 43 itself has tended to be treated rather differently in 'the literature'. It has been by some too easily – and crudely, sloganistically – adopted; and by others too quickly – and equally uncomprehendingly – rejected.[6] "Use in the language" has, by both admirers and rejecters, tended to be read as amounting to just the emplacement of a word among others in keeping with grammatical propriety; and "meaning" is then conceived – as it often is in linguistics, for example – to be merely a matter of sensefully combined strings of words.[7] Now, in work prior to the *Investigations* – especially, I believe, at certain moments in what is sometimes called his 'middle period' (e.g. in the "Big Typescript") – Wittgenstein *was* himself sometimes inclined, as Garth Hallett has suggested, to equate "meanings" with such purely grammatical regularity. Wittgenstein responded to the ghost of the *T-LP*,[8] to its purported logical atomism, with (at first) a fairly static, linguisticistic notion of usage. Here is Hallett: "having dropped atomic meanings, [Wittgenstein] did not immediately shift to use, but instead gave the following definition: the meaning of a word is its 'place' in a 'grammatical system'".[9] But the eventual shift to "use", as Hallett observes later, presses the concept of meaning beyond the limits of any purely grammatical or logical accord. Thus in a sense it radicalizes "the principle of the *Tractatus* . . . that a word has meaning only in a verbal context. But [this appeal to "use"] might be worded just the same way . . . It must be understood that [the "context" in question] is a vital context . . . 'Only in the stream of life does a word have a meaning. '"[10]

It is worth noting that Hallett explicitly remarks that we might use *the very same words* to refer to what the *Tractatus* is about as to what the *Investigations* etc. is about, with regard to "use" and "verbal context". The final (nested) quotation in the passage just quoted is from Malcolm. He and Hallett are 'doctrinal' commentators who have nevertheless recognized the difficulty in the static 'place-in-a-grammatical-system' model of meaning – but in attempting to render the 'position' that Wittgenstein ends up with in the *Investigations* an advance on the *Tractatus* 'position', they find themselves having to resort to vague metaphors, to gestures at the ineffable. But, famously, *that is exactly what these same commentators (among others) accuse the 'Tractatus' of having ended up in* (rather than in statable theory, or simply in silence)! Malcolm and Hallett thus oscillate uneasily between taking a theoreticistic 'positivist' line on Wittgenstein on use, and making gestures towards something more than that – but *gestures* that appear to be: only that.

My fear, and my polemical contention, is that in fact very few of Wittgenstein's commentators and followers (Hallett included) have actually managed to make the leap to Wittgenstein's deepest concept of "use", the concept implicit in *PI* etc. (but *also* arguably implicit in *T-LP* – see e.g. 3.323–3.3, and 5.5563), which Hallett envisages. In the *name* of use, instead, they mostly remain with at best a notion of "usage" – with a picture of the record of use of a linguistic community, or, what is relevantly similar in terms of its philosophical problematicalness and limitations here, of place in a *Satzsystem*. Instead of having a concept of use which can do justice to Wittgenstein's remarks in the *Investigations*, they are stuck with a relatively static version of language, of context,[11] and of use. My contention will be that only a genuinely dynamical conception of use – which I will detail below – enables one properly to understand the meaning of the remarks from Wittgenstein (on the consequences of meaning) with which I opened this Part, and thus to be able to apply Wittgenstein's method to (everyday) language, let alone elsewhere.

As already intimated, Malcolm's metaphor of "the stream of *life*" does at least suggest a rather intriguing and different reaction (different from the reaction, outlined above, of Wittgenstein's 'followers' and 'opponents', including at times Malcolm himself,[12] who take Wittgenstein to have had a 'use-theory of meaning') to *PI 43*. Malcolm's 'gesture' here perhaps implies that the "use" which constitutes meaning is not merely beyond grammar but beyond any intelligence that could be considered properly linguistic, something mysteriously integrated into "*life*". And thus the problem is polarized: if meaning is not a matter of the word's "place in a grammatical system" – not a matter of purely intra-grammatical relations or connections – then it is a matter of putative 'vitality' which may seem entirely beyond grammar's reach, and beyond un-metaphorical description as well. Again, we find Malcolm and co. *oscillating* uneasily and often unconsciously between and across these two polarized (and clearly incompatible) possibilities.

These two possibilities are what one tends to find, similarly, in the huge amount of talk about '*form* of life' that goes on among 'Wittgensteinians' (and also in some of Wittgenstein's critics).

In other words, 'form of life' is often taken to be theorizable (e.g. to be the basis for a sociological theory), to be the keystone to unlocking the secrets of Wittgenstein's 'theory of language / of practices'. To treat the term 'form of life' in this way, as a quasi-technical term, as part of a theory, is manifestly to go against Wittgenstein's intentions; and moreover, we should bear in mind that 'form of life' occurs only five times in *PI*, and less often than that in the entire remainder of his now-published works. As Putnam has said, the volume of the secondary literature on 'forms of life' is out of all proportion to what would appear to be its importance in Wittgenstein's actual work, and the sense its invocation makes often in inverse proportion to the claims made for it in any given instance as the lynchpin of Wittgenstein's philosophy.

Less commonly, 'form of life' is taken not as a 'technical term', but as a quasi-mystical marker, a name for something which cannot be theorized. This, while it cannot be ultimately satisfactory, is in some ways preferable to the theorization of the term.

(Incidentally, why can't it ultimately be satisfactory to take 'form of life' (or 'stream/flow' of life, somewhat similarly) as a gesture at the ineffable? I hope the reason is obvious. It would leave the later Wittgenstein in the quandary of the *Tractatus* on the 'ineffabilist' interpretation of that work (the interpretation according to which Wittgenstein was trying to 'whistle' something which he was quite clear could not be said); gesturing, *in words*, at something it itself seems to claim is unwordable. I am claiming, then, that the mainstream interpreters of the later Wittgenstein, where they do not 'positivize' him (by sociologizing him, or psychologizing him, or biologizing him, or at best linguisticizing him by means of taking him to be literally depicting for us the grammar of our language (ironically, or perhaps naturally, this is the route down which Baker and Hacker, great scions of contemporary linguistics, including of Chomsky, take Wittgenstein)) . . . where Wittgenstein's interpreters do not positivize him, they ineffabilize him. Thus, unless the *Tractatus* was simply (philosophically) right, which no-one who reads it positivistically or ineffabilisitically claims, then the later Wittgenstein cannot have hit the philosophical nail on the head either (though quite a number of people claim he has) – *unless* there is a way of taking his work which is truly neither positivistic nor ineffabilistic. It is the search for such a way of taking *PI* etc. which I am engaged in here.)

In any case, the point, again, is that I find on the one hand a popular project of integrating Wittgenstein with mainstream philosophy, a project of facilitating the treatment of his 'cryptic' turns of phrase as simply the clothing of a theory. This in practice normally is held to license a 'positivistic' construal of Wittgenstein on non-linguistic and linguistic practice, on the use of language etc. So, for example, one gets quasi-positivistic treatments of the supposedly fundamental concept of 'form of life': it gets theorized as referring to the way of life of a given culture or community, or of a given species, and sometimes Relativistic consequences are then deduced from it.

On the other hand, we have those who would gesture at something ineffable by means of using the term 'form of life', and would have our use of language and our practices generally thus be for principled reasons both efficacious and mysterious(!). The ineffabilistic version of 'form of life' says that what the positivists are trying to capture is something uncapturable, that 'the stream of life' always evades philosophical theorizing. Its trouble is in how it can say so much – or indeed anything at all – about what it says is unsayable.

Thus while the way that Wittgenstein is usually taken on the question of "use" might be said, perhaps polemically but not unilluminatingly, to be 'Positivistic' in nature – to be an Anti-Realist would-be reduction of meaning to use, where use is understood as place in a substantial and static grammar (even if it is allowed, as Pragmatist readers of Wittgenstein for example stress, that this grammar itself may change, such that different meanings become possible at different times) – this rarer and, as I explain below, in some ways preferable (though ultimately flawed) alternative to such a conception could not unreasonably be construed as ineffabilistic: holding that there is a Truth to what 'use' is, but a Truth that we can only gesture at, or perhaps think but not say. Interestingly enough, these – 'positivism' and 'ineffabilism' – are, as parenthetically suggested above, *precisely* the options usually presented to readers of Wittgenstein's early masterpiece – the *Tractatus* – for how to understand that work and its conceptions of 'sense' and 'nonsense'. Many commentators on the *Tractatus* take the 'ineffabilist' reading of that work to represent in a certain sense an important advance of the 'positivist' reading of it (for it can at least understand in a sense the way *T-LP* ends, while Positivism – from Humians to Carnapians – is usually just silent on its inability to understand itself, on its 'self-mate'), even if these commentators often still (rightly) take 'ineffabilism' too to have a troublingly – utterly – paradoxical or contradictory character. Yet many of those same commentators, who normally present themselves as admirers above all of Wittgenstein's later work, taking Wittgenstein in it to have advanced upon the conceptions of meaning etc. that they locate in the *Tractatus*, prefer what I have polemically characterized here as 'positivistic' renditions of his later work. They present Wittgenstein, for example, as having one or another variety of 'use-theory' of meaning; or as rooting use in sociologically describable and definable 'community practices'.

I take this as evidence that something is seriously awry in the reception of Wittgenstein's work. If most of the commentators on the *Tractatus* are not completely wrong, then it follows that what they say about Wittgenstein's later work has that work be in certain important respects a *backsliding from* the insights of his early work (those insights being, furthermore, so they say, beset themselves by a flaw, a paradox!)![13]

I have argued this case elsewhere with regard to Wittgenstein's most scholarly exegetes, Baker and Hacker.[14] I will prosecute the general argument a little further, here.

I believe that it is true to say that, its metaphorical character and vagueness (and its ultimate sheer incoherence) notwithstanding, the mysterious suggestion of Malcolm's – ineffabilism, applied to Wittgenstein's later work, to action, to the use of language – must indeed be somewhat preferable to the more mainstream view. For Wittgenstein was almost always clear, even from his earliest notes, that "meaning" was not just a matter of grammar in the 'static' sense indicated above. In the *Notebooks 1914–1916* Wittgenstein discusses a sketch of two figures fencing: "If the right-hand figure in this picture represents the man A, and the left-hand one stands for the man B, then the whole might assert, e.g.: 'A is fencing with B.' The proposition in picture-writing can be true and false. It has a sense independent of its truth or falsehood."[15] I take it as obvious that the "proposition in picture writing's" truth or falsehood is something that would be discovered in its use or application, in its representation of some actual state of affairs, in which case it would be *either* true *or* false. But, as this "proposition" is unapplied, it has, independently of any such use, a more neutral "sense", which one might conceive of as its purely grammatical "form", that one might say *can* be 'both true *and* false'. This is to say that the "proposition in picture writing" is not truly a proposition at all, but is instead an example, an exposed and exhibited expression that *would* be a proposition only if and when it *were* applied to or held to represent something. This application can seem to be always *beyond* the grasp of any staticist theorization.

My discussion of the passage from the *Notebooks* above should indicate clearly that Wittgenstein was never a positivist about "use" – unless one actually does take the highly uncomfortable line that he actually did backslide in his later work,[16] and even perhaps that *PI* is a retreat from, a flawed and inferior version of, *T-LP*.[17]

Was Wittgenstein then perhaps an ineffabilist about use? The hazards of ineffabilism, as already indicated, are clear: a severe risk of obscurantism; a terribly ironic movement away from the very concretion (emphasis on actual examples of practices, on 'looking and seeing') that concepts like 'use' were supposed to yield for us in the first place; above all an unavoidable paradox in the pronouncements of the ineffablist – the necessarily unsatisfactory nature of any *philosophical* mysticism.

What I will now seek to demonstrate is that, thankfully, *one need not read Wittgenstein that way either.* There is a way to understand his remarks on logic, grammar, use etc., such that, in the later work at least as decisively as in the early work, he rejected not just the substantial theorizable notion of 'sense' which most commentators attribute to him, but also the particular substantial conception of nonsense – 'meaningful' nonsense, nonsense 'gesturing at' a sense – which 'ineffabilism' argues for. I will look not just at the pull towards staticist theorization of use, but also at the real attractions of ineffabilism with regard to (reading) his later work – and see where they *actually* lead one. I will, in short, read Wittgenstein resolutely so as to begin the task of applying his thinking to render visible, perspicuous, the actuality of the working of language, in its ordinary condition.

The distinction between the merely formal "sense" of expressions and the "meaning" of their actual uses made in the *Notebooks* was maintained throughout Wittgenstein's career. Even if we look for instance at some of Wittgenstein's reachings and graspings in the 'middle' period, we still see him recovering himself. For instance, the following remark in the *Philosophical Grammar* risks (the word "want" is perhaps already an indication that it does not actually do so) confusing static grammatical relations with meaning: "I want to say the place of a word in grammar is its meaning." But Wittgenstein follows up that expression of his inclination directly with this remark, which at least partly remedies the matter: "The use of a word in the language is its meaning."[18] As I have argued elsewhere,[19] from around this point in his work onward, Wittgenstein was progressively more and more inclined to conceive "meaning" as a matter of the actual and dynamic application (and even (re)construction) of (local) grammar; whereas any more static recognition of purely grammatical relations, of senses, became merely what was liable to be mistaken for meaning: "The confusions which occupy us when language is like an engine idling, not when it is doing work" (*PI* 132).[20]

In the *Investigations*, the denial that language in such an "idly" senseful (rather than actually meaningful) condition might give us any intelligence of how it actually means begins early; for it is at least implicit in the rejection of the "Augustinian picture" of language-learning, where the recognition of isolated *names* plays so foundational a part:

> One thinks that learning language consists in giving names to objects. Viz. to human beings, to shapes, to colours, to pains, to moods, to numbers, etc. To repeat – naming is something like attaching a label to a thing. One can say that this is preparatory to the use of a word. But what is it a preparation *for*? (*PI* 26)

The act of giving or knowing names may appear so "fundamental" to learning and even to using language just because it is transparently an example of a "purely grammatical" linguistic condition, with all the apparent flexibility or capacity (to be "true *and* false", for example) of expressions in that condition. Naming is through-and-through 'grammatical' because it is 'about' language, rather than yet being language-in-action. As Wittgenstein says, it is a preparation (much as one sometimes prepares the ground in a pedagogical situation by telling one's audience how one will name certain things not entirely familiar to them – how one will use certain terms). Wittgenstein considers such business merely "preparatory"; he clarifies his point by saying that "naming is so far not a move in the language-game – any more than putting a piece in its place on the board is a move in chess. We may say: *nothing* has so far been done, when a thing has been named" (*PI* 49).

But if this diminution of the role of purely senseful or grammatical relations and rules – of mere linguistic preparation, or of a *Satzsystem* (or somewhat similarly of Saussure's *langue*, or Chomsky's 'grammar') – is so necessary, according to Wittgenstein, to an investigation of meaning, what is it about such inactive grammar that continues to tempt many philosophers and linguists, even supposed Wittgensteinians, to insist upon the overwhelming importance of our grasp of it? It is the fact, I believe, that such grammar is so evidently something that one *can* 'grasp'; and so it may be conceived as a stable prop for one's linguistic behaviour. Otherwise, one fears that one will be lost in the seas of language in action without a rudder. (And the theorists of language have perhaps just this fear, in spades.)

One is tempted, then, to claim that the meanings of the words, phrases and sentences of one's language are something that one *knows* (or 'cognizes') independently of one's using them. But although one may commonly use the expressions 'knowing what *X* means' and 'knowing the meaning of *X*', their form may distract one along a line against which we were all warned in *The Blue Book*:

> The questions 'What is length?', 'What is meaning?', 'What is the number one?', etc., produce in us a mental cramp. We feel that we can't point to anything in reply to them and yet ought to point to something. (We are up against one of the great sources of philosophical bewilderment: a substantive makes us look for a thing that corresponds to it.) . . . The mistake we are liable to make could be expressed thus: We are looking for the use of a sign, but we look for it as though it were an object co-existing with the sign. (One of the reasons for this mistake is again that we are looking for a 'thing corresponding to a substantive'.)[21]

Thus expressions like "knowing the meaning of *X*", involving a "substantive", may fool one into looking for a 'substance', and meanings may then seem static objects or contents. Hence for some philosophers and more linguists – many of them again following Chomsky's lead – the knowledge of these 'meaning-objects' is itself dangerously hypostatized into a kind of "possession" of them, characterized as a mental – or some relevantly similar kind of – "state".[22]

Of course, some meditation upon linguistic expressions as if these were objects in space is reasonably frequent in one's experience of language; it is something that one often practises, for example, in reading poetry. But one goes quite wrong when one supposes that the evident substance of such objectified expressions is an answer to the question, "What is the meaning . . . ?": if one mistakes a real 'language object' for an unreal 'meaning object', and confuses one's relatively static "knowing" of such a language object with understanding how it actively might mean.

In this connection, Hacker has shown – in what can I think be interpreted as a reasonably effective rebuttal of the relevant Chomskyan positions – that knowing the meaning of a linguistic expression is normally best regarded as a knowledge not of *what something is* but of *how to do something* (see below) – of a technique – and so it should be least misleadingly considered an *ability* rather than a "state".[23] And the grammar of abilities tends to be altogether different from that of the mental (e.g. "depression") or physical (e.g. "headache", or "stomach-ache") states of a person. The criteria for a person's "states" tend to be different from the criteria for their "abilities": the former, for instance, are much more subject to temporary variation, or have a different sort of 'duration', than do abilities, and the latter tend to be more strongly dependent upon the behaviours that manifest them than are states; and so on.

But the distinction that Hacker draws, though I think it is in the final analysis fairly helpful, is slightly more problematic than he suggests, for the difference wanted between "abilities" and "states" may often be intrinsically difficult to mark, and this difficulty is not without significance, in my view. It signifies the hard-to-grasp and easy-to-mistake nature of 'ability-concepts' more generally (as discussed in all their difficulty in Wittgenstein's *Brown Book*); and it instances the inevitable absence of a proprietary philosophical vocabulary with which to describe language.

"Knowing what 'hammer' means", for example, ideally – i.e. if one is to maximize one's chances of avoiding serious philosophic confusion – should probably be considered an ability, and thus equivalent to "knowing how to use the word 'hammer'". Even if abilities would seem obviously more 'active' than states, the ability to use language is nonetheless 'static' when compared to its actual manifestations or exercises.

I have brought "knowing meaning" a little closer to Wittgenstein's conception of meaningful linguistic action. But I have not reached it; for again, meaning something, or understanding someone to mean something, has a more clearly active/dynamical aspect than "knowing how" to mean or understand, which may well continue to seem quite "static" (state-like).[24]

But not – and this is why at bottom I tend to agree with Hacker's distinction – 'simply' static, in the way of a persistent depression or headache (or indeed stomach-ache). Underlying states of the organism for sure are in some sense a necessary condition of the kinds of abilities I am interested in here – a human being cannot use meaningful language unless it has a nervous system (and indeed a digestive system) in one of a certain range of states – but linguistic ability nevertheless is not best construed as identical with any of those underlying states.

For a clearer understanding of how an ability may be regardable as a "state" of affairs concerning a human being, but not as a mental *or* a physical state,[25] we might usefully consider one of Wittgenstein's most interesting remarks concerning "aspects": "The expression of the aspect is the expression of a way of taking (hence a way-of-dealing-with, of a technique); but used as a description of a state."[26] As an object of comparison, then, I would propose this analogical 'model', which I hope may lessen one's mental cramps hereabouts: *an ability is a description of an action(s) used – presented – as a description of a state.* Of course, again, this does not in the slightest rule out the consideration that some person, after all, or some living thing, is implicated in both the action and the state! But it indicates that the attributed ability is a 'hypostatized' action *presented as* a description of a person, rather than simply an actual description of the states of that person. Wittgenstein proposes that the "logical form" of the "expressions of aspects" – and, I would add, the logical form of the attribution of abilities as well – finds "room" in another "dimension": "In this sense there is also no room for imaginary numbers in the number-line. And that surely means: the application of the concept of an imaginary number is radically different from that of, say a cardinal number . . ."[27] And while that thought deserves much more explication than I can give it at present, at the least one may infer from it that, like imaginary numbers, attributions of ability do not simply apply to any empirical state of affairs, and have a special "grammatical role" in the language. Or, to take a further step: these expressions might be said to have a role which is perhaps surprisingly *strongly* grammatical (or logical) rather than empirical. Attributions of abilities might then helpfully be said to amount to logical projections from and to actions, rather than to descriptions of facts about individuals' states.

Now it might look as though I am denying that people really have abilities at all. But of course I don't mean to deny anything. I am only denying that people have abilities if one has in mind a prior and confused notion of what it would be to have an ability – for example, if one is conceiving of "ability" simply and exclusively as a mental or physical state of the organism, rather than as a concept relating actions to states of affairs concerning human beings.

"Knowing a meaning" (or "knowing a language") may perhaps seem more 'active' than any mental or physical state when one considers it as an ability: "knowing how to mean" (or "knowing how to use a language"). But this only shows, once more, that meaning is something "known" (or linguistic ability something "possessed") only by virtue of the 'hypostatization' of *an action*. Thus it is towards that action that any further investigation of meaning must inevitably turn.

The general conception that Wittgenstein offers to indicate the activity of meaning, as is well known, is often to be found under the heading of "language-game". "The language" in which a word is used (*PI* 43) is not simply our grammar at large, but is always *both locally and dynamically constituted*. By which I mean that one is least likely to be confused if one deliberately thinks of language-games as occurring always in some specific though not static situation in which there is the inclination to activity, to *doing something* with words.[28] As Hallett has at least said, such local limits therefore do not comprise merely a "verbal context", but an actual set of living circumstances in which the "use" of words often exceeds their "correct" and even their quite specifically defined senses.

This must be stressed: it is the action, the dynamics, of meaning that the concept of the "language-game" is meant to illustrate. To take any such game merely as a particular closed "context" would be to remain within the narrow "grammatical relations" construal of "use" which I earlier raised serious questions about. Language-games are not occasions merely for the specification or refinement of more general rules of grammar. And even when such grammatical specification is in place – as a set of particular senses for certain 'syntaxes', for example – it is still just a set of rules. Such rules must be 'applied', must be acted on or from. Before that, one does not as yet even have a language-game, but only the preparation for such a game. Any meaning that might occur with the putting to use of such preparation will not yet then have occurred, and will not so far have been considered.

However, there will be nothing wrong with conceiving a particular language-game as a sort of "local grammar" so long as we understand that, in any actual language-game, grammar is complicit with its application, 'internally related to' the activity of its use. As hinted earlier, this is of course to suggest that the move to a genuinely dynamic, action-oriented conception of "use", via thinking of "language-games" as genuine and unclosed interweavings of actions and words, may suggest to one a dynamicized version of 'grammar', too. Rather than grammar that at least at any particular moment is conceived of as stable, such that the "language-game" involves always the work that language does (that we do with language) *beyond* its grammar, no matter how particularly that grammar has been specified, one may then wish to think of the "language-game" instead as a term partially replacing and radicalizing the earlier terms, "calculus" *and* "*grammar*". Such that the grammar/the language-game would, like an ability, be always an idealization: in this case, *a description of our interleaved linguistic and non-linguistic actions in all their dynamicness, used – presented – as a description of a set of interrelations of the sentences etc. in question.*

But even if this is right, we are again confronted by what may be beginning to seem an unresolvable dilemma, a dilemma which could pull one towards 'ineffabilism'. For no matter how particularly we conceive the rules of a language-game, its meaningfulness seems to be something further, something beyond it, which no grammatical considerations – and even no linguistic ones, no descriptive ones – could illuminate. Something of this predicament was evident in Wittgenstein's own handling of the language-game 'model':

> It is a rule of grammar dealing with symbols alone, it is a rule of a game. Its importance lies in its application; we use it in our language . . . We can only prepare language for its usage; we can only describe it as long as we do not *regard* it as language. The rules prepare for the game which may *afterwards* be used as language.[29]

Here once more is revealed Wittgenstein's acute distrust of "idling language" in which even the description of language – to say nothing of more emphatic modes of its exposure, such as citation or artistic presentation – creates a picture so misleading that with what some might see as logical awkwardness he must insist that to "describe" language is not to "regard" it *as* language.[30] But such insistence is of course exactly what I have been suggesting – and again, here, one feels the pull towards 'ineffabilism' concerning language and what can be said about it. And 'ineffabilism', though it is incoherent, has at least this much right about it: while it's at best very odd to think that the right way to think of the use of language is to stress its ungraspability and unsayability, it simply is at best very difficult even for Wittgenstein's acute remarks to 'capture' language in its lived activity. "Language-game" and the other words he coins apparently to help him to do so can seem destined to fail, if this is Wittgenstein's task.

When the rules of the game and their actual use are considered so divided as in the above quote from Wittgenstein, then that use must of course seem to occur "afterwards"; as if the *employment* of grammar, once more, were always something further, something beyond, and even as if that employment were somehow separable from what it employed.

This is not – I want to emphasize – the way Wittgenstein mostly treats of "language-games" later, in the *Investigations,* where their rules have usually to be conceived to be *already in action* in order for them to be "language-games". But the difficulty remains of how we are to understand just what is being described by Wittgenstein when he describes such "games", and of whether there can *be* a description which 'captures' language in action. I believe that Wittgenstein's mature conception of "language-games" – where a grammatical rule that is not "in action" is not functioning *as* a rule, and therefore is not so much as a rule at all – is more likely to cure us of delusions of staticity and of determinacy of sense than his earlier use of the concept (and of the concepts of 'calculus', 'satzsystem', and even 'grammar'). But even in this later treat-ment, where rules and their applications may begin to seem inseparable, the most important questions must remain: what is the action that these rules govern or in which they participate? If grammar is to be read now as through-and-through 'complicit' with its use, what and where is that use? (And, how exactly can we hope for these questions truly to be understood and answered?)

Cora Diamond's work provides, I believe, the essence of an answer to these questions.[31] She has something to say about them which manages to be less merely metaphorical and gestural than Malcolm's "stream of *life*", while ener-getically and convincingly avoiding producing a philosophical theory. In pursuing Rush Rhees' directive to "show how rules of grammar are rules of the lives in which there is language",[32] she initially appeals to the particular: "[Wittgenstein] thinks that, when we raise philosophical questions about meaning, we are for various reasons inclined not to attend to the place words have in our lives: to the very particular places."[33] If these "particular places" still sound too much like "contexts", like specific grammars statically conceived, which may constitute or invite local theorization (of "usage"), it nevertheless soon becomes clear that Diamond has something else in mind, for the "place" of a word in a people's language is a matter of what they *do* with that word. Examining an imaginary tribe of language-users in relation to "private language"-type examples, she writes that:

... we may say that they have a word which is, in a sense, a word "for pain", but what kind of public character their word has is seen in such things as the place that different people's remarks about someone's pain are given in the commerce with the word in question. In the commerce with the word, we see what it is that "publicity" of sensation language comes to in the particular case of this concept.[34]

This conception of "the commerce with the word" may seem at first to have certain disadvantages. "Commerce", as a name for linguistic behaviour, remains here a metaphor; will Diamond turn out to be just an ineffabilist, a 'mystic', about language and its use? And though "commerce" does at least seem a more analogous and practical metaphor than Malcolm's "stream", it may continue to suggest that the meaningful use of language is something that one does *with* it, some activity whose description must be separate from a description of language itself. If it is, again one asks whether it will be describable at all? And may this not leave too much of a gap ultimately between language as such and (language-in-) action?

It soon becomes clear, however, how "commerce" and "linguistic behaviour" may be names for the same activity: "It is only in the give and take of language, the relation between what one person says and what others say, that you see the kind of public character that different sorts of concepts in it have."[35] In this way Diamond appears to conceive the "commerce" with language, and the meaningful use of language, as *dialogical*: the difference that meaningful use makes, the way that such use matters, may in a sense be discovered in how people subsequently *respond* to their own and to others' "sayings":

> [H]ow do we tell that some people distant from ourselves are telling the time? It is not a matter of their glancing at the sun and saying something; rather, on the supposition that they glance at the sun and say things, it is telling time if they coordinate their activities by such means, or refer to such matters in their narratives in certain ways. Or they say such things as "he left at dawn, it is half a day's trip; he should be back by now", and then they begin to prepare a meal for him, or start worrying about why he is so late.[36]

I want to narrow the focus of these last remarks even further: to try to show that, however widely (or narrowly) one might conceive the consequences of meaningful linguistic use, certain consequences still should be observable just in the "give and take" of speaking itself. Diamond's "commerce" is not only what occurs *with* one's expressions; one can also see it occurring *within* one's expressions. Whatever consequences accrue from or by language use, there occur also, and in the first place, consequences to language as it is used. And so when Wittgenstein says that the meaning of a word is its use "in the language", I take him to be pointing away *both* from standing grammatical considerations *and* from any merely pragmatic utility to which meaningful expression might after the fact be put; and *towards* what actually happens to our expressions in their dialogic and sequential development.

I must now endeavour to be more concrete in setting out exactly what this means.[37] Let us start by returning to "description", via "names" again.

Having asked of the "preparatory" act of "naming", "but *what* is it a preparation *for*?", Wittgenstein several sections later at last answers, "naming is a preparation for description" (*PI* 49). And the most obvious examples for an investigation of how meaningful language works would perhaps seem to be such descriptions: empirical observations of facts. But it is both odd and important, I think – and I think that Wittgenstein's philosophical development after his return to Cambridge centrally involved an ever-increasing estimation of this importance – that this mode of expression is not so obviously amenable to the criterion of "consequentialness" as certain other modes. It may often be easy to see the actual changes in situations made by "performative" or by "imperative" utterances, for example; but what difference does a description of fact make? Having made such a description one may use it to do something further, of course; this is often the sense of "use" upon which Wittgenstein seems to rely: "What we call '*descriptions*' are instruments for particular purposes" (*PI* 291). But that important remark should not give us to suppose that the meaningfulness of descriptions depends only upon the realizations of their pragmatic instrumentality. The blueprints for a building or for a new machine do not *become meaningless* or fail to achieve meaningfulness if we do not set to work upon construction *the moment* they are drawn. (Though it is important to see that this might happen after a *sufficiently* long interval, with enough cultural or conceptual change, etc.) So the way in which descriptions "work" does not have to be immediately "actual" in some concrete or physical way. But what then is to distinguish such "plans" from idle grammatical "sense", from any "description" composed according to the rules of grammar but which in a given set of circumstances has *no* application?[38]

What I am suggesting is that whatever is 'done' by operatively useful descriptions should *not* be limited to the alterations they might accomplish upon a physical world (which might seem an 'extra-linguistic' sort of "use"[39]). Such descriptions of course *may* be extended to further, and more evidently practical, activities than they themselves constitute, but their meaningfulness, if it is indeed in a sense an active '*intra-linguistic*' (where this would mean 'intra-grammatical' only on the genuinely action-including dynamic version of "grammar" I sketched above, and will detail below) *meaningfulness*, must be discoverable in another, prior, and more constant sort of "operation". I am looking, then, for a sense of meaningfulness, of "use", which is immanent to language-in-action, to language interwoven with non-linguistic action and with the world, but *not*, in either case – and this is crucial – as any kind of outside to that language.

One may begin to understand what this operation that we are looking for must be by insisting again upon Wittgenstein's phrasing: "'descriptions' are instruments for particular uses", rather than "*in* particular uses". A meaningful description is thus one that has the capacity *for* some particular use; and this particular capacity must somehow have been achieved just in the development of the description itself. Now this may seem dangerously close to saying, "meaningful descriptions operate on themselves", and so be troubling to those who rightly distrust the all too frequent appeals to language's "self-reflexivity" in contemporary language studies.[40] But these appeals – and the problems they are meant to solve – would seem, at least in large part, once more to be the result of a too static view of linguistic behaviour, in which everything is imagined quite literally to be surveyable,[41] or even is imagined to happen 'all at once'. Yet this is surely not how language, in the most obvious way, actually works. And if the differences that meaningful descriptions make – the consequences they have – *may* be said to be changes in themselves, these changes must occur as and where all descriptions operate: in some linguistic sequence.

Such a sequence, once more, is most easily and probably least misleadingly imagined as a dialogue. And now I turn to applying a genuinely Wittgensteinian approach directly to language. For example, someone ("A") comes into the house from a walk and says, "The leaves have begun to change." [42] In these circumstances, this remark would in all probability count as an "empirical proposition". By virtue of its timeliness – which is signalled by its following upon one's change of position (and the position of one's co-conversationalist), and by the tense of the verb, and so on – it marks a difference: a difference from what one had been saying lately, or could have said, especially about the leaves. And a listener ("B") *could* 'sensically' respond to such a difference with further (non-verbal) action. "B" might look out the window, for instance, or look at the calendar, or recall what the weather of the past few weeks had been like, or go out for a walk themselves, and so on. Some of these responses might amount to tests of that initial utterance; for empirical expressions are potentially both confirmable and doubtable. But whether they are in fact tested or not, or stimulate any obvious sort of action, they also virtually always allow for additional discourse, for *further description.*

The initial speaker, "A", can for instance now add, "The maples, especially on high ground, are changing more than the oaks." Of course, "A" might have said just that upon walking in, without first declaring that the leaves had begun to change; but he would have done so with rather less probability of being understood, at least without pause or surprise. Thus an empirical observation – "The leaves have begun to change" – may come to function *in relation to the expressions that follow it* as, roughly, a *grammatical stipulation.* In this development the role of such expressions changes 'dialectically' from active to 'static', from a temporarily descriptive and even "referential" functioning to a new and undoubted grammatical establishment, a background or "foundation" against which one can make another empirical and testable observation.[43] Expressions that serve initially as descriptions of fact are transformed, evidently just by the onward sequencing of the discourses in which they occur, into *presumptions* that make the next description assertible; and each presumption amounts to a further articulation of the grammatical rules of the sequence, a determination of the logical "range" appropriate for subsequent empirical expression, and hence *a modification of the grammar of the entire discourse to that point.*[44] (Almost as if the development of dialogue in the present changes the past. But it only seems that way, because of the deep attractions to us of staticist versions of 'grammar'.)

This is what I have meant by a dynamic conception of grammar. A conception such that the grammar of a sequence is to a certain degree being generated and specified (though not, normally, 'defined' – that would give quite the wrong impression) as one goes along, and in which a speaker's responsive linguistic reaction to a previous speaker's action is understood not as determined, nor as arbitrary, but as interleaved, in a less or more seamless fashion, with that action.[45]

So when Wittgenstein says, famously, that "the same proposition may get treated at one time as something to test by experience, at another as a rule of testing",[46] I would amplify by claiming that the sequential progress of speech from "one time" to "another" constantly *produces* a change in linguistic status similar to the one he describes. What becomes presumed can be rendered genuinely empirical – genuinely questionable – again, only through losing its status as "presumed".

It may be that, in the original context, the segments of time Wittgenstein's remark envisages for such alterations of status are longer than those of the individual discursive sequences with which we are presently concerned, such that my remarks look more counter-intuitive than Wittgenstein's, which apply in the first instance to how propositions may change their status on a large historical scale. But even if the linguistic changes of state that occur in the smaller or narrower "histories" of ordinary, particular verbal sequences are less memorable and monumental than those which Wittgenstein mentions, nevertheless in their very dynamicity they are perhaps even closer to what Wittgenstein most frequently means by "grammar" in his *later* work. And he seems to allow for this particular and temporary sort of grammatical development and for our individual agency in it when he says, "It is clear that our empirical propositions do not all have the same status, since one can lay down such a proposition and turn it from an empirical proposition into a norm of description."[47]

Just as the transformational "laying down" of empirical propositions is not confined only to large-scale changes in what comes to be deemed "logical" or "presumptive" in linguistic activity, neither is such 'grammatical stipulation/ specification' confined to what is preliminarily or peremptorily logical to any discourse. Specific and functional grammatical foundations are of course often "laid" in that formal or deliberate way, which is analogous to naming the game – or reading out its rules – before one plays it. But what more particularly and temporarily can *then* appropriately be said – like what more particular and temporary moves can appropriately be made – may be discovered only as the sequence of the discourse or game develops, as empirical propositions or actual moves one by one become syntactic history, transforming into grammatical bases for those that follow.[48]

If these observations are accurate and to the point, then empirical expressions have at least two sorts of "consequences".[49] One of these may be conceived as an *action from words*: someone says something and we may then appropriately look somewhere, or do something, or think something.[50] But this momentary action may sometimes be in practice somewhat difficult to distinguish from what it must be distinguished from – from various non-communicative, non-meaningful effects that words may have on us: for example, effects of nuance and connotation consequent upon non-communicative particularities of expression in poetry.[51] (For present purposes, I want to reserve the word *"effects"* for "consequences" such as this latter type.)

'Action from words' (and *its* – meaningful – consequences) may *seem* remarkably evanescent, since the 'syntactic' onwardness of our verbal behaviour may very quickly transform what were cues for action into the foundations or backgrounds for further cues. But the obvious, measurable, and special "consequences" of meaningful linguistic developments – what such developments always accomplish, unless there is some drastic failure in communication – is a continuing change of grammar. We may see, think, and act from these expressions; but as we do so they work to adjust what *might* always be said anywhere to what *may* – what properly can – be said here and now. So when Wittgenstein insists that meaningful expressions must make a "difference", we should understand that this difference is initially and always indicated in the development of our empirical assertions *into local and timely* presumptions *that enable further assertion*. The consequences that meaningful developments have – which no "process" could have because, be it as 'dynamic' as one cares, since even then it cannot "process" its own rules as language-in-action continually does – are in this sense well described as *grammatical* consequences. (And such grammatical consequences – meaningful consequences – must, I repeat, be distinguished from the 'grammatical effects' and the mere psychological associations and effects which attend particular verbal formulations, and which are so vital in literature, and in relation to the difficulty of adequately translating one natural language into another.)

That Wittgenstein never himself explicitly made such a 'claim' in the *Investigations* may seem reason to doubt the accuracy of attributing it to him. (And in the end I am much less interested in whether it can be justly attributed to him, and much more concerned with whether it helps us 'to go on' in understanding – in pre-empting our tendencies to misunderstand – the workings of language.) But I think it may be justly inferred that he would not have thought the suggestion in the least wrong-headed from this remark in the *Blue Book*:

> I want to play chess, and a man gives the white king a paper crown, leaving the use of the piece unaltered, but telling me that the crown has a meaning to him in the game, which he can't express by rules. I say: "as long as it doesn't alter the use of the piece, it hasn't what I call a meaning".[52]

One may allow that the crown may have had a "meaning" to the man, in the same kind of way that (say) the word "crown" may have a "meaning" to someone – or less misleadingly, a grammatical or psychological effect: perhaps it "means" "authority and wonder", or perhaps it "means" – systematically reminds one of – some particular person. To this man, the crown may have been of immense personal significance. It may have "meant" a lot to him in the kind of way that (say) the words "America" or "Great Britain" mean an awful lot to some people. (But the answer to the question, "What does 'America' mean to you?" is nevertheless very different from – both much more than and much less precisely – what even a good dictionary will give as the meaning – the use – of the word, "America". In the dictionary sense, in use, "America" is *meaningful*; while in answer to the question, "What does 'America' mean to you?", it rather has effects upon one, which is as much as to say: it is (only) *"meaning-full"*, full of meanings, associations, etc.)

What the crown did not have – and this is I think Wittgenstein's point – is a meaning *in the game*. Wittgenstein's imaginary opponent appears to mis-conceive as a "meaning" some strictly personal – and therefore indubitably communicatively and practically non-functional – quasi-grammatical appre-hension, which I have suggested would be better characterized as an "effect". For Wittgenstein the "alteration" accomplished by a *meaningful* gesture either with or in regard to the king would be altogether different: it would amount to a change not simply, as we might have expected, in the facts of the situation – for example, in how the chess game might stand at any moment after the king had been moved – but in the "(permitted) use of the piece", in its very capacity for further movement.

The paper crown would have been meaningful in just this way right from the outset, of course, if the changes it was to make (e.g. changes in the king's powers of movement) had been preliminarily posed and accepted. And one might, once more, want to discriminate between that sort of use-altering re-definition of the king's capacities and those that occur subsequently in virtue of the actual moves of the piece in some actual playing(s) of the game: to say, for instance, that the former would comprehend the "whole game", and thus comprehend the more specific 'grammatical modifications' that were produced by the actual and particular development(s) occurring in each playing of the game.[53]

But those subsequent occurrences/developments are in an important sense just as grammatically consequential as any preliminary considerations. What is "presuppositional" with regard to any language-game, in other words, is only so since and as the particular grammar of that game must continue to develop with its progress. And each of these developments is as 'comprehensive' as the grammatical 'stipulations' with which one began, just because it governs the entire range of what moves can next be made.

The grammar of an actual language-game, then, is necessarily dynamic. Grammar is not maintained by fixating on what seems obviously general or permanent about it – nor even (for those Pragmatistically inclined) by concentrating on what seems particularly central or determinative at any one time (e.g. the formative and distinctive elements of a 'vocabulary'), while mutable. And our employment of grammar is not like looking again at a table in the imagination, nor at a picture on the wall, nor like meditating over a poem, nor like our attention to any other sort of exhibit. Nor is it – and nor are we humans – usefully analogized hereabouts to a machine, with mechanical processes at the forefront. The better analogy is perhaps to *our behaviour with machines*: with an automobile, for example, which cannot be well maintained unless it is used. Thus we should measure a grammar – any particular set of linguistic rules – by the same strict criterion by which, as we have seen, Wittgenstein identifies a language as a language[54]: what is a grammar that is not used, that does nothing? It is not "nothing" in its effects and static implications, in how one may experience it; but neither is it a grammar.

1.3 Distinguishing 'Meaningful Consequences' from 'Grammatical Effects'

To sum up the argument thus far: I am suggesting that it will most likely be useful – philosophically illuminating – to see things roughly as follows: processes have *effects* – including "grammatical effects", effects upon one which result from systematic aspects of the language, such as we are much subject to in the operation of most good prose and poetry, and these effects can be more than mere individual psychological associations – but it is meaning – it is actual use – which has consequences, which is *consequential*.

Wittgenstein does not have a Positivistic conception of "use". The trouble with the work of many of his admirers, as of many his detractors, is that this fact is obscured from view if one thinks of Wittgenstein as having a "use theory" or even a "pragmatic change of use theory" or a "naturalistic theory" of meaning. That is the trouble with many moments in the work of such diverse admirers of Wittgenstein as Stephen Hilmy, Norman Malcolm, J. C. Nyiri, Richard Rorty, Stanley Fish, and, despite certain appearances, in Baker and Hacker.[55]

Even the Pragmatist version – which appears to allow, indeed to pride itself on, conceptual change, and thus might appear to be of a piece with the Wittgensteinian approach that I have – remains 'Positivistic' at heart. For the change is conceived of as a change in something definite and quasi-scientically theorizable. The Pragmatist version of dynamicness in "use" tends to retain a notion of there being at least notionally/momentarily stabilizable and theorizable meanings or uses in "vocabularies".[56] Whereas I have intimated that *even the very idea of "language-game" ought to be recognized as itself an idealization*, as itself a transitional move needing to be overcome, and therefore the term "language-game" as, if a quasi-technical term, then one which Wittgenstein hopes his readers will be able to lay aside, to be silent about, eventually.

"Use", one then perhaps feels inclined to say, 'goes beyond' anything which one can say about it, or philosophically account for, even in allegedly

'Wittgensteinian' terms.[57] But the reaction away from a 'Positivistic' conception of "use" (broadly construed: e.g. a Carnapian, or a Pragmatistic theory, or even a Scientifically Naturalistic theory such as Quine's) . . . the reaction towards an ineffabilistic conception – a conception that makes of use literally a mystery, by placing it within 'the stream of life' in a manner defying further saying, further description – such a reaction does not actually *succeed* in looking in the right place for rules, meaning, use. 'Ineffabilism' is right to think that there cannot be any effective theorization of "use", be it Verificationist, Pragmatist, or whatever. Ineffabilism is wrong however to think that then there must be profound Truths about "use" which are hidden from us but which we can gesture at. The opportunity which the work of Diamond, Conant and their followers offers is the opportunity to see this clearly. They lead one beyond the ineffabilist moments in Malcolm and others, to seek, resolutely, not to have *any* 'substantial' conception of use at all. This is the difficult thing, perhaps the hardest thing: to really have and give no theory at all, *to make no claims.* And to see that it is enough, rather, to make 'transitional' remarks such as I have essayed here; remarks which, drawing upon actual or coherently imaginable examples, seek only, as I have done, therapeutically to suggest and enact and point up certain ways of thinking and of *not* thinking about meaning. Specifically, I have suggested that it will cause least confusion to *reckon meaningful consequences as part of grammar, though only upon a genuinely dynamic conception of 'grammar'*, and to distinguish pretty rigorously between meaningful consequences on the one hand and 'grammatical effects' and 'psychological effects' on the other.

Such a suggestion is then not a claim, a theory, or even a thesis. Nor is it a gesture at an ineffable 'beyond', to a fantasized bird's or God's-eye view. Again, it is a suggestion articulated primarily for negative purposes, a suggestion that I hope will eventually 'self-deconstruct' rather than be read as having a 'substantial' character. If and when my remarks serve their purpose, I happily then give them up – I *hope* that they will be transitional, in just that sense. I would be happy indeed then for them to go without saying – the way Wittgenstein often went without saying them.[58]

So my conception here should not be mistaken for a post-positivist (and post-ineffabilist) '*theory*' of meaning'. The trouble with theories about language's "general form" – as we may now understand from Wittgenstein's work – is that there is no such thing, that nothing about how language generally *is* can be said. (As Conant and Diamond have argued, this was established by Wittgenstein at least as early as the *Tractatus*.) Whereas relatively abstract descriptions about how language characteristically behaves or acts are not inexpressible, as ineffabilism would have us believe, but *redundant*. I have not exactly offered such abstract descriptions, only specific exemplifications (and prophylactics against theorization) – and such exemplifications I do not intend as the basis for a theory, but as the basis for their own redundancy. As soon as they have served their purpose, give them up, as nonsense, or (sometimes better) as quite trivially obvious.

1.4 Towards a Dynamic, Applied Conception of Meaning

"If one tried to advance theses in philosophy", Wittgenstein says, "it would never be possible to debate them, because everyone would agree to them" (*PI* 128). I understand this as follows: because such a "thesis" ought to be a general description, or even one of a bunch of specific descriptions, of how our language works, it would simply amount at best to an exposure of something that – as competent language-users – we all already 'know'. And 'know' must be placed firmly within quotation marks here just because our purchase on such fundamental 'rules' ('procedures', and 'norms', might be better) for linguistic activity goes much 'deeper' than anything we might, ordinarily, empirically, have 'knowledge' of.[59] Much 'deeper', that is, than anything we might be said to observe or doubt. As 'deep', and as utterly surface, everyday and ready-to-hand, one might say, as most human practices and actions.[60]

Along these lines, I would say that "meaning makes a difference in what next can be said" – which might seem a laborious philosophical "theory" or "thesis" – is, rather, no less (and no more) an elementary grammatical 'rule' – 'citable' when someone is in the grip of some very particular confusion *(and otherwise quite nonsensical)* – than "red is a colour". A young acquaintance of mine is learning the language, and one of his temporary modes of action is to insist on what he learns, or even, one might say, on "definitions". A vehicle approaches on a deserted stretch of road and he says, "That's a truck!" And one nods; and then he says, "That's a truck" again, and again. And sooner or later someone has to say, "Yes?", or "And . . ?", or Wittgenstein's own, "Well, and what of it?" Just to show him, as it were, that it doesn't matter when the right hand gives the left hand money.

This, then, is the status I would claim for my 'thesis', my (hopefully redundant) non-thesis, here. The 'proposition' that meaning should be in the first place conceived neither as merely senseful grammatical relation nor as some 'extra-linguistic' use of language nor as a complete mystery, but as the use of language in and for particular 'grammatical developments' – speaking in the service of speaking, speaking as doing – is nothing more than a fundamental 'rule' of linguistic behaviour that should go without saying. It is 'learned' and presumed and *needs* no saying: save sometimes to children, and, sometimes, to ('we') philosophers. Sometimes, on occasions, transitionally.[61]

1.5 What does "Signify" Signify?

A key area in which grammatical effects become *confused* with meaningful consequences is in the psychoanalytic interpretation of everyday utterance, such as parapraxes (slips of the tongue). The psychoanalyst holds such utterances, wherein one 'tellingly' reveals an 'underlying' intention, as a candidate for interpretation and thus *consequentially meaningful.* Instead, following Guetti, I hold such instances to be a result of our perpetual access to, or *ear* for, the grammatical potentialities inherent in language, for I believe that the word "signify", much like the word "mean", is extremely prone to be misunderstood. More precisely: I submit that a widespread failure to distinguish between meaning and the consequences without which it is not meaning on the one hand and what I have called (following Guetti) 'grammatical effects' on the other is echoed by a failure to disambiguate between significance in the sense of sense and significance in the sense of connotation, echo, etc.

One reason it is worth making this point, which I will enlarge upon below, is that, while English-speaking philosophy has tended to focus on the word "mean", French-speaking philosophy (and, especially, its English-speaking advocates) – hugely influential in the last generation or two – has tended to focus on the word "signify". I believe that leading recent French philosophers, notably Derrida (and 'Deconstruction') and Lacan, have been led (perhaps initially by Saussure) into ramifying error on this point. Once one has looked carefully at what one wants 'signify' to signify, I suggest, a *gulf* opens up between the Wittgensteinian way of applying philosophy to language and meaning on the one hand and the Saussurian/Lacanian (and to a considerable extent similarly Lévi-Strauss and Derrida[62]) views on the other. As I hope to render more perspicuous here, the signifier/signifier basis for theorizing meaning *is incompatible with arguments and 'reminders' which take sentential and contextual holism more seriously* – i.e. with Wittgenstein, especially.

This incompatibility is generally concealed in those influenced by the 'Continental' tradition or by Literary Theory beneath the very – almost 'congenitally' – vague word, "signify" and its cognates/derivatives. This word conceals a vast difference in 'depth grammar' between: ordinary linguistic meaning (use); 'implicatures'; 'special' literary (e.g. metaphorical) significances (which of course themselves come in many varieties); purely personal psychological associations; and portents, etc. I now wish to illustrate what I mean here, and the dangers of seeking to look at language in its ordinary condition via the mind, via 'psychosemantics'. In particular: the dangers of failing to separate the kinds of items just listed.

An interesting example to take – interesting for reasons that will shortly emerge – is the sometime attempts to use philosophical psychoanalysis as a basis for such application. Take for instance the distinguished would-be Wittgensteinian (and also Lacanian) commentator, Grant Gillett. At one point in his suggestive essay, "Signification and the Unconscious" (Gillett 2000),[63] he makes some effort explicitly to distinguish between different meanings of "meaning", different significations of "signify", different aspects of use; in short, between different kinds of 'thing' that language effectuates and creates. But the metaphor he uses to express the distinctions, rather than highlighting the importance of context and the various kinds of differences between everyday language and its others, only muddies the waters: for the metaphor employed by Gillett is 'layers' of meaning. Gillett writes that "[E]very signifier carries layers of meaning", and this makes it sound *as though these are all layers of the same kind of 'stuff'*. Whereas my suggestion thus far in Part 1 has been that one has to see, minimally, that there is a deep difference between the use of the word "salt" in "Pass the salt", on the one hand . . . and the way the word "salt" could work on one if it featured in a poem at some particular point, or again if one had traumatic childhood memories associated with salt, on the other. In short: the term "layers of meaning" *preserves* the systematic ambiguity (concerning the meaning of meaning/signification) that one finds in Gillett (just as in Lacan, and Derrida, and so on).

For a better way forward – to understand what of value there may be in the likes of Lacan (and Freud himself) for thinking about "signification" – I recommend the following two (Wittgensteinian) guides: David Finkelstein and James Guetti.

Finkelstein's paper, "On the Distinction between Conscious and Unconscious States of Mind", is in my view the most significant effort by a Wittgensteinian philosopher of mind – perhaps by any recent philosopher – to understand what discourse about 'the unconscious' – what psychoanalysis – can actually be. Finkelstein's paper has the virtue of presenting talk of the unconscious rather as something which people actually engage in, as a practice, rather than as a set of theoretical gambits. In short, Finkelstein offers a sophisticated understanding of how one can understand 'the unconscious'[64] without violating Wittgensteinian precepts.

A number of pieces by Guetti are relevant, but especially the opening of his *Wittgenstein and the Grammar of Literary Experience*. It is worth quoting at length from pp.19–20 of that work:

[T]he logical problem of Freud's argument concerning slips of the tongue and the like – in which 'unconscious' processes are unsatisfactorily distinguished from 'conscious' ones – goes very deep. For it bespeaks his own actual unrecognition of the unconscious itself. There is nothing free or wild or irrational about the unconscious – attributes that Freud will claim for it elsewhere – in its function in Freud's 'literary' cases. It traffics in the same sort of meanings and purposes as do the conscious operations it sometimes interrupts and replaces. It is not revelatory of associative possibilities, but rather of "meaningful" chains more determined and foregone – and, of course, more boring – than anything the conscious mind has to offer.

It should be noted that I am not proposing that the "unconscious" does not exist, but only that the modelling of it upon processes and motives that are if anything hypermeaningful is nonsense. More importantly, I am certainly not objecting to the notion that an "unconscious" might be composed of *some* sort of language. Rather, I would suggest . . . that 'accidents' in speech are the results of our assimilation of and access to the grammatical possibilities of our language. This is a recognition that some of Freud's revisionists – most notably Jacques Lacan – sometimes seem to approach. Lacan considers, for instance, that phrases like Freud's 'unconscious thought' are not contradictory precisely because 'the unconscious participates in the functions of ideation, even of thought', and it does so just because it is itself composed of language – as if the unconscious might be figured as the entire learned totality of the possibilities of language – which I have called the 'grammar' – unrestricted by any immediate and particular applications or intentions. Here one may be so gratified to discover that the importance of such grammatical possibility is acknowledged by a psychologist that Lacan's formulation may become too eagerly accepted. But we should proceed with caution here, for this agreeable assumption of 'the omnipresence of human discourse' – in which even the unconscious mind should be considered as somehow 'structured like a language' – often reveals itself as a much more restrictive conception where language is not present as a system of possibilities but working, even unconsciously, as a secret but quite meaningful code. A 'subject' is introduced by the analyst into a 'primary Language in which, beyond what he tells us of himself, he is already talking to us unbeknownst to him'.

This conception of 'unconscious language' as a source of meanings and knowledge to which only psychoanalysts are privy may be indistinguishable from Freud's own. The powerful influences and effects of the body of language, of the grammar, within our speaking behaviour that I am describing [here, in this book] are neither so occult as this nor, when discovered, so revelatory, exactly because they are merely a matter of language's complex and variegated texture, of its surface of possibility as we learn it. And if they seem magical – or 'significant' beyond anything we might say in a meaningful way – this is not because they are varieties of some sort of hypermeaning, but because they are not meanings at all; rather, they are signs of our very *capability* of, and of our language's *potential* for, meaningful expression, exhibitions of verbal power and freedom that in fact can never be realized since they *are* meaningful only in restrictive applications, when we know what we must say . . .[65]

Guetti provides us the resources not only to worry about but to get beyond (for example) Grant Gillett's phrase "layers of meaning" – for he points out that 'grammatical possibilities', the kinds of inflections and associations found in much Modernist poetry and in some parapraxes, are not best seen as meanings (uses) at all. As I have already made clear: Guetti distinguishes, notably (though not 'absolutely' nor reificatorily), between *meanings (uses)* and *'grammatical effects'.*[66] 'Grammatical effects' and associations are more or less systematic effects of language which words and their interconnections have on us, effects of great 'significance' to us, but not well understood as 'signifying' strictly in the sense of being used to name something, or to describe something,[67] still less to accomplish some action. Thus we can avoid running together, as Lacan, following Saussure, sometimes does, what these authors call "[discursive] significations" with 'semantic content'.

Guetti thinks then that the idea that "the unconscious is structured like a language" *can* indeed be fruitful for one thinking, in broadly Wittgensteinian vein, about philosophy, language and varieties of 'meaning'. One can think about the unconscious as generating or even being the kinds of effects that 'grammar' has (more or less systematically) upon us – *without misleadingly assimilating these effects to ordinary applications of language* (or indeed to some other things that can be meant by the word "signify").

A clear place in Wittgenstein wherein one can see clearly the significance and power of the kinds of points that Guetti makes, where the 'minor theme' of 'grammatical effects' for the first time emerges in the text as a counter-point to the 'major theme' of 'meaningful consequences', is as early as section 6 of *PI*. Wittgenstein remarks that the ". . . ostensive teaching of words can be said to establish an association between the word and the thing". Wittgenstein presses himself for clarification: "But what does this mean? Well, it can mean various things; but one very likely thinks first of all that a picture of the object comes before the child's mind when it hears the word." That is classic psychologism. Does Wittgenstein repudiate it? Does he contradict it, or argue against it? Not straightforwardly; he does something much subtler: "But now, if this does happen, can it be the purpose of the word? – Yes, it *can* be the purpose – I can imagine such a use of words (of series of sounds)." The parenthetic clarification is pretty crucial. One might express it this way: using a word as a sound, or so as to create a certain picture in the mind, is not really using the word *as a word* at all. To use a word as a word is to use it to say something, to carry out some linguistic act, to make a move in a language-game. When what one has is what Wittgenstein immediately goes on to term, rather, an utterance of "a word [so as to strike] a note on the keyboard of the imagination", one doesn't yet have a move in a language-game.[68]

Now, as Wittgenstein says, it *can* be the purpose of words to work that way. When? Well, for example, in much (good) literature. Also, quite possibly, in attempting to train or control someone (e.g. a child) – one might well work to evoke certain images, so as to encourage or discourage a behaviour associated with them.

But according to the dominant pictures of philosophy of mind and language in recent Anglo-American philosophy (as for so long before), it is in the first instance *precisely* the aim of uttering words, all the time, to strike notes on a mental keyboard. This *is* what Cognitivism and Mentalism say. And Lacan? It appears to be what he says too: for the subject is to be "defined as the effect of the signifier". And this effect, presumably, is primarily one of construction through 'evocation' (of images, of atmospheres), which for Lacan is what language is essentially about.

We see here how Lacan is still rather *beholden to psychologism* – he has not made the Wittgensteinian turn away from static evocation and towards actual use. In the unconscious, 'grammatical effects' of words – not their uses – may indeed be king. But the running together of the workings of the unconscious and of aspects of language which play upon it with the dynamics of actual everyday use of most language is a recipe for unclarity.

So: 'the unconscious' may indeed be like the way that a certain word unavoidably strikes us and reminds us of certain other connected words/structures (cf. Guetti); but Wittgenstein does *not* identify ordinary language use as similarly 'non-negotiable'. On the contrary, ordinary language use is almost infinitely negotiable.[69] E.g. I can even perhaps say "Bububu" and mean "If it rains, I will go for a walk," if only a language-game is (co-)constructed to this end, only if a sentence which can be made sense of occurs in the course of an activity. We look for a sense in what others say: only as a last resort do we find their talk nonsensical, and even then not because it 'breaks grammatical rules'. Wittgenstein simply had no role in his philosophy for 'logical and grammatical truths'. Wittgensteinian philosophy leaves the use of ordinary language as it is: the *practitioners* of ordinary language can do all the negotiation and clarifying of it that is required. This deflationary approach is perhaps what is especially uncomfortable for Chomsky and Dummett and Derrida alike.

Thus, *if we are thinking of everyday language*, then Lacanian images of Language as a total system through which we are structured and in which we are 'imprisoned' surely do significantly more harm than good.

I have implied that Lacan is likely only to confuse us if we try to read him, as I admit it is (unfortunately) reasonably natural to do, as a 'psychosemanticist', i.e. as someone trying, absurdly, as Cognitive Science does, to discover things about meaning by looking at the mind. I have also suggested that Lacan *can* hint to us important things about what we might with profit now call 'psycholinguistic effects' – about certain phenomena, not happily identified with meaning, which nevertheless do have a lot to do with language in its non-transparent, non-used aspects.

The difference between Lacan and (say) Wittgenstein on fundamental issues to do with ordinary meaning/use is plain: "the function of language", according to Lacan, "is not to inform but to evoke".[70] This fits perfectly with the idea that 'signifying' – producing 'signifieds' – is what language is all about, but contradicts completely a properly Wittgensteinian conception of (very roughly) meaning as use. For sure, Wittgenstein thinks 'the' function of language is not primarily to inform – but the function *only of literary etc. language* is (primarily) to evoke.

Thus one is driven strongly to suspect that Lacan (perhaps after Freud, and certainly after Saussure and along with Derrida) is systematically unclear about what the word "signify" means ("signifies"? . . .). I am not arguing that Lacan should be ignored; on the contrary, I am arguing that, if one expects intellectually minded psychoanalysts and open-minded philosophers in the English-speaking world to take Lacan seriously, and work on bringing his ideas into creative dialogue with Wittgenstein *et al.* (who must first be adequately interpreted), then one must provide an account of Lacanian insights which does not founder on a basic unclarity about language – in particular, on distinctions between different uses of the word "mean" which we need sometimes to be reminded of.

The central thrust of my critical remarks might then be summed up thus:

evoking is one thing, *informing* another, *doing* (which, roughly, subsumes informing) still another . . . Sure, Lacan, like Wittgenstein, opposes an *informing*-
centred picture of language; but Wittgenstein's major picture of language is
doing-centred (especially as we find it in great detail in his later work). Where
there is an interesting and genuine connection (between Lacan on
the one hand and Frege/Austin/Wittgenstein on the other) is around the 'sub-
sidiary' issue of *evocation* by means of language. To put this in a capsule-like
form: if the unconscious is structured like a language, then that language
is at the least rather more like Keats' or Faulkner's or Wallace Stevens' or
L.A.N.G.U.A.G.E. poetry or Artaud's writing than it is like CliffsNotes or a
lawyer's description of a traffic accident or a car-repair manual or the dictionary
or 'The cat sat on the mat.'

There are serious difficulties with Lacan's conception of language-in-
general, difficulties which emerge into clear view only I think if one thinks and
applies the likes of Wittgenstein seriously, rather than merely translating them
more or less reductively into 'analytic' or quasi-scientific 'verities'. Wittgenstein problematizes precisely the kind of 'picture' of language (of words as
akin to names, of sentences as getting their meaning through combining the
meanings (references) of the words of which they are composed – in Wittgenstein scholarship, this is known usually as 'the Augustinian picture of
language') that in practice is shared by Millikan, Devitt, Dummett and Lacan
alike. Lacan is simply a kind of enlarged/distorted mirror-image of the Anglo-
American psychosemanticists . . . Where their bottom line is a single-minded
focus on *information*,[71] his focus is single-mindedly on information's 'other', on
evocation; what they all have in common is an unhealthy preoccupation with
bells being rung in the mind, with 'names' which – through the 'medium' of
the mind – are held to produce images, or words, or feelings, or otherwise to
yield a 'picture' of the world and of oneself in (or apart from) it. The
concomitant failure of all these thinkers is a failure to take seriously the actual
use of words (sentences) to accomplish real actions: to be, with others, in the
world.

Two closing 'Lacanian' questions:

First, *is the unconscious a network of signifiers?* We can now answer: roughly, *yes,*
insofar as one can understand and make something of the question; but *don't
be under the illusion that what actual language most of the time is like is: like this.*
Indeed, it might be happier to say rather the following: words primarily
'signify' concepts or things only in exceptional circumstances; normally, words
are transparent, and nothing at all is meant by them except in an actual situation of use of a sentence.

Second, *is the unconscious structured like a language?* Again, perhaps *yes* – *if* we
understand by "language" what Lacan asks us to. Lacan *can* help us to understand 'the unconscious' – because it *does*, arguably, operate in something like
the manner of the 'Augustinian picture', i.e. it *does*, arguably, operate through
the weighty resonance of names, through the hiding and exposing of
suspended grammatical possibilities, through, in short, the kinds of processes

long known to Freud's great predecessors, namely Shakespeare and those poets who, like him, revel in the form and materiality of language, and in the way words work on our minds. Especially then if one emphasizes a psychologistic reading of the 'Augustinian picture', one can say that 'the unconscious' *is* structured like a language. It is structured like a language – *as Lacan (inadequately) understands language.* Unlike ordinary, everyday language, wherein use and context, developed dialogically (as explicated in earlier sections of this Part) – not names and their combinations and the effects of both – are paramount.

Lacan's misreadings of the use of *everyday* language may not in the end be of much moment, insofar as he is read above all as a psychoanalyst, who is naturally therefore predominantly interested precisely in 'the pathological'. But then it will be dangerous to use and trumpet Lacan much beyond the important but relatively narrow domain wherein he deserves his fame. It is *Wittgenstein*, above all, who offers us a proper orientation towards (everyday) language, and who enables us thereby to understand the different *aspects* of language which words such as "signify" tend to run together.

And so, it is time to turn to times when it is the non-sense-centred 'significations' of language that start to take centre stage. Let us apply Wittgenstein to the most 'central' of these: to *literature.*

Part 2

Literature

2.1 'Wittgensteinian' Poetry

2.1.1 Wallace Stevens as 'Wittgensteinian'

The appreciation of the broadly connotative nature of literary language, which the discussions in Part 1 attempted to clear the ground for, is explored further in the following analysis. The recognition of grammatical effects as differing from the consequentially meaningful can aid us in our reading of poetry. For relinquishing the attempt to assimilate the literary into everyday terms enables us to *hear* the elements of the text that have been rendered inaudible by attempts at 'translation'. Beginning with a close-textual analysis of Wallace Stevens' "Thirteen Ways of Looking at a Blackbird", which shows that the 'ways of looking', the apparently *visual* aspect invited by the poem, are undercut at each instance. The illusion of meaningful expression, which the idling language of the poem evokes, is *not* the product of working language. It can *transport* us: it can make a beautiful noise; and a noise that prompts us to notice and comprehend much about it and about the world and about words and noises – but it cannot transport us from A to B.

2.1.2 The Many Meanings of 'Seeing': A Literary 'Reminder'

Here is the first of the thirteen stanzas of Wallace Stevens' famous and wondrous poem, "Thirteen ways of Looking at a Blackbird":

> Among twenty snowy mountains,
> The only moving thing,
> Was the eye of the blackbird.

Of this, James Guetti (1993)[1] justly remarks,

> [T]here may be no difficulty in visualizing the parts of this sentence, the "snowy mountains", even if not exactly twenty of them, and a small, bright eye. But there would seem to be a problem in organizing them into an entire image . . .

The simplest problem here is one of visual scale and perspective . . . One might think of a "surreal" superimposition of pictures – some extravagant sort of double exposure – but that would appear to generate more possibilities and so more problems. Is that eye in a head, and by virtue of what contrast of light and colour would it then be visible? . . . But after all, it is difficult to estimate how far this shuffling of representational techniques would go, given the problem created by the pivotal line, by the fact that the blackbird's eye is "moving".

A central question raised by this stanza of Stevens, then, and I believe it to be raised in one way or another by every single stanza in the remainder of the poem too, is simply this: in what sense exactly (if any, indeed) can we justly regard this as a description of a way of *looking* (e.g. at a blackbird)?

For sure, there are other 'ways of looking' than the ways involved in and with visual perception. And so for sure part of what is in process in Stevens' poem is the relatively straightforward task of 'reminding' readers of the many meanings, which we can crudely refer to as variously 'literal' and 'non-literal', of "looking". *But* what fascinates, what grips about this first stanza of this poem – and several at least of the other stanzas have the same feature – is that it *looks* so like it involves a visual looking. One so naturally *experiences* this little haiku-like piece of literature as generating an image. But, just as Guetti says, when one presses on this experience, when one 'looks' closer, the 'image' starts to collapse on one; or rather: either quite to disintegrate, or to become an image of such a strange sort that it is not clear we can easily succeed in imagining it, let alone draw or paint it (even if we were a very good artist indeed) . . .

Borrowing from and adapting Cora Diamond,[2] I should like to say that some of the ways of looking that appear to be natural to the implied reader of "Thirteen Ways . . .", we only imagine that we can succeed in realizing: for instance, we merely imagine that we can successfully *image* or *visualize* this first stanza. And *what* we imagine that we can thus image is itself nonsensical: it cannot be put into prose without falsifying it, and its poetical presentation remains forever strange to us. We just don't know what it would be – it doesn't as yet *mean* anything, for us – to know that and to see (that) only a blackbird's eye (is) moving, among twenty snowy mountains. It is, I am arguing, Stevens' genius to allow us to learn from gradually figuring this out for ourselves (therapeutically, self-helping), when at first the stanza seems so overwhelmingly to yield us something that can be seen, a way literally of looking at a blackbird.[3]

We imagine that we can visualize *this*, what the poem 'describes'. What is it to imagine this, at least as a way of looking at *a* blackbird, without imaging it? The poem lets us learn gradually, the hard way, that our imagination is wrong, is overreaching. Reading the poem with understanding is giving up the illusion that it is, in the ordinary sense, to be understood *at all.* This first stanza, as more obviously others, such as the second:

> I was of three minds
> Like a tree
> In which there are three blackbirds

and the fourth:

> A man and a woman
> Are one.
> A man and a woman and a blackbird
> Are one . . .

undermine one's sense, as one 'works' through them, that there is, first impressions notwithstanding, anything to be understood here:

- In what sense "Like"?! One is supposed to be able to make any simile work. But one hasn't the foggiest how to put stanza two to work.
- "A man and a woman are one": sure. "A man and a woman and a blackbird are one":? And now one perhaps looks back at "A man and a woman are one", and wonders whether one understood any one thing by it, clearly, after all.[4] One surely didn't imagine, let alone image, just one thing: or if one did, that image had little or even nothing to do with what anyone else might or would necessarily understand by the phrase. The fourth stanza first obscures and thus begs a contrast between the two 'cases', and finally it makes one think whether perhaps they *are* in some respects surprisingly alike after all.

Part of the teaching of this poem, then, is that when what we most appear to have on our hands is something visual, visualizable, something like an image, something that can be – or is a product of being – looked at in the most straightforward of ways, then in just those cases we should beware, or look out (to coin a phrase). The "reality effect", as Barthes called it, is beautifully exploited in Stevens, as (in different ways) in some of the other greatest of modernist writers, such as Hemingway (also discussed in this vein, in Guetti's book). *In this most natural way of reading the expression "looking", it is not clear that there are any such lookings at blackbirds at all, present(-ed) in Stevens' poem.*[5]

2.1.3 Invitations to Nonsense: Poetry Considered as a Therapeutic Tool

I would submit that this is the case, even in the wonderfully still and apparently least strange of the poem's stanzas, the last:

> It was evening all afternoon.
> It was snowing
> And it was going to snow.
> The blackbird sat
> In the cedar-limbs.

There is much to discuss here, much to say for instance about the peculiar apparent duration of the image apparently created here.[6] I will restrict myself in the present context only to the following three points:

Firstly, the first two lines appear to set a scene, straightforwardly. They appear to tell you simply and vividly what was happening (viz. it was snowing a lot). But the repetition of that deeply simple phrase, "It was", is deceptive: the first "It was" characterizes how things were over a long period of time ("all afternoon"). Whereas the second is actually apposite only to moments: "It was snowing" is past continuous, and applies to what was happening at some given moment in the past. We can tell this by "And it was going to snow": that is only so when it carries on snowing. So, unless it snows forever, this can only be so at certain specified times. Thus the first line establishes a time – *the whole* afternoon. The second (re-)establishes a/the time – *some particular point in* the afternoon. And now one has to ask: *did the blackbird sit in the cedar limbs for the whole afternoon? Or just at some point in it?*

Stevens' poems are full of such 'false friends' as "It was" is here: repetitions of words or phrases that crucially work to establish a rhythm or pattern that pulls the reader, *and yet* between which there is a difference in signification that subtly upsets the 'easy' effort to establish a visualizable sense of what is happening; or, indeed, to establish *any* stable *sense at all* to the words as a whole.

Secondly, we should also perhaps note a peculiar effect of the "And it was going to snow." A more natural turn of phrase here would have been "And it was going to keep (on) snowing." The line could of course be read as ". . . it was going to *snow*" – to really snow and snow. But it is (of course) referring us to what was going to happen *later*: and it is to say the least strange to speak in this way of the future when what is spoken of is something *that is already happening*. The most natural, normal context for "It was going to snow" is to refer to a time at which it hadn't yet started snowing. And yet, by hypothesis (as it were), it was evening all afternoon – it was snowing the whole time. The "And it was going to snow" somehow throws one: it somehow questions the knowledge one has as to what has been happening so far. It is almost as though what Stevens clearly gives with the one hand – that it was snowing a lot, and had been for some time – is taken away with the other – that "it was going to snow". Precisely in emphasizing just how much of a wintery day this is/was – it's really going to snow, big time! – Stevens manages to half *undercut* the sense of same, too. One is left half-wondering whether it really has been snowing, even at all, after all . . .

And thirdly, a perhaps-half-silly but nevertheless I think unignorable question: if you are looking at a blackbird up in a tree, motionless, in persistent heavy snow that has been falling for some time, do you see very much at all? Do you see, at any rate, any *black*? Do you succeed, in such a situation, in looking at – or at least, in seeing – a blackbird?

Or consider the delicately conceptual eighth stanza:

> When the blackbird flew out of sight
> It marked the edge
> Of one of many circles.

Here, the blackbird, at the moment at which the poem focuses, is *ex hypothesi* not visible. There is no such thing as seeing the horizon of what one can see, neither at the 'far' edge of that horizon, 'beyond' which is in the unseen or invisible, nor at the 'near' edge of that horizon, 'beyond' (or 'before') which is the seer. Thus Wittgenstein's discussion of just this – in this instance, primarily of the latter – towards the end of the *T-LP*:

> 5.632 The subject does not belong to the world: rather, it is a limit of the world.
> 5.633 Where in the world is a metaphysical subject to be found? You will say that this is exactly like the case of the eye [Auge] and the visual field. But really you do not see the eye. And nothing in the visual field allows you to infer that it is seen by an eye.
> 5.6331 For the form of the visual field is surely not like this:

The diagram is crucial to our purposes here. It brings out *by contrast, by absurdity,* the sense in which we might usefully characterize the visual field as *without limit* (compare also here *T-LP* 6.4311). The horizon of vision is not like the limit of (say) a football field: it makes *no sense* to 'look across' the former, while the latter is *defined* by its visibility and measurability.

Similarly, the crucial guiding words for how to read Wittgenstein, and how to understand his talk of 'limits' from the Preface to that same book:

> [T]he aim of the book is to draw a limit to thought, or rather – not to thought, but to the expression of thoughts: for in order to draw a limit to thought, we should have to be able to think both sides of this limit (we should therefore have to be able to think what cannot be thought).

As Diamond remarks, of this, "He then draws the conclusion from those remarks that it will therefore only be in language that the limit can be drawn.

And what lies on the other side of the limit will simply be nonsense."[7] The circle that Stevens' blackbird marks is precisely a circle that cannot be drawn; or, perhaps better, as the blackbird 'draws' it does so in a way that is not visible. What is blackbird-like outside the circle is, for the 'observer', nothing. It *makes no sense* for one to hope to see this invisible. Stevens teaches here a lesson that Wittgenstein too teaches. One seems to see the blackbird flying out of sight, in one's mind's eye. But in this stanza, as in the others, it would be a complete mistake to try to force what one seems to see into being a real seeing; it would be a deep conceptual mistake indefinitely to try to will oneself to suspend the disbelief that one will still probably feel in the middle of this. For belief here, acquiescence in the image – the would-be stable imagination – seemingly generated, in this poem, leads one in just the wrong direction. The *point* of the thing is to *learn* from the *collapse* of many of one's efforts to obey the poet's implied instruction, "Try out these 13 'ways of looking' at a 'blackbird' for yourself."[8] In the case of the eighth stanza, the absurdity of the effort to capture in vision *or, by analogy, in thought of any kind* the limit, the 'far' horizon, is I would submit entirely of a piece with the method of Wittgenstein's work. For this 'blackbird' at the end – at the edge, at the 'limit' – of the mind, is the same delicate deliberate nonsense as the limit drawn by Wittgenstein in Fig. 1, above.

Thus Stevens opens up for us what "looking" can mean, and undermines the prejudice that looking need be visual – but *not* in service of a merely reactive counter-prejudice (the kind of prejudice that some post-modernists or deconstructionists[9] might assume or enjoy, for instance), that (say) looking can mean just anything one pleases, or that we must entirely dispense with or suppress visualizing. Rather, one has to be reminded of and to figure out, simultaneously, what "looking" actually does mean and can mean for one / for us. One can see that roughly *this* is the teaching of the poem, by considering the following question, a question I suggest is more or less implicit in the cumulative action of the poem as one reads to its end and then re-reads: is *any and every* sentence with the word "blackbird" featuring in it a vehicle for "looking" at a blackbird, in some suitably loose sense of the word "looking"? Surely not: for instance, a mere mention of the word "blackbird", as in the sentence, "Pronounce the word "blackbird"", hardly seems well described as involving or implicating a way of looking at a blackbird. Likewise, nonsense-sentences or ungrammatical sentences involving the word "blackbird". And it is in *approximately* these ways – though of course more subtly; that is how the poetry gets to work its magic – that I claim the word "blackbird" – and *thus* the word "looking" – typically appears, in this poem. I.e. The word is more *mentioned* than used, here; or, if you prefer, it is 'used' very roughly in the way words are 'used' in nonsense-poetry, but with a more enduring *appearance* of sense. You can of course (if you wish) insist that all the same such occurrences or mentions *are* uses of the word "blackbird" (and "looking"); fine, only notice the qualitative difference between such uses and other things we call "uses". (And now we start to notice or be reminded of something of importance about the use(s) of the word "use" . . .) I suggest that an important aspect of the poem is obscured if we fail to see that the word "blackbird" in Stevens' poem tends to veer for instance towards mention more than towards use, and that the language of the poem as a whole is *"idling"* as a car engine idles: it is not working language, it is not going anywhere (except perhaps on holiday). It shows us our language and our life with it mainly *by contrast*, via absurdities. It does not show us nor even necessarily point us towards any blackbird, real *or imaginary*.

2.1.4 Wittgenstein as Stevensian?

At the start of 2.12, I quoted a Wittgensteinian literary critic, putting broadly and specifically Wittgensteinian ideas to work, as he does throughout his book (by drawing for instance on Wittgenstein on aspect-perception, and on the use of language and on there being an other to this use, which Guetti sometimes calls "language on display" (again, compare "language on holiday")), in helping to place Stevens' poetry in a light that will 'illumine' it, not falsify or reduce it. But by this point a gradual shift has occurred. We are on the cusp of a new way of looking at – or using – Stevens. There have been a number of moments, in the above discussion of "Thirteen ways . . .", wherein it appeared less that I, a (Wittgensteinian) philosopher and (I hope) appreciator of literature, were seeking to render Stevens clearly by means of using Wittgenstein as a tool with which to place or illumine his words; and more: that I was actually finding the kind of insights and therapeutic manoeuvres that are Wittgenstein's teaching *in* Stevens' poetry.[10] And that is a key point of the present discussions: to see what we can learn by trying to read Stevens *as* a Wittgensteinian; as *making*, through his 'strong-grammared' poetry, a set of moves that invite the reader to learn almost exactly the kinds of thing about themselves and about their tendencies to mire themselves in misunderstandings that Wittgenstein invites his reader to learn, through his therapeutic writing, his philosophy of delusion *and its overcomings*.[11]

I want now to try to establish this perhaps surprising parallelism more firmly, by offering a reading of a little gem over-full of riches, Stevens' "Anecdote of the Jar":

> I placed a jar in Tennessee,
> And round it was, upon a hill.
> It made the slovenly wilderness
> Surround that hill.
>
> The wilderness rose up to it
> And sprawled around, no longer wild.
> The jar was round upon the ground
> And tall and of a port in air.

> It took dominion everywhere.
> The jar was gray and bare.
> It did not give of bird of bush,
> Like nothing else in Tennessee.

The first thing I want to say here, is that you cannot place a jar in Tennessee. You can place a jar on a shelf, or in a cupboard – or even on an elephant, with a bit of planning and assistance – but there is no such thing as placing a jar in Tennessee. The ludicrous coupling of the relatively small (the jar) with the very large (a state) is integral to the entire work of the poem. It is repeated in the second line, where it is again considered perfectly normal by this speaker to note the shape of the jar (round) cheek by jowl with where it was placed (on a *hill*) . . . There is no such thing as placing a jar in Tennessee; I rather think there is no such thing as placing it "upon a hill", either. One could place a jar at the summit of a hill, perhaps, but not simply "upon a hill", surely.

Actually, of course, the above claims are not correct. If one searches hard enough for a context, one will usually be able to find one: you could place a jar in Tennessee, if you were, for instance, standing on the state-line with Kentucky, and placed the jar one side rather than the other. But this hardly helps; for the context we have now dreamed up is surely not the one the poem asks for. No such particular – sense-giving – context is provided, and any such would, I submit, somewhat spoil the poem. For this poem surely asks us bluntly, precisely to place a jar in/on a vague place: on a hill in Tennessee as opposed to (say) in a cupboard, or in some other place in which we are accustomed to placing a jar.

We try to imagine placing a jar in Tennessee. We fail. We fail to find a context for this small–large contradiction that remains true to what the poem is evidently interested in. This of Stevens is, as Cavell (following Wittgenstein) puts it, a "speaking outside language-games". There is more that can be said than can be imagined, not *vice versa* as we so often suppose.[12] There is more that can be said than can even be dreamt of, on this philosophy.

And now something *else* interesting starts to happen, beyond even seeing Stevens as a roughly Wittgensteinian philosopher doing his own literary philosophizing. We start to see how Stevens' poetry, such as the striking opening of this poem, *might be able to help us get further with (understanding) Wittgenstein* (and with practising philosophy, after Wittgenstein) than we normally do. For isn't something like this what we ought to say of some of the most crucial – *imaginary* – scenarios in Wittgenstein's philosophy, too? Take Wittgenstein's rather famous (or infamous) 'wood-sellers', who have been ably dissected in recent years by my fellow 'New Wittgensteinians': Cavell, Conant, Crary and Cerbone.[13] These characters, the 'wood-sellers', seem to have a different logic from us, for they pay more for piles of wood that are spread out, and less when the wood is piled up. Indeed, they say there IS more wood, when it is spread out, even when they witness the spreading. But what Cavell *et al.* have submitted is that Wittgenstein wants us to see for ourselves that we will, if we keep on failing to establish a context of significant use for 'the wood-sellers" talk, if we continually fail to see/understand what game is being played here, eventually cease to regard a scenario as having successfully been sketched here at all. We may, for instance, withdraw the claim that 'the wood-sellers' are really doing the same thing as what we would call 'counting' (or 'pricing'). We will not be content to say that they have an arithmetic, only a different arithmetic, if that leaves us unhappily hovering between the claim that they have something which recognizably is an arithmetic, with a comprehensible logic to it, only one slightly different from our own, and the claim that they do not have what we would call an arithmetic or a logic at all.

In other words, we 'New Wittgensteinians' urge that Wittgenstein has deceived us into the truth here. He has made us confront an unclarity in the ways we want to use words such as "arithmetic" or "logic", through deceiving us into thinking that a coherent scenario has definitely been sketched, in sketching 'the wood-sellers'. Into thinking that the life of a tribe has surely been described here, and that if we cannot understand it/them, then so much the worse for us.

The use of the term "the wood-sellers" is arguably crucial to the deceit we tend to impose on ourselves here: this term instantly makes it seem as though a group or 'tribe' *has* been indexed. So 'they' *must* be describable, we think. But perhaps this 'they' *in the form that we want to describe them* (e.g. as *buying* and *selling*) are nothing but a fiction. Or rather: a complete fantasy, an in principle utterly unrealizable fiction, *a fiction of a fiction.*

Mightn't we now, having read the "Anecdote", put all this rather more snappily? These wood-sellers are no more a stable object of our description than the jar being placed in Tennessee. Our *desires* with regard to our words must and do give out: the mistake is to imagine that we can succeed in imagining successfully the 'scenarios' depicted here. Or again: we *merely* imagine that we can imagine them. Or again: we may well withdraw the use of the word "scenario" or even of "description", on reflection. (Or again, even: a humanly attainable supreme fiction would be something that utterly appears to be a fiction, and yet that can facilitate our learning that it is 'only' a fiction of a fiction; and thus can help us to be clearer than ever about the real world: to see it aright (containing) fictions and all.)

The power of this case from Stevens is stronger perhaps than the power of some of "Thirteen Ways . . .": because here we never 'merely' make a point about what can be intelligibly visualized. Here, we are at the coal-face of what makes sense (or otherwise). Robert Frost talked of "the *sound* of sense" as integral to poetry: I believe he was right. But how much more crucial, and not only but perhaps especially in great Modernism, the sound(s) of nonsense. This is what remains, this is what endures even once one has truly learnt from poems such as these of Stevens.

Back now to the detail of the "Anecdote". I want to focus for a moment on these lines:

> The jar was round upon the ground
> And tall and of a port in air.
>
> It took dominion everywhere.
> The jar was gray and bare.

Again, we note the marvellously peculiar, almost schizy emphasis on the dimension, here indeed the alleged largeness (we learn that the jar was "tall" . . . Compared to the hill? Or compared to Tennessee's great mountain ranges, perhaps?!) of the jar. Indeed, it takes "dominion". In its simplicity, in its sparseness, in presumably its presence as a cultural/human icon, it "took dominion *everywhere*". The way the next line is sounded is crucial here: "The jar was gray and bare" is simple, brutal and short. It is interesting how much more abrupt the ending of this line reads as being than does the last line of the first stanza. That line, just four syllables following a line of nine syllables, seems to fit fine; "The jar was gray and bare" has six syllables, following the previous line's nine, but it is somehow a far blunter and more abrupt 'early finish'. What I want to suggest here is that, at this point especially, the jar, the poem, is iconic of *language's* taking dominion over nature, but not just the language 'of everyday'. Also, or indeed *rather*, the 'iconic' language that is not language – the language that is not in use – of poetry. *This*, as witness the "Anecdote of the Jar",[14] is language's second nature – its culture. Not its nature, its natural everyday meaningful consequences,[15] its existence as part of a numberless set of doings, but its culture, of 'grammatical effects': the effects that language has on us in virtue not of purely personal psychological associations, but in virtue of the various (more, or less) intersubjectively sharable modes in which (good) literature, especially poetry, works on one: through sounded repetition, through 'the *sound* of sense', through 'the sound of *nonsense*', and so on and so forth.[16]

The jar abruptly, absurdly, masters nature. The language does. Its dominion, the dominion of sparse words, in their placement in the poem, such as "The jar was gray and bare", is far stronger than the dominion of prose, for it runs on whether or not the wilderness comes to an end somewhere. The wild alienness of poetry everywhere remains strange.

I have outlined a suggestion, then: that Stevens encourages us to form a kind of belief about what we can succeed in imagining, and then facilitates our learning from the collapse of that belief under its own weight. I believe that Stevens exposes more clearly to view actual life, ordinary language and life, through exposing to us, marvellously, language as it goes on holiday. Stevens *discloses* the sensical *through 'violating' the limits of language*.[17] But we needn't think he thereby succeeds in violating linguistic rules or the limits of language, nor in saying the unsayable, nor need we think any other such *nonsequiturs*. Rather, what lies on the other side of the limit is simply nonsense. Stevens makes that nonsense fun, and a thing of beauty, as thus he midwifes our coming to find and feel where the 'limit' is. He allows us to bump our heads up against it with pleasure, and with a growing self-awareness.

The fun[18] and the glorious absurdity or almost schizoid bizarreness in Wittgenstein's discussion is less often appreciated. This again inclines me to think that Stevens can not only do Wittgensteinian philosophy, but also can help to render perspicuous – 'visible' – what Wittgensteinian philosophy *is*. Compare the opening section of *PI*:

> [T]hink of the following use of language: I send someone shopping. I give him a slip marked 'five red apples'. He takes the slip to the shopkeeper, who opens the drawer marked 'apples'; then he looks up the word 'red' in a table and finds a colour sample opposite it; then he says the series of cardinal numbers – I assume he knows them by heart – up to the word 'five' and for each number he takes an apple of the same colour as the sample out of the drawer – It is in this and similar ways that one operates with words.

Wittgenstein's blunt apparent insistence at the end here has silenced most Wittgensteinians (though not Cavell, and his 'school', including under this heading for present purposes Stephen Mulhall and David Stern, on whose work I loosely draw, here). Most 'Wittgensteinians' tend to meekly swallow that this is how language is: that this is a shop in which a practical – paradigmatic – use of language is shown us. But surely a more *reasonable* response, on re-reading, is to be struck by the unreasonable character of Wittgenstein's "It is in this way . . .", and in particular by the frankly bizarre character of this 'grocer's shop'. A moment's reflection probably suffices to show that none of us in our adult lives has seen or heard of a shop where anything remotely like this happened/happens. This is . . . a *parody* of a shop. We should instantly suspect that it yields a parody of how language works. And this is what we find. Language as it is embodied in this 'example' is not a paradigm of how Wittgenstein thinks language actually works; it is a parody of how language works according to the very picture of language that Wittgenstein is wishing to undermine in us. When one overcomes that picture *and* the parody (not: *embraces* the latter, as for instance some behaviourism does), then one can start to see language aright. One can return to the beginning of all one's philosophical journeyings, and know the place – know one's way about – for the first time.

There is then a hidden strangeness in the founding example/scenario of Wittgenstein's masterpiece. The same is true, I would submit, of his other most famous such scenarios: crucially, in his 'builders' (in section 2ff. of the *Investigations*: these builders have a 'language' that consists of just four words) and in the 'wood-sellers' (mentioned above, who pay more for wood when it is spread out on the ground than when it is piled up), among others. We learn about us, we get reminded of features of our lives with language so obvious that usually we cannot *see* them, cannot bring them into focus, not just, and indeed not best, through the plain focus on ordinary, everyday, practical examples that is the staple of 'Ordinary Language Philosophy' and allegedly of Wittgenstein, but through the collapse on us of 'imaginary' fantasy 'examples', *which at first we were much attracted/tempted by*. Wittgenstein 'exposes' or discloses ordinary language and life most tellingly when he exposes language as it is when he sends it covertly on holiday, as it passes beyond this 'horizon' that is not visible, speakable, or thinkable, the ultimate limit that limits us from nothing that we actually want, and beyond which there are *only* the glorious seductive nonsenses Stevens calls "The Creations of Sound". Creations which try their best, properly, to resist our misfiring attempts to domesticate them.

Stevens invites us to *look* 'at a blackbird' in the ways he proposes; and it seems so much as if visual looking is possible here! And then we gradually come . . . to see that it is mostly not, and that in fact we may even want to give up the claim that *any* kind of looking is. He invites us to watch him or someone placing a jar "in Tennessee", and then gradually to come to give up the absurd invitations that are the bread and butter of this 'jar'. Wittgenstein invites us to look at the scenarios, the activities he proposes (the 'grocer's shop', the 'builders', the 'wood-sellers' etc.) as if they were real, as if they were languages that we could speak, or at least understand, and then we gradually come to see that they are not – to be precise, that they are not *what we wanted them to be*. And that is philosophy, after Wittgenstein: returning to your concepts, in and with which you live, and knowing them for the first time. But the best route to where you are right now lies for Wittgenstein, as for Stevens, via the nothing that is the delusions of sense we entertain when we appear to be saying or 'showing' what allegedly lies beyond the limits of thought or language.

Many have perhaps missed many of the willing – willed – absurdities of Stevens' texts. But how many more, including the very philosophers and scholars who have claimed to be Wittgenstein's truest commentators or heirs, have missed almost entirely the absurdist atmosphere that permeates so much of Wittgenstein's best work! So much of Wittgenstein's writing, especially in the last 15 years of his life, crucially involves scenarios that are subtly (or in some cases even fairly obviously) quite 'mad'. This is an absolutely vital aspect of his method. Dusty Wittgenstein scholarship has occluded or domesticated this 'madness' – to its and our great cost. Wittgenstein has come to seem more assimilable with the philosophical tradition than he actually is: his 'arguments' have been brought to bear against those of more traditional philosophic voices – and have (rightly) been found wanting. One can only understand Wittgenstein's real point – he can only *win* – if his texts are allowed to 'self-deconstruct' on one, and if this is understood to be *the point* of them, not an argument against them!

When one applies Wittgenstein to poetry, and then turns back to understand Wittgenstein after the fashion of that poetry, then one is in a good position to understand all this.

If one approaches the *Investigations* then not from Frege or Russell but from certain poets, such as Stevens, one may be in a better mood or condition to see what Wittgenstein is actually up to. Rather than shoehorning Wittgenstein into the constraints of analytic philosophy, we should perhaps learn to see his kinship with (for instance) Stevens' educative poetry of the absurd. Less of a tired emphasis on logic, more of a journey via 'illogic' – via jars in Tennessee and blackbirds seen at the point of flying out of sight – will I think help us to understand the true, therapeutic nature of Wittgenstein's philosophy of logic – *throughout* his career. Wittgenstein believes that one has to go by the way of delusion, if one wants to arrive at truth. Stevens agrees, unlike Russell, and (on balance) unlike Frege.[19]

Simon Critchley, in his intriguing recent book *Things Merely Are: Philosophy in the Poetry of Wallace Stevens*,[20] rightly paints Stevens as transcending/overcoming Kantianism. Wittgenstein's philosophy can helpfully be seen as above all doing precisely the same.[21] Kant sought to show the limits of knowledge and reason, via his effort to set out the transcendental conditions of possibility for these things. To sum up what I have argued in this Part thus far: Stevens, as Wittgenstein(-ian), takes us to 'the other side' of language, 'beyond the limit'. And finds the 'place' then reached to contain not ineffable truths, nor thoughts that can't be uttered, nor an indescribable formless realm, nor even visions or acts of imagination, but simply: the words, the sounds, the fabulous, sensuous, delicious, sometimes hysterical, sometimes weird or mad or unpleasant delusions of sense that they produce, that they *are the creations of*,[22] together with our tendencies to over-read these. "Blackbird" and "Jar" are in the end not about imagining nor looking – they are ('about') language. The language, language 'out of use', language which iconically 'represents' only itself, and which seemingly 'gestures at' a nothing that presents itself as a something about which nothing can be said . . . language which lacks transparency and which thus, marvellously, *takes dominion.* Language's possible aspect(s) of non-transparency is wonderfully displayed by Stevens, much as it is 'displayed' and in play in the literary presentations – the 'imaginary scenarios' etc. – that are so important in Wittgenstein, and furthermore is explicitly discussed by him at scattered points, as a kind of necessary complement to what seems to be his 'philosophy of the ordinary', *throughout* his later writing, for instance at quite a number of points in Part II of the *Investigations*. That is what is presented to us by Stevens, as I read him. Language, and its fantasized other, "the signified" (as opposed to its real other and confrère: reality). Not, we might say, a blackbird(s); nor even a jar.

I have focused here on a few of Stevens' *early* poems, which I believe to be generally his best *poems*. But later Stevens also has real genius, and has I suspect just as deep a philosophical interest for his readers. Early Stevens, to generalize very crudely, tends to focus our attention most helpfully and concentratedly on the nature of our *language*, of our mindedness, and on the world as involving our mindedness. Later Stevens tends to focus our attention most helpfully on the nature of the *world*, including the world thought of as independent of our thought.[23] These are two slightly differing emphases, two sides of the same coin. Things merely are, as Critchley points out that the later Stevens 'says'. But among the things that ('merely') are, as (early) Stevens 'says', are poems and imaginations, words and their speakers, and much much more. We and our pasts and all our works – including those works that rail against mere being, against things as they are, those works that do not leave everything as it is – are real, and part of what Stevens calls "absolute fact". Thus Stevens' corpus *overcomes* the apparent tension between "where there is no imagination, there no thing may be", and "things merely are [whether we imagine them or no]", and Stevens need not be seen, as Critchley sees him,[24] as torn between these two aspects.

I have pointed up above how Stevens shows us our language – just as Simon Critchley points up how Stevens shows us the world. There is a therapeutic aspect to both (interrelated) tasks, as Critchley rightly points out.[25] But what is most therapeutic of all is seeing how the two tasks are *entirely complementary.*[26]

We could never not be nature, even though – no; in fact, *because* – nature is not there *for us.* (This is part of what one sees when one 'sees' "Jar" or a jar or "Blackbird" or a blackbird clearly.[27]) So Stevens' poetry does not ultimately fail, as Critchley claims it does.[28] It succeeds, as Wittgenstein succeeds, *in the only way one can*: intermittently (even: rarely). For non-intermittent – final – success in attaining clarity would mean and be: no more poetry. Such a 'success' would be (let us put it mildly) in many ways regrettable: it would mean that we no longer had a recognizably human life. The psychological, cultural, linguistic roots of the need to philosophize and poetize (to *write*) are so deep and widespread that we know not what it would be, in fact, to be entirely beyond them. (Except that it would not be anything like the human.)

I have not attempted here anything remotely resembling a complete reading of the two (early) poems of Stevens that I have concentrated on, still less to extend such a reading or such a treatment further into his oeuvre (though I believe that *many* more of Stevens' poems would respond well to such a treatment: including such fine poems as "Fabliau of Florida", "The Snowman", "Academic Discourse at Havana" and indeed "The Man with the Blue Guitar", not to mention most of those others which Guetti discusses in some detail in his book). I have rather attempted to display some aspects of these two poems which are I think important, and even revelatory of a number of ways in which philosophy and literature can interact and mutually inflect: for the conclusion to this consideration of 'Wittgensteinian poetry' is a perhaps triply surprising one. On the one hand, we can be helped to read Stevens through understanding and following a Wittgensteinian 'philosophy of language'. (This much, James Guetti I think already proved, over a decade ago.) On the other hand, when we thus read Stevens, at deep and crucial moments *we find him following a roughly Wittgensteinian line in the substance or 'content' of his poetry.* This is the meaning of the present section's title. But it is crucial not to read this awrong: we violate Guetti's methodological injunctions and critical discoveries/aspect-revelations, if we take Stevens to be *expressing* a Wittgensteinian philosophy. Rather, his poems remain strange.[29] They do not get successfully *translated* or paraphrased. Again: they do philosophical work *of their own*; this is poetry as philosophy, but poetry that *remains* poetry, all the same.[30] And so then, on the third hand: this sheds some light on Wittgenstein's own writing. The 'action' of Stevens' poetry, as its invitations to the reader dissolve upon that reader, makes more strikingly perspicuous what has eluded many readers of Wittgenstein: much the same method, of inviting the reader to adopt a perspective or an idea, and then seeing whether it really does/yields what s/he wants from it, or whether rather it collapses on one. And then of seeing what one can learn from that.

And, if my writing here has succeeded, these three hands will not seem separated from one another. A right hand and a left hand are one. A right hand and a left hand and a third hand are one . . .

Section IX of Stevens' "Notes toward a Supreme Fiction" opens as follows:

> The poem goes from the poet's gibberish to
> The gibberish of the vulgate and back again.
> Does it move to and fro or is it of both
>
> At once? Is it a luminous flittering
> Or the concentration of a cloudy day?

A kind of answer occurs, a few lines later: "It is the gibberish of the vulgate that [the poet] *seeks*" (my emphasis).

Wittgenstein's philosophy is an attempt at 'returning' us, via a necessarily roundabout route (via nonsense, gibberish that pretends to be something different), to ourselves, to our 'ordinary' language, to an unencumbered awareness of what we really want to mean and what we can mean. Wittgenstein returns language, we might say, to itself. Stevens' least acknowledged achievement, or at least this is what he seeks to achieve, then, is perhaps his rendering the kinds of nonsenses that are our ordinary temptation very vividly perspicuous to us, via bizarreness, that appear not to be so, such as I have exposed in "Blackbird" and "Jar". And this, I argue, is a pre-eminently Wittgensteinian endeavour.

So, these 'three things' *I* hope to have rendered more perspicuous[31]: (1) a Wittgensteinian orientation towards the reading of Stevens; (2) a reading of Stevens thus generated which displays Stevens as Wittgensteinian, as furthering the kinds of therapeutic tools to understanding that Wittgenstein majors in; *and* (finally) (3) a Stevensian orientation towards the reading of Wittgenstein. Not forgetting Wittgenstein's own remark that philosophy should properly be written as a kind of poetry.[32]

2.1.5 'Modernist' Performative Literature: Philosophy, Poetry, Prose

In the last section I showed that Stevens' poetry resists our attempts to 'decode' it, or assimilate it into our everyday way of speaking. There is no 'outside' to the strong grammar of Stevens' poetry, for what seem to be visual images in his poem do not turn out to be objects we can perceive (unless we wilfully alter the language of his poetry), nor do they *refer* to anything outside the poem. The progression of "Thirteen Ways of Looking at a Blackbird" is not *progression* in the sense of amounting to anything substantial or genuinely semantical. Its movement is instead governed by a deliberate *semblance* of sense, by connotation and the sonorous qualities of language – it is not engaged in the process of building a meaningful description, one that we can locate in a context outside of, or beyond the text. In this sense I suggested it possesses a 'strong grammar': a mode of hanging together which undercuts interpretations even as it seems to invite, and indeed, suggest them. It creates a '*sense*' of having or partaking of (a) grammar; but ultimately nothing more. The sensation that we have of speaking a language out of the ordinary, a new language, of speaking beyond the 'limits' of language, the sense that we could set ourselves apart from and above any worldly context, is consistently encouraged – and undermined. It operates as a temptation which the poetry's therapy is: to overcome. The poetry encourages one's tendency to speak nonsense as if it were sense: and resolutely (and *pleasurably*) returns us to sense, thereby.

When we read Stevens' poetry we find ourselves absorbed in something which seems to be a 'world'. However when we leave the poem and reflect upon our 'experience' we find that it produces nothing that can be adequately expressed in propositional terms. Thus, there is no *context* in our ordinary way of doing and speaking which could serve to provide the key for the interpretation of Stevens' poetry. Ultimately, we find ourselves incrementally deposited back into our everyday mode of being, with a sense of *contrast* between the way in which we use language as a mode of communication, and the way in which the poem (successfully) *does not succeed in informing us of anything*. The concentrated character of poetic 'nonsense' – poetry, as the realm *par excellence* of grammatical effects – results often in our being aware of our interpretations (or paraphrases) as tending towards falsification from the outset. There are, however, many dimensions of our practices (particularly in philosophy) where grammatical effects are more insidious, and masquerade more imperceptibly as working language.[33] As argued in 2.14, above: through the concentrated form of poetry, Stevens *discloses* the sensical *through 'violating' the limits of language*.[34] He does not suggest that there is *meaning* to be found in the poem which has somehow transcended the 'boundaries' of context. To suggest that such poetry is in fact a gesture at an ineffable 'beyond', or achieves some species of fantasized God's-eye view, is very problematic, for reasons suggested earlier. For what could it mean to approximate something which is in principle unsayable? Indeed, as the previous Part showed, there is arguably nothing that it *could* be to express the 'content' of "Thirteen Ways of Looking at a Blackbird".

Have I then arrived at a wholly negative conclusion? In a qualified sense, yes. We can regard the 'moral' of Wallace Stevens' poetry as possessing a 'negative' purpose – we are shown something about our way of speaking and doing *by way of contrast*. Insofar as Stevens' ways of 'looking' eventually (knowingly) 'self-deconstruct' we can see a strong parallel with Wittgenstein's own methods. The statements which may *appear* to be substantial are in fact transitional, a way of speaking for the moment that shows the failure of attempts to articulate the 'ineffable'. As such I may make similar remarks about Stevens as I suggested in response to positivist or ineffabilist readings of Wittgenstein in Part 1. Stevens is often considered to be a 'philosophical' poet – if this is the case then it is a species of philosophy which, austerely, operates in *not* putting forward any positive vision. (Playing with – *tempting* readers with – such a positive vision is not in the sense I mean it *putting forward* one.) If both Stevens and Wittgenstein's remarks serve their purpose we happily then 'give them up', without attempting to codify them in interpretation. But their serving their purpose is liable to last a long time, and to be repeatedly needed. I am not planning to throw away my editions of *Collected Poems, The Palm at the End of the Mind, Tractatus Logico-Philosophicus* or *Philosophical Investigations* any time soon . . .

In drawing a parallel between Stevens and Wittgenstein I have thrown into relief also the literary and *performative* character of Wittgenstein's work. The fact that Wittgenstein's work consistently resists expression in propositional terms allies him in a way more with the literary tradition than the philosophical, for we are more accustomed to speak of literature, rather than philosophy in these terms. And Wittgenstein, like Stevens, proceeds a great deal through the creative and pedagogic use of humour.

I have submitted that, in the final analysis, both Stevens' and Wittgenstein's work show that there is nothing of intellectual substance that would count as speaking 'beyond the limits' of language. What then is the appeal of such poetry? Am I not, in making this claim, dismissing its value and its appeal? Once again it must be stressed here that I am not in the least using 'nonsense' as a derisory, reductive term. (Do not for heaven's sake be afraid of wanting to read nonsense. But you must pay close attention to that nonsense . . .) Rather I venture to suggest that the temptation to look 'beyond' language is, at root, not an *intellectual* problem – at any rate if we mean by 'intellectual problem' one demanding resolution by means of the production of a theory (or even dissolution by means of a merely worded therapy).[35] The sensation of being 'confined' by the parochiality of language, without 'access' to a single explanatory principle, is not a genuine motivation for a theoretic picture. Instead, I venture to suggest that the impulse to speak beyond language should rather be honestly admitted as a matter of *mood*, or, as Cavell suggests, a mood of rebellion against the human condition or, more broadly, against the condition of actually being, existing, *at all.* This is something we see registered in a comparable form in schizophreniform conditions which I go on to discuss below. The schizophrenic's language is deeply strange, disconcerting and seemingly in possession at times of a comparable poetic quality. The utterances of the schizophrenic show the way in which the sensation of failing to mean, and being 'at odds' with language is experienced and 'lived'.

As the analysis of Stevens above shows, the blurring of grammatical effect and meaningful language is disorientating, resulting in a *mood* of detachment, which permeates not only Stevens' work, but much modernist literature in general. As Louis Sass points out, modernist literature foregrounds the sensation of failing to mean, which is at base a central motivation behind the impulse, the compulsive desire and felt need, to philosophize. Sass' project in *Madness and Modernism* is to offer a new description of schizophrenia, through a comparison with philosophical scepticism and modernist literature. Both the schizophrenic and the sceptic regard the relationship between word and world as problematic. For both there is a perceived gap between what we *can* say about the world and what we *wish* to say about the world. Solipsism, as the 'epiphany' or telos of scepticism, is demonstrative of a desire to speak beyond the 'limits' of language – again, as if we could set ourselves apart from and above any worldly context. The solipsist is confused by language, perceiving it 'inadequate' for his purposes, and thus finds himself under felt pressure to change it. Whilst the philosophical sceptic characterizes this as a problem of intellection alone, the schizophrenic (according to Sass) experiences this as of direct relevance for how one is to live in an everyday context – usually with quite disastrous consequences.

In order to examine the confluence between certain pathological states and scepticism, Part 2 now turns to examine one of the great writings on severe mental affliction: William Faulkner's *The Sound and the Fury*. Faulkner's first narrator, Benjy, can be regarded as exemplifying solipsistic tendencies, insofar as his narrative appears to offer us a dramatisation of a way in which we can imagine losing the past, in the following particular sense: the past for Benjy is it seems not *past*; it is not anything other than present memory. There is then perhaps an illuminating at-least-partial analogy here to solipsism of the present moment. Benjy's past is it seems accurately told (conceptually impossibly (at least, given the truth of what we are told is his condition[36]), and absurdly eidetically accurately, like Quentin's) in its details at least. Not necessarily in the sequence of events, but rather *each memory stands as sufficient on its own*, and in that way his narrative is like shuffled scenes from a film. But none of this adds up to actually having a *past*, and thus being able to tell a true *tale* of it; for there is no past when there is no clear distinction between past and present, between memory and lived present reality.

Using Benjy's narrative as a starting-point, I will argue that the great writings on and of severe mental affliction[37] present us with something deeply enigmatic. They have, as I have remarked of Wallace Stevens' poetry, a 'strong grammar', for when we look at these works they have a way of seemingly making sense, *which is somehow deeply different from our sense*. As such they seem to promise access to the phenomenology of a radically different way of conceiving the world, one which is divorced from practice and context. My aim here is, however, to show that there simply may be 'places' where our understanding – phenomenological understanding, understanding of 'what it is like' – gives out, and not because it is (or we are) '*merely* human', all too human. It is my contention that there is no such thing as 'capturing' some 'mental illnesses' etc. by intellection alone, or (more radically) even perhaps at all. In a similar vein to my suggestions on Stevens' poetry, the best understanding one can have of such states of derangement is purely negative (in a sense at least as strong as that involved in "negative theology", wherein 'God' is only defined by what it is not). It is for instance, I will suggest, a mythological 'mistake' to think that in the creation of Benjy's narrative, Faulkner provides us with the tools for giving an unpuzzling rendition of what had perhaps appeared to be 'another country', inaccessible to us. Rather, Faulkner's 'representation' is and remains enigmatic. To present an enigma as if it is another country, one beyond 'the bounds of reason' which we can nevertheless peek at or sidle up to *or eventually represent in plain unpuzzling terms*, is something different, and something usually very unwise. What we are left with, when we understand Benjy's world as 'outside of time' or as a species of solipsism, is at best a transliteration of psychopathology into . . . nothingness, into the relentless failure to mean that is 'solipsism' and such-like. To use Benjy's words: it is a constant 'trying to say'. Instead, I shall argue that the great writings on mental affliction, including Faulkner's *Sound and the Fury*, achieve their ends by a novel *kind* of 'hermeneutical' effort that radically subverts our prior notions of what 'understanding' must involve. As I suggested in Part 1 of the book: we must exercise subtlety in our understanding of terms such as *meaning* and *understanding*, and be cognizant of the instances in which we are using these terms in a way which radically departs from their normal usage. If we *do* want to use these words in a different sense, we must be aware of both the gains and losses that are made when we do this. Part of my analysis seeks to render explicit the qualitative difference between such 'uses' and other things we are wont to call 'uses' in our everyday mode of speaking.

I begin with a close reading of Benjy's narrative in *The Sound and the Fury*, examining the way in which it *does not refer to anything outside of its own linguistic confines*. It does not *represent*, not even a mind. As the title of the book can perhaps be read literally as implying, it is strictly speaking 'sound and fury, signifying nothing'. Thus the reading I offer here serves to highlight the problems inherent in conceiving this narrative as a description of a logically 'alien' state.

This is a problem which can be identified in the work of Louis Sass, for whom (as already indicated) schizophrenia, and related schizophreniform conditions, can be characterized as a species of 'lived scepticism'. Whilst acknowledging the humane quality and interpretive novelty of his effort, I suggest that it is ultimately[38] misguided to conceive of scepticism as a position that one could somehow 'inhabit', for as suggested in Part 1, the very idea of solipsism is a *delusion* of sense. We may think we understand it; we may think we have a clear idea of what it means to think that 'only I exist'. Wittgenstein's great achievement, in wonderful 'therapeutic' detail in his later work, was to show that we don't have a clear understanding of this; or rather, to show that there is no 'it' here. As such, 'it' cannot be straightforwardly used as an allegory for schizophrenic experience. In offering a 'negative' account of the way in which such texts may shed light upon severe mental affliction, it is important to reiterate that I am *not* suggesting such literary presentations to be redundant. Far, far from it. As Sass implies, there is something that we can do to further our understanding of what the temptation towards solipsism can mean, humanly: we can mimic going round the houses and up the ladder and hovering in mid-air with the would-be solipsist, with the person tempted by solipsism. But – that is all. Thus my analysis explores what I take to be the merits of 'creative mimicry'. The great writings on severe mental affliction invite us to engage in the mood of strangeness that pervades Benjy's narrative (and also parts of Quentin's). In doing so, we are able to get a sense of what it is *like* to experience language as inadequate, and the *sensation* that the world might be inflected through the self. This, however, is very different from suggesting that such texts allow us to experience something like 'solipsism'. Insofar as we can 'participate' in the world of characters like Benjy, we might risk saying that such literary presentations draw their strength from an evocation of a comparable *mood* – wherein the world comes to be experienced as strange and thematized, or to use Heideggerian terminology, as present-at-hand rather than ready-to-hand.[39]

2.2 'Wittgensteinian' Prose

2.2.1 The 'Strong Grammar' of Faulkner's *The Sound and the Fury*

With reference to Wallace Stevens, I suggested that we should *listen*, rather than heedlessly wandering into sensicalizing interpretation, in our approach to poetic language. Similarly, let us begin our analysis with Faulkner's words, reading closely and cautiously in order to avoid what Guetti terms the 'seeing-knowing' motive.[40]

Here then is the opening passage of Benjy's narrative, the remarkable opening of *The Sound and the Fury*: "Through the fence, between the curling flower spaces, I could see them hitting. // . . . They were hitting little, across the pasture. I went back along the fence to where the flag was. It flapped on the bright grass and the trees."[41]

We are presented here, with something that appears to be a *description*, but that is most enigmatic. In what sense is this a *description*? What the reader may want to suggest is that we are given a visual depiction, or description, of 'seeing'. Indeed, there are a number of things we could point to which would seem to render this suggestion plausible. For instance, the narrator appears to be observing through the fence, as a scene unfolds before him on the pasture. However, in what sense are we really *seeing* here? Take, for example, the particularly difficult phrase "between the curling flower spaces". In what sense are we being given something here that we are able to visualize? The reader might respond that there could be flower-shaped spaces through which the narrator is peering. Or they might suggest that there are spaces between the flowers and plants which cover the fence, and it is *this* through which the narrator is

peering. However, it is evident that we have had to do a great deal of man-
oeuvring – of manipulating – before we are able to characterize this in a satis-
factorily visual sense, or one which would justify our original sense of
something 'being pictured'. And our paraphrase seems still to fall short of the
mark – because this is *not* what the passage *says*. Instead, we are being asked to
visualize negative space not through but *between* (!) which the narrator is
seeing them . . . 'hitting'; yet there is as yet, I submit, nothing that it *could* be
for us to picture this. "To hit" is not an intransitive verb. And "between the
curling flower spaces" at first seems a wonderful evocation of direct visual
reality, but on reflection, as just suggested, it is full of 'false friends'.

It seems then, that the simplicity with which we initially accepted this as a
visual description belied its difficulty. We are reminded of the moral which we
drew from Stevens' "Thirteen Ways of Looking at a Blackbird", i.e. that some
of the ways of looking that appear to be natural to us, we in fact only *imagine*
that we can succeed in realizing. (It is significant that in both cases what we are
apparently presented with is ways of looking, or of seeing. These are the great
temptation of the reader of literature – imagined *scenes*. The greatest of
Modern writers, I think, get us to question the alleged power of our imaginations, and the allegedly centrally visual quality of 'vivid' (a telling choice of
metaphor) literary language – they get us to question this, precisely by at first
encouraging us to feel as if we easily inhabit it. In this manner, their method
is analogous to that of Wittgenstein's *TL-P*, on a resolute reading of that work.)
We merely imagine that we can successfully *image* or *visualize* what "between
the curling flower spaces" could mean.[42] Furthermore, *what* we imagine that
we can thus image is itself nonsensical: it cannot be put into prose without
falsifying it, and its 'poetical' presentation remains forever strange to us.
Benjy's own 7 April 1928: the enigma of a day.

We just don't know what it would be – it doesn't as yet *mean* anything, for us
– to know what 'curling flower spaces' actually means. We assume that what we
are being given is something which can be cashed-out in meaningful terms,
when in fact we are offered something which does not yield *a description*.

The remarks I have made here upon the first paragraph of the novel might
serve as a kind of epigraph for the entirety of Benjy's narrative, for we assume
that we make sense of Benjy's narrative by extension of something (a) that we
are *able to picture* or (b) that we already know to be true of ourselves (or at least,
ourselves as we have (allegedly) occasionally been or as we were when we were
younger).

Let us reflect too on another deeply paradoxical marvel of Faulkner's enterprise. We are seemingly given from the inside the life – the mind – of an
'idiot'. Specifically, of someone who is free of time, or trapped in the past,
depending on your preference.[43] And yet, Faulkner gives us a *tale*, told by this
'idiot'. A narrative, a story, a micro-history . . . The tale is told, as tales are, in
the past tense (as despite some appearances, especially in Jason's narrative, all
the rest of the novel is, too). To make clear that this is so, consider again a
miraculous string of sentences from the narrative's opening page: "They were

hitting little, across the pasture. I went back along the fence to where the flag was. It flapped on the bright grass and the trees." Never mind for now that there is no such thing as "hitting little", that a flag cannot flap *on* grass, and so forth. What *is* clear is that this is something that happened in the past. We have past continuous, and we have the perfect tense. Faulkner doesn't write: "They are hitting little, across the pasture. I go now along the fence . . ." This is a story told, as per normal, in the past tense . . . By someone with no sense of the past![44]

Finally, consider an intriguing easily missed feature of the punctuation of speech in Benjy's narrative, a feature strikingly absent from the more standardly punctuated speech in Quentin's and Jason's narratives (excepting those reminiscence speech portions of '2 June 1910' that lack any standard punctuation at *all*): when we are given direct speech in Benjy's narrative, it is written like this (e.g.):

> "It wasn't anything." Quentin said. . . .
> "Oh." Father said.
> [Etc.]

There are full stops placed after what is said. Perhaps this is to remind us that Benjy doesn't understand sentences semantically or syntactically. As it were: there are some words spoken. All Benjy knows of their sense is: Father said [something]. I.e. Nothing. Quentin said something. Then Father said something.[45]

But this of course should bring home to us what ought already to have been present to us: that it is at one level entirely unclear what it can mean to say that '7 April 1928' is Benjy's narrative. Because the large portion of it that consists of direct speech is necessarily in a strong sense semantically closed (off) to him. The portions 'from the past' that are there in indirect speech are even more mysterious: for, as philosophers have long emphasized, indirect speech already directly implies understanding. If you say, "He said that the party is over and so we should go now," you have to understand what he said. So what one earth are we to make of this, for instance, the first italicized segment ('from the past') in Benjy's narrative, prompted, Proust-style, by something happening now (getting caught on the nail in the fence) bringing back startlingly strongly a memory: *"Caddy uncaught me and we crawled through. Uncle Maury said to not let anybody see us, so we better stoop over, Caddy said. Stoop over, Benjy. Like this, see. We stooped over and crossed the garden . . ."*[46]

Well, there are, I have suggested, a number of seemingly intuitive ways to interpret Benjy's narrative. Firstly, we might suggest that in Benjy's narrative we are given the experience of a young child – the slightly solipsistic, omnipotent way in which the child experiences the world as inseparable from, and in accordance with their own experiences: "Caddy held me and I could hear us all, and the darkness, and something I could smell . . . Then the dark began to go in smooth, bright shapes, like it always does, even when Caddy says that

I have been asleep."[47] Benjy experiences everything in the immediate present. Like an infant, he is unable to appreciate that his needs will be met at a later point in time. Therefore, every desire is experienced as urgent and pressing, resulting in his intense frustration. In characterizing Benjy as a child, we imply that he is psychologically identifiable – that we know Benjy through an extension of what we *already know* to be true of children. In other words, we attribute the meaning of the text to a pre-existing understanding or context. In this sense, the reader feels that Benjy gives us a greater insight into what it is *like* to be a child – though at the cost of that being an insight that we already had (i.e. this way of taking the novel *prevents* it from being able to give us anything really new). As I suggested above, the reader might be inclined to say something along these lines: Benjy is *outside* of our normal experience of the world, in which we experience things as logically ordered (and by this I mean governed by cause and effect and the rest of the Kantian set-up). In his language something is exemplified in a more concentrated sense than it is in the real world. We feel that now we *have* a way for describing 'better' that real world. In order to show why this conception of the workings of the text is inadequate, I wish to expound a literary critic – James Guetti (1993) – putting Wittgenstein to work, in thinking about the work of William Faulkner. At this point I will quote extensively from Guetti's comments on Benjy:

> I want to take a case . . . of recognizing a text as "another language" . . . in which it may seem self-evident that a way of speaking is . . . "psychologically identifiable", and therefore apparently controlled by its connections with a reader's own intelligible vocabularies from beyond the text, when in fact as a language it takes much more dominion than that. The best single example I can give of this linguistic condition is from Faulkner's *The Sound and the Fury*, Benjy's narrative:
>
> > . . . I went out the door and I couldn't hear them, and I went down to the gate, where the girls passed with their booksatchels. They looked at me, walking fast, with their heads turned. I tried to say, but they went on, and I went along the fence, trying to say, and they went faster. Then they were running and I came to the corner of the fence . . . and I held to the fence, looking after them and trying to say.
>
> What Benjy is "trying to say" . . . is that he thinks he sees, or expects to see, or, more certainly, that he wants to see his sister Caddy, whom he used to meet on her way home from school; and he is trying as well to do something that he can never do, to talk to another human being. But what his "trying to say" amounts to, we also know, is a continuous loud and horrible bellowing. And . . . we know as well that Benjy now, at the age of thirty-three, is large, shambling, fat, drooling, and an "idiot".[48]

But, as Guetti goes on to observe of this "idiot", Benjy, who "bellows", and who yet seems somehow to be the centre of a semi-solipsistic (and odd, allegedly 'under-developed', sensitive – intensely sensitive, for instance, to *names*[49]), intelligence:

> [What] seems most interesting is the way that Benjy's comparative in-capacity . . . becomes his individual capacity and power . . . [H]is inability to conceive of causal sequences enables him to notice a very great deal as it happens . . . And his failures at "trying to say" . . . become his "saying" to a reader.
>
> This effect depends . . . on Benjy's continuousness to a reader over a time . . . What I am suggesting is that, sooner or later, a reader ceases to [regard Benjy's words] as the language of an "idiot": "Father . . . looked at us again. Then the dark came back, and he stood black in the door, and then the door turned black again. Caddy held me and I could hear us all, and the darkness, and something I could smell . . . Then the dark began to go in smooth, bright shapes, like it always does, even when Caddy says that I have been asleep."
>
> . . . [T]o understand the emotional force of Benjy's language, is to say that it somehow generalizes his case, and that his appeal is the appeal, and his language the words, of a "child". His vulnerability, which is equivalent to the fact that his wonderful imaginings must remain frustrated and potential, his perpetual innocence that will be hurt again and again . . . all underwrite his image as a child. And so one might say that Benjy's text . . . moves us . . . by connecting with what we already know about children.
>
> Or by connecting with what we *think* we know. For what in fact do we know about such childhood? How do we know that experiences for children are so beautifully discrete and yet so synchronizable . . . or that – when a child slept – "the dark began to go in smooth, bright shapes"? . . . I would suggest, then, that we do not recognize that Benjy is a "child" by extension from what we know about other children. If there is such a "recognition" here, it probably goes in the other direction: we know about other children by Benjy; he sets a standard; he is the child. Indeed, he so moves us because probably he is somehow more a "child" than any partic-ular child could be.[50]

The last two sentences are crucial. Benjy is perhaps a 'paradigm', a *prototype*.[51] In his language something is exemplified *more* perhaps than it is ever found in the real world; and it is described in such a way that we now *have* a way for describing 'better' that real world (or so, at any rate, we feel). This idealization of the world becomes the 'object of comparison' which we insist on *beginning* with:

> What happens as Benjy's narrative develops, I think, is rather like what Wittgenstein describes . . . when he says that "the same proposition may

get treated at one time as something to test by experience, at another as a rule of testing" (*OC*, 15). Benjy's language ceases to be dominated by the rules of the grammars we bring to it; it becomes, for its duration, itself the dominating language. And the reason why this seems so remarkable is that it amounts, again, to a reversal of what we think we are doing with such narratives. For we at least begin by feeling that we "understand" them by placing them in some sort of comparative relation with rules and vocabularies of which we are assured; and yet, sooner or later, these narratives come to exceed such presumptions and to achieve a different kind of status. The character . . . becomes "right" to say what he says not because we can explain his speech "psychologically" . . . but because through the appeal of its sustained presence his language is transformed from a sort of "dialect" or merely local grammar *into the only way of talking*, into a ['language'] a reader must speak as he reads.[52]

As Guetti holds, it is experiences *of language* that are in question here, experiences of 'grammatical' effects; not simply communications, not just meaning, and signifying. Our everyday language, and certain linguistic items (e.g. ordinary utterances in foreign languages) that we can translate into it without any worrisome violence, without loss, involve sensical 'significations'. Whereas, like poetry – insofar as it is language which exposes to our view its own form, rather than allowing itself to be translated or paraphrased into everyday prose, into (e.g.) its alleged 'meaning' or its alleged 'moral' – like poetry, discourse which must remain 'another language', *such as Benjy's*, does *not* for us involve any ordinary signification (at least, not *centrally*, in terms of the features of it which are distinctive). Contrary to appearances, it does not make *sense – even in context.*

We are led by Faulkner's 'empathy' and erudition – and perhaps by the decoding 'game' his writing naturally encourages the reader to engage in, the game of trying to identify 'what Benjy is *actually* talking about' – to believe that we understand now the psychology of someone with a serious mental disturbance, or of "the child". But, as Guetti asks: what do we really know of these things? Or rather: what does it *mean* to know of these things? I am *not* making the point that this is fiction – in fact, I have no doubt that in its way Faulkner's writing is more illuminating about real human beings' minds than many a shelf's load of psychology or psychiatry textbooks. But all we (in fact) have here is a 'language' which we can now use to 'represent' abnormal – or child – psychology; or, better, to give instances of it. When most successful, we should say that the 'stream-of-consciousness' novel generated the powerful illusion that it was *accurately expressing a previously existing but as yet ineffable phenomenon.* (Very approximately, *à la* Roland Barthes' 'reality effect', which concerns the subtle textual generation of an effective appearance of 'realism', of expressing a pre-existent reality, which partially anticipates Guetti in arguing for a non-Realist rendering of Faulkner's language.) That this could only be an illusion, in this case or in others like it (for grammar/language *is not responsible to reality*; only (some) *statements* are), we tend not to see.

I now wish to pause in order to respond to an inevitable objection to my reading of Faulkner. In pointing out that *nothing* is signified by Benjy's narrative – that there is *nothing there to be understood* – I have been read rather reductively as ruling out that some mental illness can be understood or *can even exist* on abstract intellectual grounds.[53] I am not. I am simply wishing to leave open the possibility that there may be things that some people utter or seem to experience which intellection gives us little or no assistance with.

And by extension, it may seem that I am therefore diminishing Faulkner's achievement. Not so. For if we are to pay due tribute to the way in which this superb narrative works, it is more fitting to acknowledge the way that he has created something like a 'new paradigm' (of the type suggested above) rather than merely painting more vividly something we *already knew*. In this way, I suggest, we do justice to the originality of Faulkner's writing. Whereas the type of rewriting which 'interpretation' all too often entails strips away the 'literariness', the particularity, transforming the text into our own pale reflections of it, finding ways of making sense of it such that it is no longer nonsensical, alien. We may want to have it both ways, but we cannot, and neither alone actually satisfies us: if Benjy's language *is* in quite specific ways 'responsible' to reality, if that is how coming to grips with it supposedly enables us to understand his psychology, then any translation of it into our language will eliminate that 'responsibility' to reality, and will ensure that the project of understanding the reality of this abnormal psychology fails. But if we *can* straightforwardly translate Benjy's language and understand it and him thereby, then we didn't need to understand his language 'on its own terms', in order to 'capture' what it 'depicts', in the first place. In this latter case, "understanding" so-called 'stream-of-consciousness' writing would simply be an irrelevant distraction.

The cautions I have offered with regard to the interpretation of Benjy's narrative also stand in regards to a number of psychopathologies, particularly schizophrenia, which I shall shortly go on to discuss. But first a caveat: it might be objected that it is dangerous to assimilate the case of 'the child' to that of 'the schizophrenic'. This is obviously true – finding schizophrenic thinking to be directly analogous to the alleged mode of thinking of children (and of 'primitive' peoples) is a highly dubious legacy of psychoanalytical thinking on schizophrenia, and has rightly been thoroughgoingly critiqued by Sass, among others.

What I am wanting to do is treat Benjy as a (non-compulsory) *object of comparison*, in Wittgenstein's sense (see *PI* 130–2), for schizophrenia. Thus we can learn from the similarities *and the differences* between the cases.

If pressed, I should happily for the sake of argument give up any *claims* I might seem to be making – any *opinions* I might seem to be expressing – as to the non-comprehensibility of the 'world' of the child.[54] And I would simply suggest that many of the morals of Guetti's discussion *do* apply to the 'remote' 'world' – the *non-world* – of the chronically schizophrenic person. I would suggest that the rendition of Benjy I have given here serves as a fruitful object of comparison: strictly, (much of) the language of a person suffering from schizophrenia is sound and sometimes fury, signifying nothing.[55] One must do violence to that language in order to render its sentences into our own, into sentences that successfully signify, sentences that mean, sentences that have a use (as opposed to having various 'grammatical' and psychological and associative effects upon one).[56]

I now turn from the fictional depiction of derangement to discuss the first-person *testimony* of severe mental affliction as it is manifested in works such as Schreber's *Memoirs of my Nervous Illness*.[57] Whilst I have warned of the dangers in conflating the child-like state of Benjy and the schizophrenic, there *are* a number of comparisons to be made. Firstly, the way in which Sass characterizes schizophrenia also has implications for other related conditions, such as 'autism' – aspects of which Benjy's narrative *certainly* seems to evoke. Secondly, Benjy's narrative, as I have mentioned, is riven through with solipsistic tendencies, of the sort that Sass finds in his patients. Thus it seems my remarks on how to read Benjy's narrative aright may also be of relevance to mental afflictions of a similar bearing. Thus my method is here to bring a broadly 'literary' approach to examine cases of schizophrenia, and the efficacy of Louis Sass' approach to interpretation of schizophrenic utterance. In adopting such a 'literary' approach, I follow Wittgenstein's own method. As indicated in the introductions to this book, he cautioned that we should not be too quick to assume that one could in the first place comfortably divide questions concerning aesthetics and concerning the meaning of literature from questions concerning (say) philosophy of mind, or (more specifically) philosophy of mental health/illness. As such, he very frequently moved seamlessly from (say) philosophy of mind to philosophy of maths (see e.g. the closing page of his (1958)) or from aesthetics to 'meta-philosophy' and philosophy of psychology (see e.g. pp.14–18 of his (1966)). Fundamentally, he rejected the division of philosophy into separate 'subject areas'. If we are to follow him in thinking about literature – and about psychology – then we should consider doing the same. This is what applying Wittgenstein hereabouts ought to mean.

Let us therefore take a short excursus into thinking directly about how to apply Wittgenstein to the understanding of mental illness.

Wittgenstein on Schizophrenia

The madman is not the man who has lost his reason. The madman is the man who has lost everything except his reason.

(G. K. Chesterton, *Orthodoxy*)

There have been various efforts in recent years to apply 'Wittgensteinian' methods to the understanding of various serious mental illnesses, especially schizophrenia. The most notable is that of the clinical psychologist Louis Sass. Sass' approach is most novel in its analogizations of Modern art, literature and philosophy to the form – and diagnosis – of schizophrenia. Whereas 'schizo-phrenia' is almost invariably seen these days as *a disease or disorder or phenome-non of functional or cognitive deficit*, Sass reads it instead as centrally involving *alienation, cognitive excess, hyper-reflexivity*, even '*hyper-rationality*'. Sass severely questions whether anyone has as yet developed an adequate account of the character of schizophrenic delusions. He proposes his own account, on which such delusions are like the delusions suffered by a philosopher who finds themselves drawn into absurdities (e.g. 'the solipsist', or 'the private linguist'). Sass draws to some extent on conventional work within psychology (and neurology) to found his interpretation, to some extent on his own and others' clinical experience, and to some considerable extent on biographical and autobiographical materials written on and by 'schizophrenics'. The efficacious combining of these is rare in the 'literature', but, more originally still, he also draws on a vast and thorough acquaintance with – and systematic comparisons with – Modern art, literature and philosophy. In this regard, his work can be thought of as a systematic reworking of (and thoroughgoing critique of) others' earlier efforts to understand madness through its affinities with and connections with the arts. The stereotype of the artist touched with madness, touched with fire, is one of Sass' targets – he argues instead that insofar as there is an affinity between unusual mentality and art (especially in Modern times), it runs more through the 'schizoid' than through the manic-depressive – and moreover that 'the schizoid' must, surprisingly, be understood along his 'hyper-rationalistic' lines for this comparison to work. Sass' view is that the character of a great deal (*not* all – 'the' condition of 'schizophrenia' is increas-ingly considered even within much overly scientistic medicalized thought to be not just one but a reasonably wide spectrum of conditions, and thus very heterogeneous) of 'schizophrenic' language and action can be illuminated better by comparing it to Modernism in the Arts and to the same (and to Post-Modernism) in philosophy than by means of more conventional – especially cognitivistic medical-model, and psychoanalytic – approaches. This is in part because he thinks that Modernism in the Arts etc. is itself to a much greater extent than has been normally understood a phenomenon of hyper-consciousness etc., rather than of 'Dionysian' abandon. In sum, Sass argues that we can understand the key features of schizophrenia by analogy to the character of highly inward-looking Modernism – and then by analogy to how Wittgenstein diagnostically offers an account of solipsism.

Sass' general project is expressed most fully in his *Madness and Modernism: Insanity in the Light of Modern Art, Literature and Thought.* For ease and brevity of exposition, and because of the importance of Wittgenstein not only in Sass' but also in my thought, and in this book, I concentrate in what follows on the more specific project by means of which he has effected his most detailed exemplification of his general project and thesis: a detailed consideration in the light of the thought of Ludwig Wittgenstein of Daniel Paul Schreber, the most famous psychiatric patient in history, in some respects a 'prototypical' schizophrenic, who exhibited severe 'paranoia'. This consideration is effected most fully in Sass' *The Paradoxes of Delusion: Wittgenstein, Schreber, and the Schizo-phrenic Mind*, wherein Sass tries to illuminate the *form* of the delusions central to schizophrenia.

Schizophrenia is seen by Sass not as involving cognitive deficit, but as involv-ing cognitive 'overwork' (and thus, sometimes, overload). People with schizo-phrenia suffer, roughly, from thinking too much; they think through things that most people do automatically. (This doesn't *just* apply to thought, inci-dentally: 'hyper-reflexivity' can be perceptually centred too: e.g. an excessive 'concentration' on one's kinaesthetic sensations can be relevantly similar here to an excessive cognitive scrutinization. To call such 'excessive' concentration a cognitive *deficit* would be overly expanding the extension of the in any case problematic term "cognitive deficit" – it would be making *anything* which led to unusual or abnormal cognitive function a 'deficit'.) "Hyper-reflexivity" and 'alienation' are arguably Sass' key terms. According to Sass, schizophrenia is – to coin Nietzsche's important opposition from *The Birth of Tragedy* – more essentially Apollonian (and sometimes even Socratic), than Dionysian . . . In short, people with schizophrenia *live out philosophy*: they 'think things through' that normally get presupposed. When 'philosophers' do this, it's a limited academic exercise; when 'schizophrenics' do it, it's 'deadly serious'. I.e. schiz-ophrenics *live out* what philosophers merely discuss in inchoate ways: but that's to a significant degree because the (philosophical) attempts to uncover the 'underlying structure' of our experience(s) etc. are, arguably, *themselves* very largely inchoate. That is – according to Heidegger, Foucault and Wittgenstein – the project of Foundationalism, and also Kantianism (and, let us add, the Human Sciences in their own dominant preferred self-images), which would uncover such underlying structure, are impossible projects. Schizophrenia involves actually experiencing some of the logical arguments – and the 'posi-tions' consequent upon them – of the philosophers, then, rather than merely performing them as theoretical/mental gymnastics. I.e. 'schizophrenics' tend to have experiences *akin to the thinking/feeling/experiencing of the logical arguments of philosophy* and their consequences:

> Wittgenstein's [anti-private-language] argument demonstrates the non-sensicality of a philosophical idea. To demonstrate nonsensicality is not, however, to demonstrate nonexistence. For, not only does "private language" exist as an idea, a widespread notion about linguistic meaning; it also exists as an aspiration, a very real aspiration with specific psycho-logical and linguistic effects. (Sass 1995: 257)

Sass locates that aspiration, those effects, in the life and words of Schreber.

What Daniel P. Schreber did and said – what he and other schizophrenics, including such well-known 'cases' as A. Artaud, A. Wolfli and V. Nijinsky, have written and said – can be *understood* – can be successfully interpreted – via Wittgenstein's philosophy. It is very important to understand this aright, so as not to be immediately confused: the import of *Wittgenstein* for Sass is *not* to

pathologize *him* or his thought. Rather *Schreber* is seen as living out a philosophy, *a philosophy which Wittgenstein diagnosed.* Nietzsche once polemically
claimed to have suffered philosophical problems as illnesses. Roughly
speaking, Sass for present purposes literalizes this claim – but with regard to
Schreber, *not* with regard to Wittgenstein. In particular, the peculiar structure
of the commitments of one philosophically inclined towards solipsism – the
supposed belief that one is the only person who exists – and inclined towards
related forms of philosophical scepticism and/or system-building, is importantly and brilliantly dissected by Wittgenstein, and it is this dissection which
Sass applies analogically to the case of schizophrenia. To the case of those who
utter the likes of the following: "[T]he world must be represented or the world
will disappear" (Sass 1992: 303).

Sass shows in detail how the pressures upon Schreber's thought, the various
powerful and often contradictory directions in which the nature of his delu-
sional system develops, are very similar to those that one would have predicted
finding had one begun with the notion that one was looking at someone
whose thought-processes were relevantly similar to those of a would-be serious
sceptic or solipsist, and that solipsism in turn is best understood by means of
Wittgenstein's diagnosis of it as a disease of the intellect. For it is its *form*
ultimately that is troublesome. Wittgenstein argues (as we shall explore in
detail below) that there is no stable position or belief which is solipsism, but
that 'it' is in continual internal tension. He thinks that 'the solipsist' is
confused by language, and thus finds it 'inadequate' to her purposes, and feels
herself under pressure to change it – and that, according to Wittgenstein, is
the most that the solipsist can in the end do. For example, she can insist
(pointlessly) on reserving the word "toothache" for her own toothache, and
describe others as "puppets exhibiting behaviour outwardly similar to the
behaviour that occurs when there is real ['i.e.' the solipsist's] toothache", or
such like. Immediately, readers familiar with Schreber's *Memoir* may recall
Schreber's very peculiar mode(s) of language, and his not infrequently
expressed frustration with the inadequacies of language to express what he
wants to say. And such readers might recall particularly striking coinages of
Schreber's own, such as "fleeting-improvised men". It is terms such as this
which are a starting-point for the construal of Schreber as solipsistic. For at
times Schreber apparently thought those around him were in some sense not
real, but were mere imagos, continually fleetingly constructed and destroyed
and recreated as he turned his gaze. Schreber's name for those pseudo-
creatures, *pure inventions of his imagination* or of God's, was "fleeting-improvised
men". What, then, is Sass' aim in his philosophy of psychopathology? To show
the form, the character of the *fly* and the *fly-bottle* here, to show that both are
relevantly similar to those that philosophers have deliberately (respectively)
attempted to *be* and to *inter themselves in.*

In fact, Sass powerfully argues, if schizophrenics confuse the real and the
unreal, it tends to be in the opposite direction from that typically supposed by
conventional psychiatric wisdoms. That is, they do not mistake the unreal for

real, but they mistake *the real for the unreal.* If these flies are caught in fly-bottles, it is not so much that they take their fly-bottles to be all of reality, as that they take even their fly-bottles to be unreal too! They do not act as if their delusions were reality, they tend rather to act or talk *as if* everything *were a delusion.* (This attitude, reminiscent of bizarre philosophical doctrines such as full-blown Idealism or Cartesian Scepticism, in fact dovetails perfectly with Sass' Wittgensteinian account of 'schizophrenia as solipsism', to be considered momentarily):

> Here is how one schizoaffective patient describes the unreality feeling that plagued her during much of her psychosis:
>
>> It is more like gray. It is like a constant sliding and shifting that slips away in a jelly-like fashion, leaving nothing substantial and yet enough to be tasted, or like watching a movie based on a play and, having once seen the play, realizing that the movie is a description of it and one that brings back memories and yet isn't real . . . Even a description of it is unreal and tormenting, for it is horrifying and yet seems mild and vague, although it is acute. It is felt in an unreal way in that it isn't constant torture and yet never seems to leave and everything seems to slip away into impressions . . .
>
> Similarly, the schizophrenic patient Renée, in her *Autobiography of a Schizophrenic Girl,* speaks of "the pasteboard scenery of Unreality" during her psychosis, saying "even the sea disappointed me a little by its artificiality". (Sass 1994)

"Even *a description of it* is unreal and tormenting . . ." Here we have in a nutshell much of what makes this topic so *fascinating,* and scary, and (above all) hard – to say the least – to figure out. Is this phrase supposed to imply that the description is felt to be unreal next to the reality of the phenomena experienced or some such? Possibly – but surely it looks much more like this: everything that the patient touches turns to unreality. She has become some kind of psycho-conceptual Midas, dread-fully a victim of her own mind. We have 'an impossible situation' that we want to describe in this way: here there is no reality to check an illusion by, here we cannot mount the usual and effective response against (say) a sceptical argument from illusion, that there must be a reality by comparison with which the illusion is shown/known to *be* such. Here is a lived experience of there only being illusion. Perhaps serious philosophical-ish scepticism is possible, liveable, after all: under the sign of severe mental illness.

There is also an implicit hint here that even *realizing this* may not actually help anyone in this condition. There is no guarantee whatsoever that a 'meta-move' will help resolve a 'schizophrenic psychosis'. Thus a Wittgensteinian therapeutic attempt to show the fly the way out of the fly-bottle will not help if the 'fly' feels *the attempt*, not to mention *the bottle* and of course the world, the common life, outside it – and even *themselves*, as we shall see – to be unreal . . . This, then, is Sass' claim: that 'poor reality-testing' is an utterly inadequate – and in fact *at best* largely false – model for schizophreniform actions and behaviours, linguistic and otherwise. Sass details how various phenomena characteristic of schizophrenia (though not always found there – one more time, schizophrenia is (to a significant extent) a highly heterogeneous and very complex phenomenon) can be '*explained*' by means of his method of Wittgensteinian analogy, and of hermeneutical-cum-phenomenological interpretation.

For example, the tension in schizophrenia between a sense of the self as all-powerful, all-knowing – and a sense of the self as nothing at all.

But now: the latter might seem quite obviously to contradict the idea of taking solipsism as an analogy-base, a 'model', for schizophrenia. Because the doctrine of solipsism seems to be all on the side of conceiving of the self as all. So here we appear to have an objection to Sass.

Sass however turns this objection marvellously on its head, to work as a powerful argument in favour of his reading, and in favour of the notion that he can account for the form of schizophrenic discourse etc. It will be worth quoting extensively from Sass to see how he does this, to see his method at work concretely.

A notable feature of Schreber's *Memoirs*, as mentioned earlier, is the 'scientific' – even inductivist – and in a real sense highly logicalistic character of much of his reasoning. Schreber takes a 'rational'/scientist-like approach to many matters. But this can sometimes seem to be contravened by his willingness to entertain contradictory thoughts, for surely internal consistency is a very basic mark of rational or scientific thinking. Here is Sass (1994: 55), on the matter:

> Schreber's claims seem . . . to involve a contradiction – or at least a continual equivocation – between two attitudes: one in which he accepts the essential innerness and privacy of his own claims, the other in which he assumes that they have some kind of objectivity and potential consensuality. This duality is hardly unique to Schreber: many schizophrenic patients who seem generally aware of the innerness of their claims also consider their delusions to be revelations of a truth that they assume to be in some sense, both objective and potentially public in nature. On its face, this certainly appears to contradict my interpretation: the tendency to claim a kind of truth value for delusions seems consistent with the poor reality-testing formula I have criticised; and shifting between a solipsistic vision and a kind of poor reality-testing might suggest the tolerance for contradiction so characteristic of primitive primary-process modes of thought.

So this is the worry: either solipsism is simply the belief that oneself is all, in which case it is not a good analogy for most of the features of schizophrenia which Sass wishes to bring out (such as ubiquitous unreality feelings, and systematic delusions of surveillance and persecution). Or solipsism is both, is the self as all *and* as nothing, in which case isn't schizophrenia and schizophrenic thinking (if effectively analogized to solipsism on *this* construal of solipsism) primitive or deficit-saturated, irrationally self-contradictory, after all?

Not necessarily. What Sass shows is that solipsism is indeed not all on the side of 'self as all'. But that, according to Wittgenstein's incisive analysis of it, there is endemic to it an instability, an oscillation, between self-as-all and self-as-nothing, and more besides. The contradictions 'the Solipsist' gets into are not irrational or pre-rational, but are rationality itself – or at least, an important and influential form of what has come down to us as philosophical rationality – taken to its logical/rational conclusions:

Wittgenstein's meditations can, however, offer another way [than that of poor reality-testing etc.] of viewing many such deviations or equivocations of the solipsistic mode – one that explains them not as contradictions of solipsism but as a playing out of the inherently self-refuting nature of solipsism itself. (Sass 1993: 55)

The kind of absurdity or self-refutation which occurs, for instance, when a solipsist wants to say "I have got something which you haven't." Sass quotes Wittgenstein on the matter:

"At any rate, only I have got THIS." – What are these words for? They serve no purpose – Can one not add: "There is here no question of a 'seeing' – and therefore none of a 'having' – nor of a subject, nor therefore of 'I' either? Might I not ask; In what sense have you *got* what you are talking about and saying that only you have got it? Do you possess it? . . . And this too is clear: If as a matter of logic you exclude other people's having something, it loses sense to say that you have it" (*PI* 398). The solipsist – to borrow one of Wittgenstein's many metaphors for the futility of such metaphysical claims – is like someone who tries to measure his own height not by using an independent reference system but by placing his own hand on top of his head. Schreber makes precisely this error, and it is an important source of his paranoid-grandiose sense that, as he puts it, "everything that happens is in reference to me" Schreber (2000: 197). Thus he feels he has discovered a surprising empirical fact, that experience happens only here, when in fact his experience could not on principle happen anywhere else anyway. Rather portentously, Schreber writes, "it is by no means impossible that seeing (Sehvermögen) . . . is confined to my person and immediate surroundings", Schreber (2000: 232). "I can no longer doubt that the so-called 'play with human beings' (the effect of miracles) is limited to myself *and to whatever constitutes my immediate environment at the time*", Schreber (2000: 32). His proof of this discovery is curiously circular, in just the tautologous way Wittgenstein describes. This can be seen in the following passage, in which Schreber seems to be arguing, in essence, that the proof that miracles only happen here is that they only happen here:

> In any case miracles occur only on my person or in my immediate vicinity. I have again received striking proof of this in the last few days which I think is worth mentioning here . . . [S]everal gamboling mosquitoes were . . . produced by miracle in front of my face while I sat in the garden of the inn of the neighbouring village of Ebenheit during an excursion; and again they appeared *only* in my immediate vicinity. Schreber (2000: 233). (Sass 1993: 57)

The delightful 'parody' of scientific methodology here in Schreber's relation to his solipsistic experiences is quite as clear as it is (presumably) unconscious. Crucially, as Sass remarks, "Notice the equivocation inherent in Schreber's phrase "my immediate vicinity": although he may think he is referring to the kind of place that could be objectively defined ("by the bench", for example, as opposed to "over by the wall of the garden"), in actuality "my immediate vicinity" means something more like "wherever I happen to look"" (Sass 1993: 57). The lack of an independent reference point is vital to the instability of the 'position' of the solipsistic thinker. Through his very effort to be scientifical and logical, he gets into a position of severe philosophical confusion. Now, with the same logic and scientific doggedness, albeit in a manner and within a frame that renders it unstable, the solipsistic thinker needs to pursue the question of the existence not just of things he is not looking at etc., but of *himself:*

> Wittgenstein [argues that] the usual and unrigorous form of solipsism ("the world is my world") reduces by its own intrinsic logic to what might be called a "no-ownership solipsism of the present moment" – a position that can be expressed as "whenever anything is seen, it is this which is seen". The undeniable reality of the experience one has turns out not to affirm the existence of the self one is . . . // One might still claim that the self-as-subject exists, but just not in the same way that the objects of experience exist – that "the subject is not part of the world but a presupposition of its existence" [as Wittgenstein had once put it in his *Notebooks*]. But for the solipsist who engages in a scrutinizing hyperawareness, insisting on the unreality of all that goes beyond that which is phenomenally present in a direct and almost concrete fashion, such a position would be contradictory. One might as well admit the existence of other minds, for they too can be invoked as presuppositions of observable facts (like facial expressions . . .). No, the rigorous, hyperscrutinizing solipsist must not assume the existence of the self but only of that which is directly observed: experiences. (Sass 1993: 69)

Here, then, we have the very transition we did not expect, when we thought of modelling schizophrenia on solipsism initially. A sense of the self as all, and of others as nothing, leads of its own momentum, by its own logic, to a sense of the self as nothing. This provides the essentials of an answer to the complaint that might be levelled at Sass that his account can hardly be right because Schreber is such an 'inconstant' solipsist, at best. If we look at Schreber's procedures for validating, questioning and interpreting his own experiences, we do not find the 'pure' self-fulfilling prophecy we might expect of a solipsist – but this is precisely because even *pure solipsism leads logically to its own overturning*, its own negation(s).

Such 'existential self-nihilism' is not even the end of this logic, of this road, however. Sass again, quoting Schreber again:

> "Whenever a butterfly appears my gaze is first directed to it as to a being newly created that very moment, and secondly the words 'butterfly – has been recorded' are spoken into my nerves by the voices; this shows that one thought I could possibly no longer recognize a butterfly and one therefore examines me to find out whether I still know the meaning of the word 'butterfly'" Schreber (2000: 188). Here Schreber appears to sense that the world of objects depends on him (the newly-created or "miracled-up" butterfly exists only for him) while simultaneously feeling his own consciousness to be a pawn and object of scrutiny of some other mind – namely, the "one" who directs his gaze and examines him to find out whether he still knows the meaning of the word "butterfly". Like many schizophrenic patients, Schreber combines a sense of omnipotence with a sense of abject subjugation and powerlessness. His own consciousness plays two seemingly incompatible roles: for he experiences his own mind as the hub around which the universe revolves . . . but he also feels his own experience to be limited and constrained, like something contemplated and manipulated (perhaps even constituted) by some distant and ever-receding other mind. Thus "seeing" . . . happens only "here", and Schreber's whims control the weather (though only in the mind's eye; Schreber (2000:181); yet Schreber is also totally enslaved, not only under the constant scrutiny of "one", but with his gaze being directed without his will toward those very insects that exist only for him. (Sass 1993: 62–3)

Of particular interest in the above quote from Schreber is the peculiar grammar of and around the word "one". Schreber's way of writing requires close attention just as much as Benjy's. We must note its being even stranger than it at first appears; and, perhaps, we must get used to it, and hear it as a 'language' that is in principle not understandable . . . Was Schreber 'regressing', with his strange use of the term "one", to a childhood state of being unable to use the language properly or something similar? More plausible is that this peculiarity is systematic and has something like a 'meaning', a symptomatic or perhaps 'symbolic' (as opposed to straightforwardly communicative) significance. The obvious 'meaning' now, surely, is that this grammatical peculiarity is integral to the logical oscillation between the self as all, the self as nothing [reached through hyper-scrutinization], and the self as related to (e.g. enslaved by) another [because of the perceived meaningfulness of the solipsistic revelation], *and back again*, which Sass finds in the *Memoirs*. Schreber is finding it systemically difficult (!) to know whether he has *created* God, or *is* God, or is essentially *tied to* God, or a *pawn* of God's, or even an *imaginary construct* of God's – *thus he slips more or less unknowingly at times from the first person to the third*, and back, and more.

And thus we have an account that can in a certain sense explain how Schreber's text came to have the peculiar form it does, and how he could have thought the way he did. Schreber, if Sass is right, *lived out* the kinds of pathological solipsistic etc. thought-processes that Wittgenstein has slightly more abstractly *described* and *diagnosed* for us. And sure enough, a good look at the *Memoirs* will soon show the reader Schreber on just such a not-very-Merry-Go-Round, moving continually from (for example) quasi-omnipotence through hyper-scrutinization to depersonalization, and then via slavery to another (for whom one is nevertheless terribly important) back towards quasi-omnipotence.

Sass' heterodox reading of schizophrenia – in particular, his remarkable re-reading of Schreber in the light of Wittgenstein – achieves, we might say, a detailed *fleshing out* of the lovely aphorism of Chesterton's (who, incidentally, has been much admired by a number of people in the train of Wittgenstein) which serves as an epigraph to this sub-section. Sass overturns the conventional wisdom in clinical psychology – that schizophrenia ought to be, *must* be, interpreted primarily as a disease of excess or inappropriateness of affect (and/or of object-choice), of regression, or of cognitive deficit, etc. Rather, schizophrenia is comprehensible as involving excessive self-consciousness – more generally, hyper-reflexivity – and its peculiar consequences . . .

. . . that one all-too-often finds in rarefied philosophical systems;

. . . that Kafka, and Dostoevsky (see *Notes from Underground* and *The Double*) and Nabokov (see *Invitation to a Beheading*), and others already mentioned above have documented in Modern literature;

. . . that Foucault has dissected in his archaeologizing of the human sciences (in his analysis, that is, of the creation of 'the modern human subject' *by means of* the turning of the human subject into a study-object. See particularly *Les Mots et les Choses*, particularly the segments of that book treating of 'modern man' as a 'transcendental-empirico doublet').

Sass thus 're-specifies' schizophrenia without simply re-evaluating it – which is arguably what some of the Anti-Psychiatrists do. Speaking a little crudely, and generalizing, the Anti-Psychiatrists & co. tend to accept the clinical psychologists'/psychiatrists'/psychoanalysts' *descriptions* of schizophrenia, insofar that is as they accept any essentializing of schizophrenia/madness at all as a phenomenon, and then tend towards *valorizing* it: valorizing the 'primitivity', interpreting positively the denial of reality, the refusal to accept society, the glorying in the 'excess' of emotion, that conventional psychoanalysis in particular finds in schizophrenia. While I wouldn't deny that there is something right about this – it is true that schizophrenic 'delusions' sometimes contain a troublingly large degree of truth – nevertheless the danger of romanticization (and indeed of simple failure to understand how very un-Dionysian much of schizophrenia is) inherent in such valorization is by now I think well known. Thus Sass' project is in a certain sense more *radical*, or at least more psycho-philosophically novel, than that even of the Anti-Psychiatrists. He can account better, I have suggested, for the form of schizophrenic language and delusion, than they *or* than conventional psychiatry or psychoanalysis etc. Sass' thought runs deeper, it seems to me, than his near-namesake Szasz's . . . or indeed, where they disagree, than Laing's. Sass builds on the early Laing and (all but the early) Foucault, but his thought presents a serious challenge to the later Laing, to Foucault's supposed 'followers', and to any who would resist the provocative and, I think, compelling thought that schizophrenia often mirrors the hyper-rationality of solipsism etc. more than it reflects either failure or out-siderness. Schizophrenia, Sass suggests, is not a failure to attain Enlighten-ment, nor an alternative to it or a rebellion against it, but is instead Modernity and Enlightenment and individualism *come home to roost*. Schizophrenia *à la* Sass involves not a dearth of rationality or a heightened emotionality but rather *an excess of self-consciousness* and its associated forms of *alienation*. One might say that, if Sass is right, people suffering with schizophrenia 'perish' not by fire, but by ice.

In the next section, I shall undertake a critique of this fascinating 'Wittgen-steinian' reading of 'schizophrenia', and bring into question, though not from a scientistic point of view, whether in some key cases it can actually, ultimately, be read at all.[58]

2.2.2 Delusions of 'Sense' in the 'Representation' of Derangement: The Dangers of Interpretation

I follow Sass in very largely rejecting scientific or quasi-scientific *explanations* of schizophrenia, primarily because – even if effective within their own terms (e.g. predictively) – such explanations fail to deliver any improved *understand-ing* of schizophrenia. They fail, for example, to give us an insight into its phenomenology. Understanding some of the causes behind schizophrenia, as probably we increasingly do, is not then, in my sense, understanding schizo-phrenia, understanding the people who suffer from it. Schizophrenia involves actually experiencing some of the logical arguments – and the 'positions' consequent upon them – of the philosophers, then, rather than merely per-forming them as theoretical/mental gymnastics. I.e., to say it again: 'schizo-phrenics' tend to have experiences *akin to the thinking/feeling/experiencing of the logical arguments of philosophy* and their consequences. The full incoherency of those arguments is, as we shall see, in a sense dramatically revealed by the detail of this comparison; but more important in the first (Sass') instance is that the *nature* of schizophrenic language and experience is thus arguably rendered

comprehensible, more than it ever has been before. The claim is that Sass'
Wittgensteinian 'hermeneutical description' of schizophrenia facilitates our
understanding of why it works in the ways that it does, of why Schreber *et al.*
speak and act in the ways they do, of how those ways have a *certain* logic and
sense, a certain strong 'rationality', and even a strange kind of 'scientificness'
or scientificity, and are not expressions of a mere bizarreness or primitivity or
deficit nor even an alternative mode of being or such like.

Here I am concerned with severe cases, cases which seem to require for their
possible comprehension a whole 'new mode of representation' (such as
Benjy's narrative). And what I argue in such cases is that sophisticated appreciation of Wittgenstein and of Modern Literature tends towards a more
'pessimistic' or 'negative' conclusion than Sass'. To the deflationary conclusion, that is, that we are ill advised to claim that serious cases of schizophrenia
can be successfully understood or interpreted, via Wittgenstein, or literature
(or by any other means). In a way, I am 'extending' Sass' line of argument: I
want to suggest that we have not been given good reason to think that there
can be any such thing as understanding an actual person who is thoroughly in
the grip of such absurdities as Sass describes. To do so, to be able truly to
understand a lived solipsism, would be somewhat like understanding 'logically
alien thought' – but the point, as Wittgenstein was the first to argue, is that
there isn't any such thing as (what we will in the end be satisfied to call)
'logically alien *thought*'. (*A fortiori*, there can't be any such thing as understanding 'it'.)[59] Whilst acknowledging the force of Sass' critique, and the fruit-
fulness of his alternative, I nevertheless intend to apply Wittgenstein to
develop objections I take to be fundamental (though they are without a doubt
philosophically controversial) both to Sass' project and more generally to any
attempt to develop a hermeneutic for schizophrenia and similar 'disorders'.
Instead, I suggest that a properly Wittgensteinian approach would show that,
except in some very remote and vague sense of the word 'understanding',
there probably cannot be any such thing as understanding the words, actions
and experiences of the very severely 'mentally ill', those who might perhaps
truly be worth calling deeply different from ourselves.[60]

In order to draw the difficulty in Sass' work into sharp relief, I turn to
examine Wittgenstein's important remarks on dreams and altered states of
consciousness in *On Certainty* in *PI*, drawing a *partial* analogy to hard cases of
schizophrenia. I will then refer back to Guetti's reading of Faulkner to rebut
an obvious objection to my conclusion drawn from *On Certainty*.

For Wittgenstein, it is very important to note that veridical accounts of dreams
can only be given from outside the dream context. This is, so to speak, a conceptual point, not an empirical one. It is for instance what renders the whole
procedure of Cartesian doubt so pointless and logically awry:

If someone believes that he has flown from America to England in the last few days, then, I believe, he cannot be making a *mistake*. [For that would be 'too big' to be a mistake.] // And just the same if someone says that he is at this moment sitting at a table and writing.

"But even if in such cases I can't be mistaken, isn't it possible that I am drugged?" If I am and if the drug has taken away my consciousness, then I am not now really talking and thinking. I cannot seriously suppose that I am at this moment dreaming. Someone who, dreaming, says "I am dreaming", even if he speaks audibly in doing so, is no more right than if he said in his dream "It is raining" while it was in fact raining. Even if his dream were actually connected with the noise of the rain. (Wittgenstein 1975: 675–6)

One might try putting Wittgenstein's point here thus: Cartesian scepticism is pragmatically self-refuting. If one allegedly supposes that one is dreaming, then it follows from the supposition that one is not engaged in normal potentially public talk or thought. One's 'quasi-thought' in such circumstances – in this case, the mental occurence of "I am dreaming" – is not a serious candidate for truth-evaluation, etc. One is not correctly placed to make a *claim*. (If one is correctly placed to make such a claim, contrariwise, one is no longer fully in the dream.) So: any quasi-claim one makes while dreaming, while asleep, need not be taken seriously. There is nothing that it *is* to take such a pseudo-claim seriously.

So far so good. But we can see also that Wittgenstein would be traduced were one to take such 'pragmatic self-refutation' to be somehow inferior to 'real' or 'semantic self-refutation'. Wittgenstein's point is that Cartesian scepticism cannot even get off the ground – it makes no truth-claims or truth-denials to evaluate. We have here, then, the whole mainstream epistemological tradition condensed into a drop of grammar.

Now, this does not imply that there cannot be any such thing as someone enjoying or enduring the mental occurrence, "I am dreaming", or that such occurent quasi-thoughts do not, by means of an apparently quite logical process, eventuate perhaps in a real mental confusion or paralysis, which can take on a Cartesian mode of presentation. If we think of schizoid intellectuals in certain moods, or indeed of sufferers from schizophrenia – for example, of the famous cases of Daniel P. Schreber or Adolf Wolfli – in the light of Wittgenstein's remarks, then ought we to say simply that they are confused? That they made/make clear mistakes, errors? Are they, as the influential 'cognitive deficit' accounts of schizophrenia would suggest, simply the victims of frequent or more or less permanent mistakenness?

A genuinely Wittgensteinian view, if we are to work with the vital passage from *OC* just quoted, would rather involve not just a questioning (as in Sass' work) of the crude mainstream picture of schizophrenics as *poor* 'reality-testers', and a remarking (as in Sass' work) of the analogies between their 'testimonies' concerning themselves and (say) solipsistic philosophic moments (which involve not error by a 'mythology' of language), but also a clear noticing of the limited degree which we can take seriously – or even comprehend – what they (sufferers from severe schizophrenic delusion) say, *at all.* 'Quasi-thought', thought or talk in the nowhere 'beyond' the limits of thought, consisting of quasi-thoughts which are, roughly, 'logically alien', which can only be mentally compassed through an overly hopeful and presumptuous process of analogy, or through imaginative mental projection of quite dubious status, is 'simply' not, strictly speaking, to be regarded as comprehensible. As Wittgenstein once remarked, in discussing the related problem of 'private language': "I cannot accept his testimony because it is not *testimony*. It only tells me what he is *inclined* to say" (*PI* 386). We must be wary of taking seriously – of thinking that we can *interpret* – what there is/are no clear criteria for, no clear criteria for evaluation of. And one cannot evaluate mere inclinations for their epistemic reliability. One can only evaluate (e.g.) *testimony*. We might say: what is said by a person in the grip of schizophreniform delusion is only ever: what they are *inclined* to say.

An account of a dream can be given only from outside a dream, and 'inside' the ordinary. But with severe schizophrenia, one might say, *there* is *no outside*. There is no such thing experientially (for the sufferer) as an outside to psychosis, or at least to the kind of continual oscillation between systemic quasi-solipsistic delusion and everyday reality which we find in most of the case-history of, for example, Schreber – see for instance Sass' (1994), and Schreber's own.

While: outside (ordinary) thought there is arguably nothing but the nothing that is (e.g.) psychosis. Now, we are likely to continue to want to call psychotic experience a kind of *experience* – but probably not one that can be rendered in terms making sense. After a certain point, 'moments of lucidity' cannot count for much – where all would-be 'testimony' is only more inclination to speak,[61] where *the patient themselves* is no more confident of their so-called 'testimony' than of their so-called 'delusions'. If Sass is roughly right about the analogy between schizophrenia and solipsism, and if Wittgenstein is (philosophically) right, on my reading of him, then it follows that badly off schizophrenics are *not (even) in the reality-testing game.* But this *negative* remark is *as close as we can get* to an accurate or apposite positive characterization of what game it is that they *are* playing.

For to be outside delusions (outside the 'fly-bottle', 'inside' ordinary life) is *ipso facto* no longer to be a first-personal 'authority' on this condition. A retrospective account, one prescinding from the form of the condition, of the delusions, is not authoritative. But an 'internal'[62] account is an account without authority either: it's *at best* what someone is *inclined* to say, rather than a *testimony* as to what their experience is. The 'accounts' given by the very severely mentally ill of their experiences are in this respect precisely like the 'account' Wittgenstein's dreamer gives of what is happening to him while he is dreaming. To say it again, bluntly: they do not constitute testimony. To rely upon such 'accounts' is to be victim to a deep philosophical illusion.

Ergo, there can be *no* authoritative first-personal account of what severe schizophrenic experience is like. And so, strictly speaking, any such candidate-accounts cannot themselves be anything more than nonsense. (Thus purely empathetic understanding of sufferers from chronic schizophrenia, which might be thought to be an *alternative* possibility to the kind of understanding of another's motives and reasons etc. which (roughly) I am mostly focusing on here, is (also) ruled out. We had better say: there is no such thing as my understanding what it is like to be you, if there is no such thing as you understanding what it is like to be you. 'What it is like to be you' is just undefined, we might most usefully say, in such cases.)

2.2.3 'Creative Mimicry' and the Untranslatable Metaphor

In conclusion, then, the would-be objection to the object lesson I drew from *On Certainty* fails. The least misleading thing to say about cases of severe mental illness is probably that there can be no such thing as understanding them. (And then, of course, no such thing as misunderstanding them either. They just aren't candidates for understanding.) We have no criteria via which cognitively to evaluate them, and so *whatever we attempt to say of them by way of affirmative characterization will be arbitrary*, and in a way quite misleading.[63]

Again, I must confront the objection that this is an anti-Wittgensteinian conclusion. Am I, for example, being overly narrow still, failing to treat "understanding" sufficiently as a 'family-resemblance concept' with a variety of different cases? Mustn't there be a sense in which a 'respectful', hermeneutic-ish, Wittgensteinian approach to this matter would involve us finding a way, perhaps some kind of 'indirect' way, of describing correctly the experience of the sufferer from schizophrenia? Well: no. At least not for Wittgenstein himself. I would invite those who feel inclined still to disagree with me and to answer the above questions in the affirmative, to offer their interpretation of the following remark of Wittgenstein's, a remark precisely consonant, it seems to me, with the line of argument which I have pursued here: "Suppose you say of the schizophrenic: he does not love, he cannot love, he refuses to love – what is the difference?!" (Wittgenstein 1980: 77).

The difference between saying these things of the ordinary person, is weighty. That a person refuses to love implies a kind of criticism of them not present in their being unable to love, for example. But Wittgenstein specifically rejects such discrimination, in the case of 'the schizophrenic'. It does not matter which of these we say: there can be no such thing as getting schizophrenia right. *You* can call being able to say everything and nothing – being able to say whatever you like – 'understanding', if you wish! I would prefer to restrict the use of that term to contexts in which there is a reasonably clear distinction between understanding and *not* understanding someone. What we can be intelligibly said to understand in another, in the sense of understanding what their actions are, or understanding their motives for action, or empathetically understanding them, etc., is (most of) the hurly-burly and variety of ordinary life. But most serious

schizophrenia does not fall under that heading. It is better seen as the persistent *semblance* of another language – very much like the semblance of another
language that we find in Wittgenstein's 'private linguist', a philosopher subject
to an illusion of sense, an illusion that his words, in the way he finds himself
wishing to employ them, mean anything at all.

To return to *The Sound and The* Fury, we may then suggest that getting
Faulkner right involves seeing that his novel displays to us language which,
ironically, cannot be translated or interpreted into sense . . . without irreducible 'loss' or 'garbling'. An odd kind of 'garbling', admittedly: a garbling
which inadvisedly turns nonsense into sense . . . What we *do* share with Benjy
is something far more important – the relentless sensation of failing to mean
that characterizes his narrative, and indeed our reading of it. We need to see
Faulkner's language 'clearly': as a language of paradox, of nonsense mas-
querading beautifully as sense. We should try to see Faulkner's work as exemplifying these Wittgensteinian – Guettian – points; and then we can see his art
– his artifice – clearly, as the brilliant creation of an illusion of meaning, an
illusion of sense.[64] The illusion perhaps that we can make sense of the 'life-
world' of a young child, certainly of Faulkner's 'idiot' – or, I have argued, by
(I hope) a justified extension, of a sufferer from chronic schizophrenia. If I am
right, we can see Faulkner then – now – as an artist whose art bears among
other things a very particular aspect: an exemplification of deflationary
Wittgensteinian 'philosophy of psychopathology'.

2.2.4 Wittgenstein and the 'Sound of Sense'

The decidedly 'strong' grammar of Faulkner's Benjy in *The Sound and the Fury*
can, as I have argued above, brilliantly provide us with the illusion that we are
now *understanding* (in the *usual* sense of the word) an 'idiot', or a 'schizophrenic', or what-have-you. But my suggestion was that the risk of thinking
that this is an understanding which helps us to 'capture' the psychopathological – and "capture" is the word repeatedly employed by Sass, in the works
referred to above – is in the end rather less than the analogous risk in the case
of the 'weaker' grammars employed by psychologists and psychiatrists, even
deeply literarily and philosophically sophisticated ones such as Louis Sass
certainly is. The risk in the case of the more prosaic, less resistant schema for
interpretation offered by the likes of Sass – in his case, "pseudo-solipsism" – is
that it will seem that we have indeed captured much schizophrenia, *and
rendered it in a form that we can in the ordinary sense 'understand'*. The strong,
strange grammar of the writing of Faulkner is significantly less likely than the
writings of a psychologist to be taken up as an orthodoxy for what 'schizophrenic language' or what-have-you 'really means' – and that is all to the good.
What such a work as *The Sound and the Fury* actually gives us in its 'deranged'
literature is a new *mode* or *manner* of 'representation', *not* a way of capturing
something that is waiting to be captured, to be rendered into anything
remotely like plain prose.

And the 'stronger' the 'grammar', the less akin to ordinary prose requiring no interpretative work, and the less likelihood of thinking that one has found 'the real meaning' of what is 'represented'.

What I would like Sass to acknowledge is what Freud half-jokingly allowed of his own writings on Schreber;[65] that one's own remarks have in themselves no superiority to (e.g.) Schreber's, or even Benjy's words. Sass' remarks, and indeed my own remarks, at best re-express or re-present these, in a 'weaker grammar', and are thus themselves no less nonsensical than that which they re-present. When one is trying hard to re-present aright something that is resistant even to the subtlest hermeneutic, the irony is that one can only *succeed* by *producing further nonsense*.

Sass' work is (or should be) a ladder that one *throws away* after climbing it. Or, better: the 'insight' one gets from work like Sass' *is* the coming to see that what appeared to be a key to understanding something strange is itself just more nonsense. *In* overcoming Sass' words, in overcoming the temptation to think that one now simply understands what was problematic before, one learns something. (To say this is not necessarily any criticism of Sass; it is an attempt to characterize the *kind* of text his is, the kind of writing that is actually of any use, hereabouts. Holding obstinately on to the 'ladder' of the pseudo-solipsistic interpretation, as if holding on to a key, or a Traveller's Phrase Book, is chickening out from acknowledging the full strangeness and difference and difficulty, the utter paradoxicality, of that which one is trying to write about.)

I would like to close this section with one further example. One example of mine that Sass criticizes is that of the schizophrenic girl, 'Renée'. In her pseudo-Heideggerian remarks on 'the things' around her, she characterized them as being 'alive'. Here is what I wrote on this, in my (2001: 462), in the course of arguing that 'Renée' renders her own thought uninterpretable:

> "[T]he doctors . . . thought that I saw these things as humans whom I heard speak. But it was not that. Their life consisted uniquely in the fact that they were there, in their existence itself." // This stops one in one's tracks. The chance one seemingly had of coming to understand Renée's strange world (via the concept of 'personification' [of the things], etc.) finally disappears fairly precisely at this moment. She has specifically ruled it out. Any way that she has of expressing her experience is "inadequate", and so of course she is not understood. Her confusion is irredeemable, irrevocable. // For surely there just isn't anything it can be for the *life* of objects to consist uniquely in their existence.

Their appalling 'life' wasn't for her simply (!) a matter of their being (like) malign-spirited objects, or humans everywhere in the form of objects, or just otherwise terrifyingly threatening. *It consisted simply in their existence.* My challenge to Sass *et al.* is thus to find a way of understanding this (and similar examples) that does not violate his own hermeneutical principles, and that does not impose a false coherence on the thought-processes of 'Renée' *et al.*

My suggestion is that one can only really be getting Renée right if one produces an account of her that is itself in the end plain that it is nonsense. Sass might respond by saying that *he* is not committed to the 'animism/ personification' interpretation of 'Renée', but rather to an interpretation of her as 'living' Cartesianism, as having decisively lost what J. J. Gibson has called the 'affordances' of ordinary human life. But either this is a heavy interpret- ation which does not start from what Renée herself thinks – I criticize such 'impositional hermeneutics' in my (2001) – or this is *simply a redescription of the problem.* We can indeed say of 'Renée' things like that she has lost a sense of what the world affords an active social human being, a sense of what it is to live, to be-in-the-world, and thus that she speaks of things as alive precisely due to their seemingly pointless *existence*... but does this help us to get any further with *understanding* how someone can actually feel/think of the *life* of *things* – again, it is their *life* that so disturbs or terrifies her – as consisting 'uniquely in their existence'? Perhaps it does help; the reader can judge for themselves. My question is: can we avoid imposing on 'Renée' a schema of interpretation that trashes her own, without finding her to be either irrational (not, as Sass would have it, 'hyper-rational'), or to be living a 'life' that is so utterly not our's that we are fooling ourselves if we think we can understand it in *any* positive way, or (and here our words *really* start to give out) a life that has no form, or a life- world that is so teeming with 'life' that it is lifeless, or the sheer absence of anything that we will ultimately want to call a lived world.

The great temptation that must be resisted – but without trapping us in allegedly limited or closed languages or minds or cultures – is to think that anything human must always be comprehensible. Occasionally, just occa- sionally, the greatest illusion is the delusion of sense – a delusion that itself intriguingly echoes a typical delusion of 'the pseudo-solipsist', whose 'world' is typically not blankly empty but, rather, too full of thought, of meanings, of significance – that insists there is always some sense to be found where there is something like the linguistic jingle of rationality, the *sound* of sense. This, I believe, is a hitherto-unrecognized major insight available to the applier of Wittgenstein to 'deranged' Modernist literature, and to the writings of the mad.

Part 3

Time

Time is not a new topic to us, after our extended considerations of Faulkner (and Sass, and Stevens) in Part 2. But this Part tries to apply the philosophy of Wittgenstein, read resolutely, to time as it has been considered by philosophers (and physicists, sociologists, various kinds of ordinary folk, and then returning to the psychologically and psychiatrically suffering). Some of the material in this Part is technically challenging; I consider some abstruse maths, physics and philosophy in the course of my work here. If Wittgenstein can and is to be usefully and *widely* applied, it had better be in these zones too, and not just in the kind of humanistic and everyday domains considered in Parts 2 and 1, above.

It is time to examine how the 'tale' of time is told,[1] by the cleverest of non-humanistic minds.

3.1 Dummett Challenged: Beyond 'Realist' and 'Anti-Realist' Renderings of Time[2]

3.1.1 Introduction

Philosophers typically tend to presume that time is something like a continuum of instants, or a succession of durationless 'nows'. This presumption faces some serious difficulties. It is unclear how one can possibly build up to time, as continuous, from durationless instants. It is very like the notion of building up a line from dimensionless points. There are certain contexts in which it might do no harm to think of a line as 'composed' of points – for example, in certain rarefied contexts of theoretical geometry; or perhaps, if one was trying to explain to a student how to measure a line; or, more straightforwardly (with the points now transparently *not* dimensionless), if one was wishing to paint a line 'Monet-style' or 'Seurat-style' . . . But it is absurd to surmise that a collectivity, however large, of dimensionless points could actually result in something with dimension.[3]

There seems then to be something very dubious about the idea of time as *composed* of instants.

Furthermore, "now" is a paradigmatically *indexical* and *context-relative* expression: when specified somewhat more closely, it can mean today, this year, the modern age, this instant (i.e. 'right away'); etc. It isn't any kind of temporal unit whatsoever – and hence time can't be a sequence of those 'units'.[4] Much the same is I think true, if less obviously, of 'instant'. Compare, "Come here this instant!" It would seem deeply misleading to think of this command as congenitally 'false' (in the sense of appearing to demand something ('simul-taneous' compliance) that it actually does not), or as implicitly invoking a quasi-scientific unit of time – or as congenitally vague. Rather, it is surely an adequate, ordinary, indexical, context-relative etc. utterance.

The leading philosopher of time in our time is Michael Dummett. He has argued in recent years[5] to somewhat similar effect to my points, above: he has criticized severely the 'classical' model of time, a model he notes is strongly present in Hume and after,[6] *and* which he thinks has deep 'Realist' pretensions (actually, he goes so far as to speak of a *super-realist* metaphysics here (D1: 497)). That is, the notion of time as composed of durationless instants:

1. presumes that there is always a completely precise answer to the question, "When did *x* happen?", even if such an answer is entirely and in principle beyond our cognitive powers. Furthermore, it:
2. invites the postulation of seemingly 'conceptually impossible' scenarios.

Dummett proposes a series of *alternative* models of time (of which his favoured one is, roughly, 'Anti-Realist', while all are at least Anti-'super-Realist'). If one wishes to apply Wittgenstein's thinking to (the philosophy of) time, in our time, as I do, one shall have, then, to reckon with Dummett's model. We shall get to its details in the course of the following discussion. But I want to begin by remarking that we need to be very careful, from the beginning, not to buy into latent nonsense here, if we are inclined to agree with Dummett's (terms of) criticism – if we are inclined, that is, to agree that there seems something abhorrent or nonsensical about the classical model. I will take (1) and (2) in turn, and we will see that Dummett's manner of dealing with them leaves his own philosophy of time in an unstable and potentially nonsensical condition. (In the process, he fails to recognize the possibility that there may be ways in which 'the classical model' of time can be rendered as harmless.)

3.1.2 Using Nonsense to Combat Nonsense: Different Conceptions

(1) If we are inclined not to agree that a 'completely precise' answer can be given (by God) to some (or any) "When did *x* happen?" questions, we should not rush to the conclusion that this is because *x* happened, for instance, *at a vague time*. Rather than rushing to give an alternative answer to the 'Realist''s question we should instead ask whether any sense has yet been attached to what the 'Realist' asks and then asserts (for others to deny).

The Realist seems in the grip of an attractive picture. A picture, we might say, of the universe as everywhere and everywhen just as it is, and not another way.

But that now sounds tautological. Can the picture be made any clearer than that, and controversial enough for someone actually to disagree with?[7] I am not sure it can. But the point is: Dummett does not stop to find out. He instead assumes that the Realist picture is intelligible and contentious, and presses immediately to provide an alternative picture, a picture he thinks less 'implausible', more 'parsimonious', or something like that. It is hard to know how one can actually assemble *criteria* for judging between these pictures, for saying that there is an alternative to Realism that is "more satisfactory" (D1: 505), or "better" (D1: 505). It is unclear whether Dummett is using a philosophical *method*, one might say. Unless he is simply 'doing metaphysics'. But didn't we learn anything from Wittgenstein? Can we just presume that the question "What is time?" is well defined, or that the question "When did *x* happen?" must always have some kind of definite answer, even if that answer attributes indefiniteness to *x*?

But am I being unfair to Dummett? Doesn't he actually understand at least somewhat well a central Wittgensteinian objection to metaphysical Realism, namely that it is not a coherent picture at all? That it yields various conceptual impossibilities (see e.g. D1: 503, 505)? This is where (2) comes in:

(2) We should be alarmed that Dummett seems to have no problem describing *exactly what the 'conceptual impossibilities' are* that he claims follow from 'Realism' about time. Dummett claims that there is something unintelligible about the 'Realist' picture of time, that it involves the postulation of phenomena that ought "to be rejected as impossible on pure conceptual grounds" (D1: 505); but he acts and talks as if he *understands* it perfectly well.

Again, the worry here is that Dummett goes far too quickly. He tends very quickly – without giving any philosophical (let alone sociological, or linguistic, etc.) justification – to cite certain features of 'our concepts' (see e.g. D1: 499), and just as quickly wheels them in to attack 'Realism' about time. Take the following example (from D1: 503):

> [Consider] a pair of objects which, throughout a certain interval, were exactly 2cm apart, save at one particular instant in that interval, when they were 4cm apart. *Our conception of physical quantities is plainly such that this supposition makes no sense.* Yet the classical model allows it a sense; according to it, it is barred, if it is barred, only by the laws of physics, and not *by conceptual necessity.* The classical model supplies descriptions for states of affairs which, *being conceptually impossible,* should admit no description. (Emphases mine)[8]

This example does indeed seem to bring out something 'unsatisfactory' about the picture of time as a continuum of *durationless* instants. (It is not clear that anything at all has genuinely been pictured, if we are asked to imagine something being somewhere only for an instant that has no *duration.*) I have already suggested that we need to go right back to the 'start' of that picture, to what Wittgenstein would call "the initial move in the conjuring trick". We need to ask ourselves how we could ever have imagined in the first place that you can 'develop' continuity, time, change, out of changeless points alone. I don't see how the picture gets off the ground; it's as hopeless as the fantasy of getting perception out of empiricist sense-data. But it seems incoherent to let the picture get off the grounds, and *then* counter-example it, if the way that the counter-example you describe supposedly proves your point is that . . . the counter-example has not described anything! Why shouldn't the Realist respond to Dummett simply thus: "Given that it is obvious that you and I both understand the plain English used in your example, it is a self-refuting 'counter-example'"?[9]

In a nutshell: one self-refutes, if one conceptually *describes* something that one has claimed to be "conceptually impossible". The conceptually impossible is not a genuine candidate for description. ('It' is, rather, not anything at all.)

The 'conceptually impossible' does not (as Dummett seems to be committed to saying it does) have a 'senseless sense'. It is simply a lack ('as yet') of sense.

A route that Dummett could have taken here, rather than insisting that classical mathematics does 'develop' "the continuity of the one-dimensional real line out of dimensionless real numbers" (D2: 389), would have been to have raised worries, worries that he undoubtedly has strong sympathy with (for he is sympathetic to Brouwer's Intuitionistic critique of classical mathematics), concerning whether it actually makes sense to think this way.[10] My own Wittgensteinian (rather than 'Intuitionist') way of raising something like this concern would be as follows: do we really know what we are talking about, when we talk of the classical model being of time as "*composed* of durationless instants" (D2: 390)? Doesn't this picture inherit all the dubiety of thinking of "the classical mathematical continuum [as] composed of real numbers" (D2: 390)?

To compose a line out of real numbers is to imagine an actual infinity of real numbers that, by means of a kind of infinite pointillism, *form* a continuum. But the idea of assembling all the numbers in order to do this is an idea repugnant to a Wittgensteinian.[11] No sense has yet been given to such an 'idea', in our view.

Dummett speaks freely of "the rational line" and "the real line" (see especially D3, *passim*). That's fine, so long as we never forget that these are abstractions. This is *obviously* so, in the case of "the rational line". Geometry can mislead us here.[12] If we can draw something, then it must exist, yes? *No*, not in the relevant sense. That we can speak of "the rational line" or "the real line" oughtn't to be seen as having any revisionary *consequences*. A line is continuous, and is formed out of the *marks* that make it up; that of course implies nothing about the character of the continuity of the rationals or even of the reals; recall that a line is not literally composed of points, in the mathematical sense of that word.

If by "the real line" we mean nothing other than a set (a set of points, we might accurately say), then that is fine. But a set is not a line. Thinking of the real numbers as *forming* a *line* gets us off on the wrong foot. As soon as Dummett allows that wrong start, he is hobbled in preventing it from 'developing' further. And then he ends up depicting something that appears allowed by the Realist picture of maths, and yet that must be 'conceptually denied'. But the depiction undermines the case for denial. One needs to issue one's philosophical challenge earlier: one ought to question the metaphysical Realist *picture* of numbers that appears so naturally to generate a metaphysical Realist picture of time and reality, through our illusion that we have been already told something about what (e.g.) a line really is, from the Realist picture of numbers.

At page 409 of D3, Dummett asks, "What is the point of asking whether the real line is made up of or composed of individual real numbers? What is the point of asking whether time is made up of or composed of durationless instants?" He answers that he has tried to cash out these metaphors. I submit that the metaphors here have not been and as far as I can tell 'cannot' be cashed out in any way that the casher-outer *will accept as fulfilling the totality of his original purposes in putting forward the metaphor*. Dummett, in allowing that the metaphors *can* be cashed out successfully, already concedes that the 'position' that he is attacking makes sense. It is thus nonsensical for him to criticize it as nonsense, or as 'yielding' nonsense, *as he does*. This is his main criticism of the 'classical' view. But he has already deprived himself of the resources for making it . . .

Better, then, to say simply this, and stop the rot before it starts: there is just nothing that it is to 'develop' continuity or change out of durationless instants. Just as there is nothing that it is to 'develop' a line out of geometrical points (of numbers), no matter how many of them there be.

To sum up, then: Dummett thinks, apparently, that he sort-of understands the classical model of time. It has enough sense, he thinks, for him to understand why it is 'ultimately' nonsense, what it is 'trying to say'. I think that *that* 'thought' of Dummett's is nonsense.

Dummett goes on to explain *what it is* in the classical model that he (thinks he) *does* understand: namely, the 'continuum of real numbers' (D2: 388–9): "[A]ny segment of the real line . . . has a length." Yes; but not a length *in numbers*!![13] In any given representation, it has a length in centimetres or whatever. It has a length *incomparable with* the ('infinitude' of the) real numbers.[14]

So: I do not accept that the real number continuum could possibly give us any model at all of anything in the real world in the way that would be necessary for classical maths to allegedly underpin an understanding of (say) time. It (the continuum) is strictly speaking best described as incomparable with real things. (Unless we re-picture such a continuum as a kind of true *flow* – as prescinding altogether from its 'elements' or 'constituents'.) One can of course measure things in the world by means of a ruler, or by means of any device that in effect uses (rational) numbers as its gradations. But I do not see that or how it could mean anything to speak of a collectivity of dimensionless points accumulating into anything with a length. The reals get you precisely nowhere, in this connection.

3.1.3 How to Discuss Matters with a Realist

One key aspect and moral of the above discussion was this: one has to have a way of 'dialoguing' with the Realist that does not *first accept* his terms and *then* (as he will not unreasonably see it) beg the question against him.[15] If one is genuinely reducing one's opponent to *absurdity*, one must not *accept* his terms; one should at most 'entertain' them, and make perspicuous that they were not terms anyone could ever intelligibly accept and use (as opposed to mention) in sentences of one's own.

If Dummett wants to employ the 'scenario' he describes, he should either:

(a) endeavour to get it to be patently or latently 'self-deconstructing', from the start, merely a rhetorical device, a piece of nonsense to bring out the latent nonsense of 'Realism'. (Otherwise there will clearly be a latent contradiction in what he has done: *describing* something (e.g. take his example involving "a pair of objects . . . 2cm apart save for at one particular instant . . .") that he precisely wants to argue *is indescribable* (at least, 'for us').) Or, better still:

(b) he could actually take the risk of allowing us to think for ourselves about the topic, to think about these difficult matters in all their complexity. What do I mean? I am thinking of the striking difference between the examples and scenarios which Dummett employs, and those which are invoked in Wittgenstein's texts. Typically, the latter are more 'open-textured'. We have in a way to decide for ourselves whether or not a scenario has actually been depicted at all, in most of Wittgenstein's 'examples'. Take for example the 'builders',[16] the 'wood-sellers',[17] 'pain-patches' and 'pain in stones'[18] etc.; do we really know what to say (in advance of thinking them through in a potentially almost endless dialogue) about any of these? Or do they rather engage with our profound temptations to mire ourselves in nonsense? (I will return to this matter below.)

Anti-Realist (e.g. Relativist) interpretations of Wittgenstein tend to short-circuit all that is most profound and potentially therapeutic in his thought. When one encounters a teasing 'example' in Wittgenstein, one will perhaps inevitably at first work with the assumption that it makes sense, that something possible in another culture or at least in a world with different natural-scientific 'laws' is being described. But Wittgenstein's writing then tends to bring out features of the 'scenarios' he has apparently described which induce those 'scenarios' to collapse in on themselves. One way of expressing what Wittgenstein's examples tend to show is that we are deluded if we think of what can be thought, of conceptual possibility, on anything at all like the model of physical possibility. 'Conceptual possibilities' are not, as they seem to be for Dummett, 'impossible possibilities'[19] – they are simply expressions which delude us into thinking we know how to use them. Whereas we are far from having found a use for them *at all.*

But one could equally express the tentative, situation-relative, confusion-relative 'insights' that working through Wittgenstein's 'examples' yields in ways quite different from the above, even in ways apparently contradictory to it. For the thing is, not to establish any philosophical thesis; the important thing is to resolve the contradictory impulses one already has, probably latently, in relation to the seemingly underlying 'questions' (e.g. "What is language?", in the case of the 'builders'; "Is there only one possible 'system' of logic, or of arithmetic, or are there several?", in the case of the 'wood-sellers'; and so on). The important thing is to face honestly the difficulty attending any wish we might have to speak of 'something' that seems 'conceptually impossible'.[20]

Dummett, by contrast, knows exactly the answer he wants us to reach, the philosophical thesis he wants us to enunciate along with him; the devices he uses to get there do not essentially interest him, and that is perhaps how he misses *their* incoherency – how he misses the respects in which, evidently, he himself does not have a good grip on the words he is using; the respects in which he is only mirroring the absurdities of the 'Realist', not in any way 'correcting' or transcending them, not perspicuously bringing them out. In short: it is just no good to state just what it is that one's opponents impossibly conceptualize. (Have we learned nothing from Frege's wrestlings with this? Nor from the central difficulty of the *Tractatus*, which Wittgenstein thematized throughout that work?[21])

My view, then, is that we should ask ourselves with the utmost seriousness whether it is wise to think as Dummett does. He replies in the negative to the question, "Is time a continuum of instants?"[22] I am pretty sympathetic. But he seems to think that this negative reply entails giving an alternative theoretical account; he nowhere canvasses the possibility that there is something amiss with the *question*; or rather, with what we want when we raise such questions in the first place. In other words, he thinks that he still has to reply to the question, "What (then) is time?" He canvasses some possibilities, and appears most sympathetic to the anti-classical model of time which he terms "constructive". Here are his concluding remarks on this alternative model:

> The constructive model does not represent time as composed of durationless instants corresponding to determinate real numbers, as the classical model does, nor of small constitutive intervals, as the unmodified fuzzy realist model does. Rather . . . it represents time as a continuum which we can dissect into intervals whose end-points are the initiation and termination of physical processes. We can determine the end-points of such intervals as themselves much smaller intervals, these being our approximations to the instants at which they occurred. Such instants are indeed representable by real numbers, and it is on them that are defined the functions giving the magnitudes of other quantities at different times; in this respect all is as in the classical model, and we may [in this sense] say that time is composed of such instants. But the constructive model

differs from the classical one in that these instants are not precisely
located . . . (pp. 514–15)

What I want to ask about passages like this is what the character of the debate
is supposed to be here; how are contests between the different 'models'
supposed to be decided? Or even argued, at all?

3.1.4 Realism *versus* Anti-Realism?

Participants in these debates, the Realist vs. Anti-Realist debates, typically try
to speak as if the debate between them is *a genuine question of a matter of fact*, as
though the question is not whether their opponents' view is *coherent*, but about
whether their opponents' view is *false* (and their own, true). The difficulty, as
hinted earlier, is that it is hard to come up with arguments – with criteria – for
the falsity or truth of such abstract claims as we are here dealing with.
Dummett and his opponents do not wish to fall victim to properly scientific
refutation or ridicule. But they want to have something to say against each
other more than just, "I don't like your picture." So they tend periodically to
fall into making 'logical' or 'conceptual' claims against one another after all –
thus leaving themselves open again to meta-criticisms such as that that I
essayed in consideration of point (2), earlier.

What I shall increasingly argue for in what follows is that the unclarity in
what the character of the debate is supposed to be, as indicated in the above
paragraph, ramifies: such that in the end the most perspicuous thing to say
is, in fact, that 'Anti-Realism' is invariably *a form of Realism*, just an odd,
subtly inconsistent form. Anti-Realism keeps the fundamental metaphysical
picture of Realism intact; it does not radically alter but only slightly
broadens the structure of options, of categories, that are open to one. I
suspect that deep down, rather than merely thinking of itself as the most
coherent and helpful available way of talking metaphysically, Anti-Realism
still thinks that there is a Reality . . . *settling whether Realism or Anti-Realism is
correct!* We might say that 'Anti-Realism' is never anti-Realist *enough*, or not
consistently anti-Realist. It inevitably tends, as a matter of rhetoric, towards
regarding its dispute with Realism as one *about a matter of fact*. Among other
things, this enables it to be philosophically 'respectable'; it does not seriously challenge well-established philosophical 'games', it does not raise
questions about philosophy itself, or even about philosophical method. It
appears to be in the game of stating 'how things are', when it falls back from
its incoherent criticisms of Realism as nonsensical, incoherent, into a criticism of Realism as 'false'.

If I am right, Anti-Realism is essentially conservative. Who really cares
whether one rallies behind the flag of super-Realism, of 'fuzzy' Realism, or of
Constructivism; Realists *should* acknowledge Dummett as, on the points that
really count, one of their own. The disagreement between classical Realism
and Dummettian Realism (it perhaps matters less now whether we include the

prefix 'Anti-' or not) is like the disagreement nowadays between the Conservatives and New Labour; most of the non-rhetorical differences between the two sides are within their accountants' margins of error.

But, as yet, some of the above may appear to remain mere assertion. I need to do a little more philosophical work, concerning the work that 'the philosophy of time' (allegedly) does, concerning its 'cash value', in order to *convince* anyone sceptical of my claims, and so as to lead up to my conclusion – which concerns the very limited degree to which the activity that Dummett is engaged in is anything different from traditional (more or less pre-Kantian, certainly pre-Wittgensteinian) metaphysics.

Perhaps Dummett and a Realist opponent of his would *jointly* object to my arguments, at a high level of generality, roughly as follows: "You are trying to evacuate the philosophy of time of content and significance. But the questions we are trying to answer are important. You have still offered no good reason for *us* to think that there is not an issue between us, between Dummett and his target and critic."

After all this discussion, it is possible that I am not alone in wondering, rather by contrast: "What *is* the point of all this Realist and Anti-Realist contestation about time? What could really *turn on* the answer to the questions that Dummett is considering?" If *these* questions are in the reader's mind at all, then I am evidently very sympathetic. For what *is* the 'cash value' of disputes between 'Realist' and 'Anti-Realist' hereabouts? (And this puts into doubt the value too of what Dummett seems sometimes to be offering: a 'compromise solution' or 'middle ground' between the two.)

Does *physics* need these pictures, these metaphors? Possibly they might help, they *might* provide ways in which physicists might want to think about time; but it is hardly as if physicists are going to let themselves be instructed by philosophers as to how they ought to think about time.[23] If the point is to offer potentially helpful images of time to physicists, then at the very least the tone of the debate between Dummett and his opponent should change rather. In fact, it would become rather unclear whether there was really a *disagreement* between the two, at all. If I paint one picture or compose one piece of music, and you paint or compose a discordantly different one, are we *disagreeing*? If I come up with one idea that might prove heuristically helpful, and you come up with a different one, are we even yet *disagreeing*?

Is it perhaps rather psychology, or sociology – human science as opposed to natural science – which needs help from the philosopher in understanding time? Is it time as lived / as experienced which is actually at issue between Dummett and his opponents? This seems even less likely – for, unlike many in the 'Continental' tradition (e.g. Bergson, Heidegger, Schutz), Anglo-American philosophers seem extremely uninterested in the 'secondary' question of how time is lived.[24] Even most philosophical 'Anti-Realists', who might have been expected to have been gripped by the phenomenon of time-for-humans, actually show little ostensible interest in it. (Though it is worth remarking that many human scientists, practitioners of anthropology, sociology, etc., who work on 'time' can I think be reasonably described as 'Anti-Realistic', as implicitly more or less 'Dummettian'.[25])

Are there questions lying 'behind' questions like "Is time a continuum of instants?" – questions which *do* have a more genuine or weighty interest, or use? For example, is one perhaps really trying to understand *how change is possible*, when one asks questions like Dummett's? Well, if one is, one is unfortunately pursuing an entirely unproductive route of approach to that question (a metaphysical question, a question whose level of generality is such that it is admittedly unlikely to be a productive question to ask in the first place). For the point is that Dummett's 'theory of time' does not actually help us understand how change is possible in the slightest, being itself *entirely parasitic upon the phenomenon/phenomena of change.* The 'grammar' of change – in fact, the 'grammar' of temporality in general – is already presupposed by Dummett's apparatus (see e.g. D1: 509): the apparatus of constitutive intervals (of time) of varying lengths, etc. These units, of which time is 'composed', already presuppose *the passage of time.* Some might want to regard this as an improvement over the 'classical' model of time, wherein it seems impossible to constitute time at all, given that all we have in that model are durationless units.[26] But the 'improvement' is very fishily bought – rather than have no understanding of time result from one's model because one has quite deprived oneself of time (of duration, of continuousness), one has an understanding of time . . . because one has *presupposed* time, has presupposed what time is!

Dummett's own 'model' appears to me, then, not actually to offer any assistance at all to anyone, be they scientist, layperson, or even philosopher, in understanding what time 'really' is, or in understanding apparently related matters, like 'how change is possible'. In contrast I believe to our presentation in section 3.2, below, it certainly does not offer insight into the philosophical dilemmas and temptations posed by the phenomena of time and change; in contrast to some moments in Part 2 of this book, it does not offer insight into psychopathological time (and thereby into ordinary time). One is inclined to think that it offers no assistance to anyone at all.

Except perhaps: a pure metaphysician might be 'helped' by Dummett. Someone who thinks there is simply an autonomous subject: 'the theory/metaphysics of time', orthogonal to physics, or to psychology, or to (post-Wittgensteinian) philosophy.

In the end, it appears that Dummett may in fact be happy to self-identify as such a metaphysician:

A [charitable] realist will say that [Dummett's] is a good description of our imperfect methods of determining instants and magnitudes, but that we must believe that the limits we cannot attain exist in reality, though known only to God. The constructivist asks why we should believe this: he does not think that reality contains, or that God creates, anything of which His rational creatures cannot in principle become aware. (D1: 515)

This fits *precisely* the line of argument which I have pursued in this section. Dummett is, in the end, still I think playing a quasi-medieval game: he is still trying to figure out what reality contains, or what God creates, and so to answer the allegedly 'straightforward' question, "What *is* time?" Dummett is engaged in a metaphysical – or 'ontotheological' – debate, ineliminably, and (at this key point in his text) self-confessedly. His ultimate motivation for his philosophy of time is avowedly theological in nature; it is motivated by a particular conception of God, as having created a Universe designed for comprehensibility.

The Realist says that the World contains more than we, constrained as we are by our alleged 'finitude', can understand or know. But the Realist thinks that we can look beyond those 'limits', in philosophy (metaphysics), to say something about what there is beyond what we can actually understand or know. The Anti-Realist (e.g. the 'constructivist') says that the world contains nothing more than we find, within our 'limits'. But the Anti-Realist thinks that we can look beyond those 'limits', in philosophy (metaphysics), to say something about what there *isn't* beyond what we can actually understand or know.[27]

When one puts it like that, isn't it obvious how very much the two 'combatants' share, how barely differentiable are their positions? Anti-Realism does not really question the big Realist picture of things *at all* – it merely denies its truth. Or, to put it much less grandly, 'Realists' and 'Anti-Realists' just differ about how words like "world" should be used. The difference between them seems, from the point of view of one who is not attracted by their games, to be above all *a **merely** semantic difference*.

We who do not see/feel a compulsion any more actually to do metaphysics are not content to let the Realist picture stand in the first place. We 'throw away', we endeavour to *overcome* the picture of limits,[28] the picture parasitic upon the picture of the Realist notion of the world beyond those 'limits'. Whereas, again, 'Anti-Realism' does *not* in the end question those pictures.

That is why I said, earlier, that it is reasonable to characterize 'Anti-Realism' as a (deviant) form of 'Realism'. Depending on one's taste, one might say that it is a poor man's Realism; or that it is Realism groping its way towards a tenable alternative. But, either way, anyone in search of a genuine alternative to metaphysics, to Realism, needs to look considerably beyond it.

Even such a one, finding perhaps what they were looking for much more in Wittgenstein (and perhaps also in Cavell, Diamond, Conant, some McDowell, and recent Putnam[29]) than in Dummett, might still ask whether I really mean to deny that 'constructivism' is any progress at all away from/beyond Realism. Doesn't constructivism help one to give up 'philosophical theism'? Isn't it a partial cure, a way-station on the road to abandoning a God who isn't *required* as 'super-realists' (D1: 497) and Lewis and Davidson and Chalmers and Colin McGinn and a thousand others throughout Anglo-American philosophy still arguably require God?[30]

Maybe so. But it seems just as likely to me that 'Anti-Realism' simply drives the illness deeper underground. That it is a neurotic condition resulting from repression of the illness' starker symptoms. 'Anti-Realism' can appear to have more philosophical acuity about it than 'Realism' – I have suggested that this is only because it rather hides its *own* 'Realism', partly through *systematically failing to choose whether its criticism of standard 'Realism' is that it is* false *or that it is* nonsensical. Where 'Anti-Realism' is in my opinion potentially most acute, where it appears to have something to say beyond the alleged 'implausibility' or 'unhelpfulness' of 'classical' Realism, is where it looks to characterize 'Realism' as nonsensical, but this cannot be done *coherently* except in the genuinely Wittgensteinian style of philosophizing that I have tried to essay in this section, a thoroughgoingly 'negative' style which Dummett, the great theoretical Anti-Realist, is, it would seem, not prepared to embrace.

As Dummett notes (D2: 392), I think that the questioning of whether it makes sense to claim that time is a continuum of instants does *not* entail "giving an alternative theoretical account". (To give any such account appears to me to necessitate 'standing outside time',[31] viewing it 'from sideways on', as McDowell puts it. I do not think that this is something which cannot be done (Anti-Realism), but that no sense has yet been given to the thought that there is something here that we can *or* cannot do. That is why I question both Realism and Anti-Realism. To suppose that the notion of viewing time as if from outside has something like a senseless sense is simply to deepen one's embeddedness in confusion.)

This scepticism of mine about the project of saying what time is does not mean that I am "indifferent to philosophy" (D2: 392) . . . unless Wittgenstein, Austin, Hertz etc. were similarly "indifferent". Dummett says of 'the question of time' that "it is a problem that has perplexed me for a great many years. It perplexed St. Augustine, too." I urge that we must not assume that the 'existence' of time (which of course I do not *deny!*) brings with it a well-formed philosophical question. The love of wisdom demands we be ready to question the questions that philosophy has bequeathed to us. I think that Dummett's refusal to consider questioning those questions has unfortunate consequences. It leads him to unknowingly enunciate some 'subtle' nonsenses.

Sometimes, then, I would rather deal with the honest and plain metaphysics – the visible absurdities, the patent nonsenses – of the likes of David Lewis and Timothy Williamson and Roy Sorenson and Colin McGinn, than with the subtle latent nonsense of 'constructivism'. Though, ironically, at least Dummett's position has this going for it, this clarity: he states absolutely explicitly the theological motivation for his philosophical (Anti-)Realism.

3.1.5 An Intermediate Conclusion

I offer no answer whatsoever to 'questions' such as "Is time a continuum of instants?" Rather, I ask what it could possibly mean to say that it is (and by extension, whether it can mean anything at all to say that it isn't).

In physics, 'time' is whatever it is, and philosophy will never second-guess physics successfully or even, I suspect, remotely usefully.[32] In normal social life

– in the alleged 'domain' of the 'human sciences' – people generally have no trouble being in time, and would in most cases I think regard as utterly absurd and pointless any effort to say whether their experience was, for example, 'really' continuous or not.

Until we *question the questions* that metaphysics has bequeathed us, questions that we can I think bring ourselves and others to see as pointless and empty, questions that 'Anti-Realism' just as much as 'Realism' purports to have clear answers to, we will never achieve philosophical peace. And we will never achieve even the level of understanding arguably native to one and all of us, as masters of the language and as competent social actors: the understanding of time, as lived, as a ubiquitous tool, a variegated *organizational* phenomenon, saturating our conceptions, our experience, our interactions, our activities. To the applier of Wittgensteinian philosophy, it is clear that time is in the end no more mysterious than other more mundane organizational devices: such as maps or tape-measures or rulers. And so: asking "What is time?" is actually no more likely to result in philosophical advance or clarity than asking (e.g.) "What is a metre-ruler?", while breathlessly expecting some theoretical or deep or revelatory answer to one's question . . .

My therapeutic notion of questioning of questions intimates roughly how I think we should understand the justly famous quotation from the great philosopher-scientist, Heinrich Hertz, that I give below, a quotation, an idea, whose influence upon Wittgenstein's conception of philosophical method was profound. Hertz in the original text is discussing chiefly difficulties around the concept of 'force'; I have taken the liberty of substituting the word "time", to which I think highly parallel considerations apply:

[W]e have accumulated around [the term "time"] more relations than can be completely reconciled amongst themselves. We have an obscure feeling of this and want to have things cleared up. Our confused wish finds expression in the question as to the nature of [time]. But the answer which we want is not really an answer to this question. It is not by finding out more and fresh relations and connections that it can be answered; but by removing the contradictions existing between those already known, and thus perhaps by reducing their number. When these painful contradictions are removed, the question as to the nature of [time] will not have been answered; but our minds, no longer vexed, will cease to ask illegitimate questions.[33]

I hope here to have made a small contribution to something like Hertz's task, by showing some respects in which "What is time?" and related questions are 'illegitimate',[34] *and do not address the vexations whose dissolving is our real need.*

3.1.6 Methodological Reflections

Let me summarize the state of the argument at this point. Dummett and I agree that the absurdity of 'the classical model' of time[35] lies *most crucially* in the notion of a quantity possessing a certain magnitude such that it is logically independent of the magnitude at any other instant. We agree that this conception of the logical independence of the 'basic quantities' in terms of which 'time-slices' are to be characterized is no less absurd *vis-à-vis* position, mass etc. than it is *vis-à-vis* (e.g.) velocity. We agree that taking time simply to be continuous in its essence is in general much to be preferred to taking time to be composed of dimensionless instants.

The primary difference between us might then best be described as *methodological*. But this methodological difference has real effects. Dummett has by my lights a poor intellectual motivation for his practice, and so does not succeed in applying his would-be ideas adequately to his chosen subject-matter. My sense remains, that is, that Dummett does not have a fully thought-through *reason* for preferring a 'continuist' appreciation of time to an 'atomistic' version of it, for preferring something like what Bergson was striving for to what Hume's picture of the Universe provided. Dummett's main arguments against classicalism *still buy into its very absurdities and nonsenses*. Thus, those arguments self-refute. They unwittingly retain key elements of the very Realism which Dummett is attempting to challenge. For this reason, they are entirely unpersuasive. We ought, I am suggesting, not to seek to *prove* to the Realist that he has to concede that he is mistaken. This *cannot be done*, in philosophy. Rather, we should do 'therapy'. One should attempt to *persuade* his opponent: that he is not clear about what he himself wants to say.[36]

My criticism of Dummett has had at its heart then the worry that he appears to conceptualize states of affairs that he then goes on to characterize, crucially for his argument, as "conceptually impossible". At D2, page 387, Dummett writes that "Latent nonsense contains enough sense for it to be possible to derive consequences from it." He hopes therefore to have intimated a way in which one can deduce from some of one's conceptualizations that they are conceptually impossible. I question his suggestion. Surely latent nonsense only *appears* to do what Dummett says it does. The notion of its having a 'senseless sense' – or enough sense for us to know what it would say if it actually made sense – is itself senseless/nonsensical (see *PI* 500. Wittgenstein's entire career is in significant measure devoted to rejecting the thought that latent nonsense can genuinely have consequences derived from it.).[37] Latent nonsense is *simply nonsense in disguise*.

Dummett speaks of finding "enough" sense that one can *work out* from some sentence(s) that it is nonsense. The image of a half-full bottle perhaps comes to mind; but sense isn't like that. A half-full bottle still contains something; its contents are still usable. A sentence 'containing' half a sense (!?), by contrast, is no use at all (at least, not for making sense with). One just doesn't find /

hasn't found a (satisfying) use, a use of the kind one wanted to find, for the sentence(s) in question.[38]

If Dummett really agrees that latent nonsense is nonsense (and the only conceivable alternative would appear to be the uncomfortable – not to say bizarre – view that the word "latent" in the expression "latent nonsense" functions in much the manner that the word "decoy" functions in the expression "decoy duck"), then he must give up the claim to be able to "operate" (D2: 387) with it (unless that means only: to go through certain operations/manoeuvres that *ape* what can be done with sensical utterances etc.[39]). E.g.: if classical mathematics were really at base unintelligible (D2: 388), then it would be *unintelligible*, and that's that. (See my discussion above of the unintelligibility as I see it, not unsympathetically to Dummett's own 'intuitions', of the way classical maths is often represented.) We can perhaps understand the utterer of it in psychological terms;[40] but not *what* is said (for nothing is).

Dummett's choice of words, in phrases such as "operate with" and "derive consequences from", appears telling. These phrases hover quite unstably between meaning that we can genuinely understand the words in question, and meaning only that those words seem to 'gesture at' something beyond themselves (to use the term incoherently used to try to describe what the words of the *Tractatus* do, by 'ineffabilist' readers of that work). This instability, this hovering, is a sign of philosophic fatality. It must be emended.

3.1.7 A Better Picture of Time(-Statements)

Beginning from the starting-point of the number line, which starting-point Dummett shares with his philosophical 'opponents', Dummett is inclined to represent time as though his representation were a picture of a *(some-)thing* rather than (roughly) a picture of a *conception*. I.e. Dummett does not take seriously *enough* the ineluctable sense in which time is *conceptual,* and not *simply* something which we *find* in (the fabric of) the universe. Here, once more, I find Dummett's position (as one might put it) *insufficiently* 'anti-Realist'![41] It *underplays* the degree of difference between time and space, or indeed matter. Much as Descartes underplays the degree of difference between mind and body, by making them into two substances, two kinds of stuff . . .

Let us try something different. Something that might actually be therapeutic. This picture of time as a picture of a thing might best – with most profit – be dissolved by thinking of time as at base involving *comparative* statements.[42] Thus our regular time-telling might be therapeutically paraphrased roughly thus: as she walked[43] from Norwich to Oxford so the Sun moved through x degrees of the sky, or of its apparent orbit (or whatever). Similarly, with contexts in physics: whilst y started and stopped, the atomic clock made zty thousand vibrations.

Isn't worrying what time is made up of rather like worrying what the orbit of a planetary or stellar body is 'made up' of? And the latter seems just not a very good worry.[44]

3.1.8 On *Still* Wanting to Ask, "What is Time?"

The therapy I have just outlined is an actual way forward. Dummett does not take such a route. What Dummett does, so he says, is ". . . to take a mathematical function that can readily be described in classical mathematics, and then try to describe a change in physical magnitude that would be represented by such a function, in accordance with the classical representation of time and change on the model of the classical continuum; when the result proves to be nonsense, I take that as a good ground for saying that the classical model is not an *intelligible* conception of physical time" (D2: 389) emphasis added). As noted above, I believe that Dummett unhelpfully (or even incoherently) represents the classical continuum. The key question, though, that we still need to investigate, to clarify a little further, to attain therapeutic and charitable completion, is what we can intelligibly hear Dummett as meaning by words like "intelligible".

How are we coherently to understand Dummett's terms of praise and criticism? For he *wobbles* or *hovers* on the question of whether or not the views he wants to criticize are nonsense. One might say that he wants the Realist views on time that he criticizes to make (patent) sense and yet at the very same time to be (latent) nonsense. But that is a patent case of wanting to eat and not eat one's cake at the same time.

Dummett tries to suggest that he is not trying to accomplish as grand a project as I claim he is. He writes: "To say that *time is a continuum of instants*, or that *[time] is not [a continuum of instants]*, is not to attempt to say what time is" (D2: 390) emphasis added). This seems a somewhat bizarre claim. Surely to say that time is a continuum of instants is *trivially, obviously* to say something pretty major and definite about what time is.[45] And, *contra* Dummett, it surely doesn't help to substitute the expression "the structure of time" (D2: 390) for "time" here. To say "what structure time has" is just a fancy way of saying something about the nature of time, about 'what time is'. (Unless, as considered below, it is rather just a fancy way of talking about the *grammar* of time. In other words, talk of the 'structure' of time might be successfully deflated into talk of ways of doing and talking (of) time.) Questions such as whether there is a time between each two times, however close they are to each other, are not answerable *through* mathematical or physical *or* metaphysical enquiry. They are rather either questions that are responsible to the *way* in which some genuine enquiry is conducted, or they are not questions at all.

Dummett attempts to defend his approach here with the following comparison: "To say that time is a continuum of instants, or that it is not, is not to attempt to say what time is, any more than to say that a language is a system for assembling small given units called 'words' into larger units called 'sentences' is an attempt to answer the general question, 'What is language?'" (D2: 390). It is intriguing that Dummett chooses as a comparator precisely the 'object' (language) that Wittgenstein therapeutically investigates more than any other, teasingly questioning or dissolving our sense that we know what we are doing when in philosophy we ask, explicitly *or* implicitly, "What is language?", and expect a definite answer of some kind[46] – *or, entirely similarly, when we make statements such as "Language is a system for assembling small given units called 'words' into larger units called 'sentences'."* What does Dummett imagine he is *doing* when he makes that assertion about language? Whom is he informing of this, and on what occasion? And does the assertion consequentially settle questions such as whether there can truly be one-word sentences or not, or whether they are elliptical for longer sentences, etc. (cf. e.g. *PI* 20)? It is striking that Dummett does not realize that the comparator that he himself cites *raises just as many questions as it quiets*, or answers. He hoped to get out of my accusation of his wishing to settle the question, "What is time?", by means of his analogy with language. But he merely shuffles, and leaves us perhaps inclined to wonder what language is, just as badly. Unless, that is, we apply *Wittgenstein's* methods, and are able to get some further clarity about our words and our often incoherent desires in relation to them . . .

Dummett claims that "it is very far from absurd to suspect a language of embodying an incorrect metaphysical idea" (D2: 396). On the contrary, we 'New Wittgensteinians' strongly suspect it *is* absurd, and that Dummett is unclear about what he actually wants to do with these words. For one believes that a culture or language can *embody* a metaphysics only at the cost of Relativism.

Still less is the human form of life as a whole constrained by language (which would entail a version of 'Linguistic Idealism'). It is not at all clear that the project of giving an intelligible account of how humans could so much as be constrained or limited or distorted by language[47] has ever been successfully started, despite much effort having been expended on it. All that can embody incorrect ideas are things which people say, moves they attempt to make in some 'language-game'.

Actually – and this is crucial – I am doubtful that anyone can get so far as actually saying something metaphysical, or purveying a metaphysical idea. I think that people can only actually say things that appear to be metaphysical, things that they themselves would withdraw if they saw them more clearly. I think 'metaphysical idea' is ultimately an empty category.[48] Once we were clear that roughly this is the least misleading thing to say (if it is), then eventually we should have no need of speaking of 'non-metaphysical ideas'.

However, I do not claim to know that the question as to the nature of time is senseless. That is the kind of thing that Carnap might have claimed to know; he or his followers might have said that any such question can be shown by rigorous logico-philosophical methods to be meaningless; but Wittgensteinians are far from such (post-)positivism. My attitude to philosophical questions is resolutely 'therapeutic' – but it may well be that *sometimes* the best therapy is to admit that the question one is looking at is genuine (or at least can 'contain' deep and perhaps perfectly sensible questions). For instance, one may conclude that it is on a borderline with physical science, and therefore cannot untendentiously be '*ruled out*' as 'metaphysical'.

This attitude – rather than being "quietist", let alone "philistine" (Dummett's words, in D2) – is one of exploring what it is that people wish to do (including, sometimes, me) when they try to answer philosophical questions. I am not trying to rubbish anything or silence anybody or nihilate any real topic. Rather, I want to understand what it is that such people are doing, and to engage in conversation with them. I have a reasonably open mind about where I will end up, in that conversation. To dogmatically take up a 'nihilist' or 'quietist' view, would *not* be to hold to Wittgenstein's method-ological injunctions to give up all explanation, to give up all opinions – to state as theses *only what everyone will agree to* and withdraw anything else.

3.1.9 Conclusions: What *is* it to Apply Wittgenstein to Time? Or: What is a Grammatical Investigation?

My recommendation is, in a *way*, just as Dummett says, to get on with our "normal social life"[49] – but that recommendation is NOT to be taken as 'quietistic' or 'nihlistic'. Philosophy leaves everything that is not nothing (in particular, everything that is not agreed to be nonsense) as it is. Our normal social life includes everything; e.g. it includes physics, for some of us at least. The only 'things' it does not include are nothings, such as what we ourselves agree to be nonsenses.[50] Whatever interest or concern some person or com-munity has with time and exactitude (or otherwise) is from the philosophical point of view being presented here just fine, providing they can in the end (i.e. after thinking things through, perhaps with a philosopher as interlocutor) satisfy *themselves* that their interest hangs together/makes sense. I am urging that certain would-be-interests – in particular, those of some philosophers – can be shown to the philosophers themselves not to make sense. My efforts fail as long as the philosophers in question do not agree. But the *various* actually non-nonsensical interests in time of physicists, of referees (e.g. of people trying to determine when the match should end, or trying to determine who won a race), of prisoners etc. are of course *absolutely fine*. I do not yet under-stand what interest one can have in the real nature of time above and beyond the totality of natural-scientific and human-scientific and practical interests. On D2, page 395, Dummett writes, "So there is a question to be answered about what form a maximally accurate specification of the time of occurrence would take: a question not to be brushed aside by saying, "We all know perfectly well how to say when something happened."" But I mean that we all know this perfectly well most of the time and for all practical purposes[51] *in ways specific to the domain* in which we are operating at any given time. Crucially, for instance, *don't scientists already have ways of sorting this out?* I remain quite unclear what Dummett takes himself to be contributing to those/their debates or procedures. Once again, we should ask whether Dummett's work (or alternatively his opponents') be of use to physical (or other) scientists? If he could show me how it might, that would considerably deflate the power of my criticisms. But I don't see that a role for THE maximally accurate specification of the time of occurrence of an event has been laid down or clearly defined, and I don't see scientists needing Dummett to help them in their thinking about the explicit and 'implicit' margins for error[52] which they actually have.

Dummett puts to me (D2: 396) the suggestion that I ought to get on with the clarification of the logical grammar of our language-games, if that is what I really believe in, rather than criticizing his asking the question "Is time a continuum of instants?" But Dummett may have an idea in mind of what I think 'logical grammar' can do that is not my idea. Not only do I not believe that the clarification of logical grammar can be carried out once and for all, *I do not believe it can be carried out 'positively', at all.*[53] I take some inspiration here from *Tractatus* 6.53, which I think intimates an aspect of Wittgenstein's *later* methods that is too often ignored: namely, that they are resolutely negative, and dialectical/dialogical, and *not* participative in the sub-Fregean, (post-)Carnapian, Rylian projects of 'logical geography'. (Ironically, as I have already suggested, it is I believe *Dummett* who is covertly committed to participation in such a project! This is a rather rich irony – to find Dummett applying in his own reflections on time the very sub-Wittgensteinian philosophizing that he claims to find (or to desire) in *my* work, whose nature is actually quite different!) I think there is no *positive* task to be undertaken of saying in general what it is that "we mean . . . when we ask at what time an event took place" (D2: 396).[54] I think the only task to be undertaken is *to 'return' us* to the actual 'language-games' in which people ask, specifically, questions like that.

The 'clarification of logical grammar' in respect of such contexts is just a making clear to (particular) people that their language etc. *is* clear,[55] so long as they do not look askance at it through the spectacles of an inappropriate 'paradigm' (e.g. 'Realism', or 'Constructivism'). And what I have tried to do in my applying Wittgensteinian thinking to philosophical questions around time and by extension around philosophy itself is to ask what it could be that is meant by Realism and Anti-Realism hereabouts, and to urge in particular that the latter is (in fundamental respects) best seen as a deviant form of the former. So, I can undertake 'logical grammar' only by working within and at the borders of concrete contexts where people are actually putting words like 'time' to use, *and* by questioning those who would say (as Dummett says) that there is something more to be done by way of making clear what they ('can' or 'should') mean.

But I can help present the grammar of time perspicuously also by making clear just how much of it is already clear even in Dummett's own modelling – *and*, sometimes even more so, in that of his opponents. For: just as Dummett sometimes *reminds* us of features of our[56] lives in and with time (such as the 'endless' possibility, usually, of further precision/narrowing of the 'margin of error' in a measurement of time – what Dummett says is just fine, so long as it can be cashed out as *itself* constituting the clarification of logical grammar that he challenges *me* to provide, and in this regard, Dummett's work *can* assist us all); so, albeit through a glass darkly, the classical model can be seen *as a large fragment of our grammar(s) of time*. The problem with the classical model would then be that it presents itself as a (complete?) model of a thing, not as a picture or possibly perspicuous presentation of something not well characterized as a thing (though not as a nothing either). But, rather than as a theoretic tool, it *can* be read as an accurate reflection of (*most* of) what we say about time. For, while it risks occluding the 'flowingness' of time; and its application may be restricted by innovations (e.g. Einstein's) in physics; it *captures* pretty well the concept of the 'time-line' that in so very many contexts we do and perhaps must take for granted. For instance: time, like the numbers, is transitive.

Dummett emphasizes that the classical model is a *model*; but in arguing for its inevitable incoherence he misses its possible harmlessness if it is taken not as a general truth, nor even as gesturing at a truth at all, but rather, as a (latent) piece of grammar. Thus Dummett's revisionism is on balance unhelpful: it would arguably be better to stick with Realism, which is by and large closer to our grammar. (Dummett is insufficiently anti-Realist in his latent Realism; *and* he is overly anti-Realist in arguing against the grammar of time. Compare *PI* 402 – Dummett attacks the normal form of expression as if he were attacking a statement, a claim.)

If the advocate of 'classicalism' insists that they are not to be understood as noting our grammar, but rather as stating facts, then, like Dummett, I cannot agree with them. Dummett claims that the absurdity of the classical model then lies in basic quantities (e.g. position, mass) being allowed to have values that are utterly independent of one another from one instant to the next. That this is indeed absurd can be determined with relative facility by an inspection of everyday ways of talking and being in time and space. But Dummett does not allow himself the resource of any appeal to the everyday.[57] His main argumentative resource is rather the (nonsensical) argument addressed earlier about the alleged incoherence of the descriptions (of imagined discontinuities within physical processes) that he himself gives. But if one *is* prepared to allow the whole machinery of dimensionless instants to get off the ground at all (as Dummett, unwisely, is), then there would surely be nothing to stop such descriptions from being perhaps correct. As I say, they are evidently not at present everyday descriptions; but maybe they might find some use (e.g.) in some revision of quantum theory. What is *Dummett's* argumentative resource against such a possibility (the possibility that a physical scientist might find it useful or even necessary to speak of particles as existing only for dimensionless instants)? He appears to have none whatsoever; yet he thinks he is entitled to proclaim that such a possibility is "incoherent".

In his writings on time in recent years, Dummett has done a sparkling job of setting out powerful reasons for believing there remains a philosophically consequential difference between Realism and Anti-Realism. He and I agree (see his D3: 409) that our dispute is in the end perhaps more about the nature of philosophy (in particular, about what terms of philosophical criticism are coherent and workable) than it is specifically about the nature of time. Its ramifications thus go far beyond the terrain on which we have conducted much of the discussion. Realism seeks to provide an account of time as if from outside (the language and practice of) time. Anti-Realism seeks to provide an account of time as if the viewpoint 'outside time' is (more or less regrettably) unavailable to us. The deeply different conception of philosophy that I urge would rather we give up the attempt to conceptualize ('the' structure of) time, whether from a fantasized 'unlimited outside' or from the allegedly 'limited inside' of our life.

The fantasy of limits, 'limits' that constrain us or that we can notionally escape, is – as McDowell has powerfully argued – still exercising a nefarious influence on Anglo-American philosophy. I urge that that fantasy be overcome, and then the debate – between Dummett and his Realist 'opponents' – will no longer exist.[58]

3.2 (Dis)solving the 'Time-slice' Conception of Time

3.2.1 Introduction

Imagine[59] that 'space-time'[60] is a piece of Brighton Rock. A very variegated piece of Brighton Rock, naturally, with the words written on it transforming as one works one's way through it. Each slice one takes from the stick of rock represents an instant. The words one can read on that slice might conveniently be taken to represent the state of affairs at that instant. Thus time is 'a sequence of 'nows'', and this sequence along with the states of affairs obtaining at each is 'space-time'.

A picture of time along these lines is I think very common among philosophical analysts – e.g. it is the very picture assumed by and popularized in David Lewis' influential doctrine of 'Humean supervenience'. Lewis combines in this picture of the Universe – roughly, as always at any time t having a nature which does not metaphysically necessitate its nature, its state at time $t + 1$ – a (roughly) Scholastic Realist vision of Metaphysics along with the inheritance of Early Modern Empiricism. This feature of Lewis' position is helpful (to me), because it makes clear that my target in this section is not narrow.

In slight sum: that target is certainly not restricted to Empiricism, nor to Anti-Realism in general, nor (obviously) to Realist Metaphysics; nor indeed, as we shall see below, to the Anglo-American wing of philosophy; nor indeed, even, to philosophy.

3.2.2 How Not to Represent Space-time

Now, if any given slice from the stick of rock just imagined has any thickness whatsoever, then the 'instant' in question still has duration. To really understand time as a succession of instants, as 'a sequence of nows', one will need to take infinitely thin slices.[61]

In fact, to understand '*succession*', infinitely thin time-slices won't be good enough, unless we can say how they are *related*. This point it seems escapes the

likes of David Lewis, though it is hardly a new point. To quote from William
James:

> [Thomas] Reid justly remarks that if ten successive elements are to make
> duration, "then *one* must make duration, otherwise duration must be
> made up of parts that have no duration, which is impossible . . . I
> conclude, therefore, that there must be duration in every single interval
> or element of which the whole duration is made up. Nothing, indeed, is
> more certain than that every elementary part of duration must have
> duration, as every elementary part of extension must have extension."[62]

This remark of Reid's roughly anticipates a number of the arguments that
Read makes below . . .

   And the problems with the 'slice-theoretical' view ramify; for, if a slice of
Brighton Rock is infinitely thin, then one certainly cannot read what is written
on it, no matter how powerful one's microscope . . . (For '*infinitely* thin' is surely
not different in meaning from 'of zero thickness'). Conclusion: what we know
as 'space-time' cannot after all be coherently and yet consequentially represented in the manner in which this section commenced. For nothing whatsoever can be learnt about the state of affairs that obtains at a time that has no
duration, at a point in time considered completely apart from any before and
after. An infinitely thin time-slice, a dimensionless quasi-Dedekindian 'cut' into
space-time, does not, *contra* some conventional wisdom, yield any intelligible
account or picture of space or matter (or anything), at all.

   One might object here that my picture of the time-slice is prejudicial, in that
I ought to treat of time-slices as analogous, not to an infinitely thin shaving
from the piece of rock, but to the *surface* of one side or other of it (or of a
broken piece of it). For instance, perhaps time-slices should be (held to be)
akin not to the products of a film-movie camera, but to those of a kind of
super-video camera that produced, not a strip of film with separate frames, but
a continuous jelly. One could slice this just where one liked, look at the surface
so exposed, and see what the camera viewed at the corresponding time, with
times now corresponding say to points on the Real-numbers line. Using such
an image, is it now so obvious that one could see nothing, if one looked only
at the slice (at the surface?)?

   However, it is hard to see how *this* new picture of time-slices is to be de-
metaphorized. For, in this jellyfied version of my 'Brighton Rock' thought-
experiment (my self-deconstructing 'object of comparison', via consideration
of which I hope to 'recover' the nature of time) the rest of the jelly – the rest
of space-time – is literally, physically, 'standing' behind the surface at whatever
point one makes one's cut. But, clearly, *that is not so for time.*[63]

   So we are seemingly forced back then, if we are to think of *time* as consisting
of time-slices, to thinking of time as consisting of infinitely thin slices that may
be considered each apart from the others. And so, again: how can it be that
there is anything to see, on such a slice?

My target in this section is any philosophy which, to the contrary, supposes that, as a matter of methodology, or indeed as a matter of metaphysics, one can intelligibly and consequentially picture time (including the present) as essentially involving a continuum of 'dimensionless' time-slices. I believe that among those whose views fall within this target (though in most cases I will only gesture at the reasons for thinking these figures actually do fall within the target-range), are to be found most self-avowed metaphysicians of time (including for example Michael Tooley), plus (supposedly on the 'other' side) most of David Hume's many intellectual heirs (including crucially David Lewis, and also, I think, Quine) and leading contemporary 'Anti-Realists' (including crucially Michael Dummett[64]), some 'human scientists' (including for example Anthony Giddens), some popularizers of physics (including some moments in Stephen Hawking), and even some important moments in the texts of major Continental philosophers (in such as – surprisingly – figures as diverse as Bergson and Derrida).

3.2.3 Are we Limited Beings?

I suggest, then, that the 'popular' notion of infinitely thin time-slices cannot be made sense of. Or to put that point more carefully: that nothing has as yet been coherently proposed for 'infinitely thin time-slices' to mean.

But is this because of a regrettable limitation on our part? Is it perhaps only because we are 'only' three-dimensional beings,[65] unable to see time (and space) 'as it really is', stuck as we allegedly are 'on the inside' of time? I have already suggested that we can make no sense of this proposal – but I would like now to show why, to the satisfaction, one can even hope, of one's would-be opponents.

So: are we 'stuck within' the human form of life – are physical science and human science *alike* able to give us only an account of 'time-as-it-seems-to-us'? It is sometimes said that time could only be fully understood by one not 'bounded' by time, not *in* time. That, just as *we* can understand something three-dimensional intruding upon a two-dimensional (planar) world, a phenomenon which would seemingly be incomprehensible to the denizens of that world, so a truly four-dimensional being *could* understand space-time as a whole, as a 'block' – roughly, as a stick of rock. (Such a being could then purportedly understand what we cannot. Such a being could, one might say, see our 3-D world as 'flat', and what it moves in – past and future, time – as 'up' and 'down'.) Each instant, each 'now', is supposedly an infinitely thin slice of this 'block', and can be seen as such by this (imagined supra-human) being.[66]

Let us risk coquetting with this mode of expression somewhat further – for, after all, if it clatters down in nonsense, we will have lost nothing . . . For the mode of expression in question is not one any of us needs in actual life; it is only a mode favoured by certain theorists. Perhaps going along with the 'thought-experiment' somewhat further will in a *way* be illuminating. So then: it would seem that if, *per impossibile*, we could master four dimensions, and not 'just' three, perhaps we could then have a perspective on the whole stick of rock, and look at whatever slices of it we wished to, for the details. Much as we actually can have a perspective on (the whole of) a two-dimensional – planar – universe?

But the same problem presents itself. For actually there is no such thing as us seeing a two-dimensional universe *at all.* The world of truly two-dimensional beings – *being infinitely thin* – cannot be 'read', either. It is, I venture, entirely 'hidden' from us.[67]

Compare these astute 'explanatory' remarks, by the denizen of 'Flatland' who is its narrator:

> [A]ll my Flatland friends – when I talk to them about the unrecognized Dimension which is somehow visible in a Line – say, 'Ah, you mean brightness': and when I reply, 'No, I mean a real Dimension', they at once retort 'Then measure it, or tell us what direction it extends'; and this silences me, for I can do neither.[68]

Is this not just another way of saying: that *we* ('Spacelanders') can't conceive of (really being in, living in) Flatland? For one has to conceive *of not missing another dimension!* And we surely cannot do that. Or, at best: if we can conceive of doing it, it is not by means of as it were Whig history that we can do so.[69] We cannot do so by means of our 'conceptual superiority'. We can only do so if we succeed in *giving up* all sense of having any conceptual superiority.

In this connection, we should note the ironic 'mistitling' of this wonderfully thought-provocative book: 'Flatland' is precisely what it is not, to its inhabitants. For calling it thus already assumes that one is thinking outside of it. The opening sentence of the text (p.3) is, "I call our world Flatland, not because we call it so, but to make its nature clearer to you, my happy readers, who are privileged to live in Space." But to really be able to conceive of Flatland, of what Flatland is like, of what it means to live there, one has entirely to transcend this crude starting-point. There is a sense in which we might rewrite the opening sentence of 'Flatland' as follows: "I call our world Flatland, in order that you should be able to obtain the illusion that you understand that world, you who happen to live in Space." Or even, "I call our world Flatland, to make its nature systematically unclear to you, my readers, who fantasise that you are *privileged* to live in Space."

But what is the alternative? How else should Abbott have entitled his book? And how could the 'Flatlander' have done better than he did? These are very good questions. Luckily, *I* do not need to answer them. For my case is simply that the way – *if there is one at all* – to understand 'Flatland' is *not* through the sense of superiority exhibited in that story by the Sphere. My suggestion is a merely negative one: that it makes no sense to think of seeing the world of two-dimensional beings from above/outside.[70]

My critique here of (the normal way of taking) the popular science-fictional 'Flatland' scenario is perhaps of particular moment in that contemporary

Anglo-American metaphysicians are very fond of such scenarios.[71] My remarks however might seem to leave me open to the charge of Relativism. I appear to be saying that there is something – a potentially lived world – alien to us, even incomprehensible to us . . . a world, which makes sense, and yet is entirely inaccessible to us. *We* cannot, I seem to be saying, make sense of the sense it makes. Am I then committed to 'us' being 'epistemically bounded' from 'them'; am I committed thereby to much the same *kind* of mistake as I find in, for instance, 'Humean supervenience', and in those pro-time-slice views which (e.g.) afflict discussions of 'personal identity', where one 'time-slice' of a person need not comprehend and is in principle cut off from the next? Am I committed, thereby, to the nonsenses of Relativism/Anti-Realism: to saying that there is a 'senseless sense' to remarks about this world that is 'hidden' from us?

Well, I *am* in a way reversing the conventional wisdom: rather than having a privileged perspective on existence in two dimensions, I am suggesting that we have *no* perspective on it at all. The third dimension *as it exists for two-dimensional beings*[72] – the dimension, if you like, that their universe subsists in, that they *live* – is thus similarly 'hidden' from us. We can look at a plane from a good elevation on it, gain a privileged perspective on it compared to someone with a view from a lower elevation; but if we are interested in what happens to those living as it were *in* the plane, rather than (as in the cases we are actually familiar with) on (top of) it, then elevation above it confers not privilege but radical otherness, and complete lack of understanding.[73]

By parity of reasoning, the thought that four-dimensional beings[74] could perceive our universe from the outside in complete clarity is the complete reverse of the truth. Which is that they could not see our universe *at all.*[75] And thus that there is no such thing as them perceiving or understanding the dimension in which we subsist, the so-called 'fourth dimension', *as it exists for three-dimensional beings.* Namely, time.

Indeed, there is something fishy from the get-go in thinking that we can certainly sensically think of four-dimensional beings[76] – except of course insofar as this is just a poetic way of describing *ourselves*, beings whom we can usefully describe as inextricably and saturatedly subsisting in / being in 'the fourth dimension'. I.e. Beings who live (etc.). I.e. *Beings*. No more is being in time perspicuously presented if it is represented as a *limitation* – e.g. a cognitive limitation – *at all*. We are limited only in a (very roughly) 'Pickwickian' sense by being in time.[77] Thus Nagelian notions of 'higher' beings with added sensory modalities and/or enhanced cognitive powers 'who' could 'solve' philosophical problems that to us are allegedly mysteries – such as the nature of time – are incoherent, or will fail to deliver what their proponents hope for from them. There is an ineluctable tension *between* the seriousness and usefulness of the added powers and the degree of alleged insight into something that can allegedly be better seen 'from the outside'. I submit that Beings with higher powers that make a difference, by giving one a view from outside, *lose their capacity* to understand time in a synchronized fashion with – in direct proportion to – their gaining those powers . . .

What I am saying is that there are important respects in which there are things to understand on and in lived worlds that are not, as philosophers, being intellectuals, like to think, entirely accessible to ordinary intellection, to cognition within the 'conceptual scheme' that one is used to.[78] One sometimes needs to *alter* one's way of thinking significantly to understand another; or indeed to *live* in the 'world' in question; or, at least, to *imaginatively apprehend* it, after the fashion invited by the seminal work of Kuhn and Winch.

3.2.4 Continuity

So: there cannot be anything second-best about the 'position' yielded by our own embeddedness in time. (I.e. 'Anti-Realism' starts to look no more genuinely attractive or necessary an option hereabouts than 'Realism'.) Why then does it seem to some as though there is something second-best about our epistemic relation to time, and as though there are real difficulties in our coming to understand what time is?

Go back to the tempting initial 'scenario': the picture of time as 'a sequence of nows'. It was this which was largely to blame, so far as the mythological errors hereabouts are specific to 'time',[79] and – providing also that one does not allow oneself to treat the concept of 'infinity' confusedly – it is *this* picture and the fantastic Brighton Rock analogy which is supposed to encompass it which must be abandoned, as not amounting to anything that means anything at all. For in order for the initial scenario actually to be a picture of time, the 'nows' will have to follow each other . . . 'infinitely fast'. But that is another way of saying that all our 'scenario' presents us with, if it is to be coherent and comprehensible, is *time*, as, I would suggest (see also below), we actually already know it. I.e.: *continuous*, 'flowing', *not* 'a 'sequence' of (static/ snapshot) 'nows".[80]

A further remark on 'now': part of the mythological mistake made hereabouts both by more or less Empiricist *and* by more or less Bergsonian-cinematic renditions of 'time' may be this: a failure to recall that "now" is a paradigmatically indexical expression: when specified somewhat more closely, it can mean today, this year, the modern age, this instant (i.e. right away); etc. etc. "Now" isn't any kind of temporal unit whatsoever. Wittgenstein is extremely clear on this, in the *Blue and Brown Books*: "The function of the word "now" is entirely different from that of a specification of time . . . // One has been tempted to say that "now" is the name of an instant of time, and this, of course, would be like saying that "here" is the name of a place . . ."[81]

Hence time can't be a sequence of any such 'units'. Thus my suggestion is that philosophers especially tend crudely to assume the intelligibility of an objective 'atomization' of time into units, failing to realize the 'irremediably' indexical nature of (ascriptions of) time; and that even some apparently better Continental approaches, such as Bergson's, *risk implicitly contradicting or obfuscating the very phenomenon (e.g. 'la durée') which they wish to present us with.*

Take for example the following passage from Bergson's *Creative Evolution*:[82]

> We take snapshots, as it were, of the passing reality, and, as these are characteristic of the reality, we have only to string them on a becoming, abstract, uniform and invisible, situated at the back of the apparatus of knowledge, in order to imitate what there is that is characteristic in this becoming itself. Perception, intellection, language so proceed in general. Whether we would think becoming, or express it, or even perceive it, we hardly do anything else than set going a kind of cinematograph inside us. We may therefore sum up what we have been saying in the conclusion that *the mechanism of our ordinary knowledge is of a cinematographical kind.*

Bergson deserves credit for trying really hard here; his philosophy certainly appears to offer more hope for avoiding the misunderstanding of time than do most Anglo-American efforts. But my point, once more, is this: however fast you run your cinematograph (unless it be 'infinitely fast'), you are not going to arrive at a *durée*. What is really needed, is the *durée, always already*. I am suggesting then, really, not quite even '*durée*', but once again, simply . . . *time*. It is just time, in its manifold manifestations, that needs to be recovered for our attention, if anything does. (And, of course, in most of these manifestations it is potentially misleading to speak in a reificatory manner of 'time' being 'manifested'; doing so is already dangerously abstract, compared to (say) simply inhabiting, or noting – or at most attempting to disentangle analytic confusions about – the way in which (say) factory-workers organize their day (or deal with the way it is organized 'for them').)

In short, there cannot be any such thing as – and does not *need* to be – an explanation as if from an 'external' (let alone 'eternal') point of view of what 'time' is, for three-dimensional beings.[83] But *nor* are we condemned to a second-best, 'merely internal' explanation either. (The idea of, for example, a sociological – social scientific/theoretic – account as providing a (perhaps 'as objective as is possible for us') picture of what time-is-like-for-us, absent a certain kind of (previously) hoped-for account of the absolute nature of time, preserves the (incoherent) *ideal* of a perspective on time as if from outside.[84] To think of our form of life as a limitation, as a fall-back given the unavailability of a 'view from nowhere', is still to think in a manner constrained (!) by the categories of traditional philosophy. A Relativist is just a poor man's Metaphysical Realist.) We understood time perfectly well to begin with; we 'inhabit' it, and what better understanding of something inhabitable could one wish to have than that got by inhabitation?[85]

No role has been provided for what an alleged explanation of time's nature would be. A picture of time – a would-be intelligible/explanatory exercise in 'imagination' – as a sequential stack of infinitely thin slices of Brighton space-time rock helps in understanding time further not one jot (and in fact: not at all).

3.2.5 Real Time-slice Talk

Consider by contrast a place in our lives – at least, in some lives – where explicit talk of time-slices *is* useful and perspicuous: geology. Geologists speak of the 'time-slices' indexed by rock strata, by the thickness or thinness of particular layers of rock, passages of time. Here, in fact, we see a very vivid sense of the word "time-slice" – we *see* it *vividly*, due to the apparentness of the visual/spatial metaphor that geologists are employing. There is little or no danger *here* of metaphor being projected on to reality.

What is strikingly different from the mythic example – featuring a different (imaginary) kind of rock – that we have been considering in this section earlier is that *these* 'chunks', these 'slices' of time – of geological time – have, of course, *duration*.

A master-myth hereabouts, the founding error to the attractive pictures we have deconstructed, is the perhaps inevitable but almost inevitably *dangerous* attempt to represent time . . . in spatial terms (e.g. as a 'dimension').[86] In the case of geology, no harm is done by this practice, for the metaphor is obvious and perspicuous; but in the contexts where philosophers invoke 'time-slices', it is usually a very different matter. As long as we seek to explain time, to get 'back behind' the time that we *inhabit*, using terms drawn from our under-standing of *space*, time will be crudely reified – and yet, ironically, will remain frustratingly out of reach, unperspicuously presented, even so. We must learn not to seek to get beyond or behind (the full range of) our ordinary tempo-rally saturated discursive practices (e.g. our use of expressions such as "Are you ready to go yet?", "They both arrived at the door at the same time," "So many years, and yet he has hardly aged at all," and "You will need an atomic clock for that purpose"), or else 'the problem of time' will forever seem to demand analogies with which to help solve it: analogies which will always fail just at the point when we try to take them at all *seriously* . . .

We might then hazard that the efforts of analysts to say what time really is (metaphysics of time), and/or how time is really experienced (some phenomenology, theoreticist psychology or sociology of time), must fail, insofar as they fail to take as their data and resource actual understandings-in-action of time. Of *time*, not of mythic 'instants'.

That is, what we need is not theorization of time on the basis of unanalysed 'intuitions' or 'assumptions' about it, nor even people's lay or professional reflections upon time, but just: time, as it is observably and accountably lived – by scientists, philosophers and laypeople alike.[87] Compare the ethno-methodologist Harold Garfinkel's remark in "The Rational Properties of Scientific and Common Sense Activities",[88] where, building on Schutz's work, he writes of how, "In his everyday activities [each] person reifies the stream of experience into "time slices"." Is Garfinkel here committed to dubious views about the slicing of time, or committed at least to dubious views on the com-mitments of ordinary persons to time-slices? Not at all, as a fuller perusal of his text (which would take us too long in the present context) clearly reveals to any attentive reader. For, in brief, the difference between standard theoretic approaches to time such as those which I have criticized and the ethnomethodological approach is that the latter:

(0) treats slices of time neither as objectively determinable nor as infinitely thin, but *as having duration*, of either a 'vague' or 'precise' amount, depending on the person, context, etc.;

(1) treats such reification as is done by persons as continually undone in practice;

(2) thus does not ironize or reify the person's experience of or enactment of time; and

(3) does not, when done right, understand decent sociology of time (e.g. these very ethnomethodological remarks, etc.) as theoretical or even assertoric in nature, but as practical; i.e. as in Wittgenstein's sense reorienting ('reminding'),[89] and as methodological recommendations.

What Garfinkel, like Wittgenstein, points us towards is the almost inevitable tendency (due to the pressure of surface grammar, and also of the scientific impulse – see the whole of Garfinkel's "The Rational Properties . . ." essay) to reify time . . . and of how, in our actual lives, though often not in the content of Theory, this is worked through, or essentially temporary, or 'unimportant' (because essentially practical), etc. This understanding of time, this recovery of time as it is already understood and lived by people, is not a second-best; it is what there is to say (in a way: nothing) about time. Alternatively put, it is (the truth about) time; unvarnished, unsliced and undiced.

If we compare Bergson with Garfinkel, the differences are pretty stark. The former focuses our attention on a 'cinematic image', which 'seems' continuous but is 'really' discrete. This naturally evokes the questions: "Is time really continuous or not? Of what units is it constructed?" Bergson then has us ponder whether our experience – "the mechanism of our ordinary knowledge" – reflects the real nature of time (Metaphysical Realism), or only our own 'limitations' (Anti-Realism). Bergson implicitly (and unwisely) opens a space *for the very forms of theoreticistic inquiry into the nature of time which he seemingly hoped to enable us to overcome.*

Garfinkel's point of departure is quite different.[90] There is no longer the question of whether a Realist or an Anti-Realist rendition of time is to be preferred; rather, there is the relentless and near-endless (but relatively 'mundane') question of how time is sliced and unsliced in diverse *actual* human practices.

3.2.6 Metaphysicians' Time-slice Talk

Let us look now, and in a little more detail, at the place in philosophy today where notions of 'time-slice' are most ubiquitous and detailed. Not, that is, at time-slices as surreptitiously, perhaps even against his better judgement, entering into someone's philosophy (as in the case of Bergson), nor at a more successful, non-theoreticist version of lived durationful time-slices (as in Garfinkel), but at a sliver of the huge 'literature' which explicitly debates the ontology of time, space, objects and persons, with a concept of 'time-slice' at the very heart of the debate. Some readers, for instance some Wittgenstein-ians, might be surprised to learn that such ontological[91] and metaphysical enterprises are still popular. But their popularity – including with major philosophers of our time such as Quine, Kripke, Lewis, Armstrong, Jackson, Mellor, van Inwagen and Parfit – is indeed such that a dissolution of the time-slice conception of time is . . . timely.

For our purposes – to bring out how the diagnosis of problematic and wide-spread urges concerning the nature of time that I have so far made is directly relevant to central debates in contemporary metaphysics, to apply Wittgen-stein in pointing clearly beyond those debates and back to 'time itself' – it will be enough I think to focus primarily upon some remarks by one of the leading participants in such debates, one of the leading Analytic philosophers alive, Frank Jackson:

> The dispute between three-dimensionalism and four-dimensionalism . . . concerns persistence, and correlatively, what change comes to. Three-dimensionalism holds that an object exists at a time by being wholly present at that time, and accordingly, that it persists if it is wholly present at more than one time. For short, it persists by *enduring*. Four-dimension-alism holds that an object exists at a time by having a temporal part at that time, and it persists if it has distinct temporal parts at more than one time. For short, it persists by *perduring*.[92]

'Three-dimensionalism' may sound relatively sane. But lurking within the view of the 'three-dimensionalist' is a tacit risk of commitment to time-slices: for an object persists by enduring through a 'stage' of time made up of infinitely many 'slices'.[93]

Now, Jackson's three-dimensionalist *may* have a harmless 'view'. (It depends on what gets *done* with the picture sketched here.) But my reasons for doubting that this is at all likely (reasons borne out, I believe, by a closer inspection of 'the literature', such as I have engaged in, and such as I advise any sceptical readers to engage in, in tandem with this book) are as follows: imagine someone defending 'three-dimensionalism' by arguing that, since the three-dimensionalist believes that each object is located 'in whole' at each of the times at which it exists, it therefore follows that there is no part, no slice, of such an object corresponding to those times, only the whole. Thus there would be no temporal slices of persisting objects, according to the three-dimensionalist. Does this mean the three-dimensionalist is invulnerable to my central charges in this section?

The key problem with three-dimensionalism is this: the three-dimensionalist speaks as though the debate with the four-dimensionalist *makes sense.*[94] Thus he speaks for instance of objects being "wholly present" at particular times. This seems tacitly to commit him at the *least* to substantive and philosophically consequential time-slice-talk making *sense.* And just that is what I am disputing in this section.

In the view of the 'four-dimensionalist', we see a stark example of what happens when metaphysically minded philosophers worry about (in this case) whether what the three-dimensionalist says is enough to 'account' for the endurance of objects, or for change: the four-dimensionalist spatializes (or 'materializes') time in an astonishingly direct fashion, by claiming that part of what an object *is* is 'its temporal *part*'.[95]

These two alternatives that Jackson offers us reflect precisely the mis-moves I have already dissected, above. The 'three-dimensionalist' may seem the preferable alternative – but only to one who already allows that the 'four-dimensionalist' has something to say. I have tried to suggest that what the 'four-dimensionalist' has to say is radically incoherent, that we can make nothing of it of the kind that he evidently wants to make of it. That the four-dimensionalist has incompatible desires with respect to his own words.

And this leaves 'three-dimensionalism' equally badly off. For the negation of nonsense is not sense, but rather just more nonsense.

It is worth noting that such 'ontological'[96] debate as that that Jackson is here presenting is particularly popular in the philosophy of personal identity. For instance, there is long-running debate about whether a 'time-slice' analysis, or a 'temporal parts' analysis, captures the supposed essence of what makes a person the person they are, continuous over time, or solves puzzle cases such as those made famous by Parfit. David Lewis' work is thought by many to have made a decisive contribution to the problem of personal identity, in just such a fashion.[97]

If I am right, by contrast, then it follows that all that alleged philosophical progress is . . . moot.

3.2.7 Dummett on Time-slices

Finally, what of Michael Dummett's 'post-Anti-Realist' conception of time? Can *this* at least be considered progress? I have subjected Dummett to sustained critique in the previous section of this Part of this book. But are Dummett and I not allies at least in moving beyond the kind of debates that Jackson and Lewis and the other metaphysicians of time are? Surely, Dummett's rejection of time-slice talk[98] makes he and I very close?

I have telegraphed my answer to these questions already. It is: no, not really. Dummett is unfortunately locked into metaphysical argumentation over the nature of time in a manner that quite fails to apply Wittgenstein *et al.* to the matter under consideration, for all Dummett's pretensions to be a philosopher who has learnt from Frege. The reason, once again, is this: Dummett *shares* in common with his 'opponents', those who advocate a conception of time as consisting in dimensionless time-slices, the presumption that it at least *makes sense* to think of time in such a way. Or rather, that, if it does not exactly make sense thus to think of time, the reason for this is that the sense it would make to talk of time thus is nonsensical . . . (see for detail the previous section, on Dummett, especially section 3.1.2 on "Using Nonsense to Combat Nonsense" and section 3.1.6 "Methodological Reflections"). *If one is applying a resolute reading of Wittgenstein, such reasoning cannot possibly be accepted.*

I submit that the reason why one 'cannot' picture time as a continuum of dimensionless time-slices is simply that it is not (at least, not yet, in the history of human thought) the case that speaking thus succeeds in meaning anything. What those who speak thus are trying to say (as *opposed* to actually succeeding in saying) is not yet clear. It hovers, or flickers; it is not yet anything. But Dummett *inherits* that hovering, unfortunately, when he seeks (as he sometimes does) to argue the case as to why what they (his 'opponents', who in a certain sense are mine too) are trying to say 'cannot' be said. He commits himself to a Carnap-like picture of language, in which the manner of speaking of the time-slicer is condemned as engaging in something like categorial violations. Dummett sees the time-slicers as making enough sense for us to see that what they are saying is incoherent. But *that* philosophical picture seems to me, following Witherspoon and Conant, just nonsensical. Or, better (so as not to inherit in my turn Dummett's hovering!): I simply cannot inherit Dummett's use of "nonsense" and "incoherence" as terms of criticism. Something is not nonsense because the sense it would make is nonsensical. Something is not incoherent because the coherence it would yield is incoherent. 'Something' is nonsensical, or incoherent, because it is just not yet clear *what* ('something') it is. We simply need to go back to the four-dimensionalists *et al.*, and press them to tell us more. And we fear that they will not succeed in telling us, however long we are able to give them. We cannot, as Dummett allegedly/supposedly does (aspires to do), *prove* that 'the time-slice conception' is *wrong*. Rather, we have to interrogate the assumption that 'the time-slice conception' *has even been defined*, yet. The therapeutic move, the key to applying Wittgenstein, as I am endeavouring to practise that, in this book, is to ask and ask again for clarification on the part of those who wish to put forward (e.g.) the time-slice conception of time, until such point as one either has it explained to one's satisfaction, or feels entitled to give up trying (because one has something better to do; because one cannot necessarily devote one's whole life to seeking to understanding 'something' that just obstinately never shape-shifts away from apparently being nonsense, nothing, only a hovering presenting itself as sense – a *delusion* of sense, only).

One needs to try, *ceteris paribus*, to make sense; so I must draw attention, before leaving Dummett, to a moment in his intentions with which I am in full

sympathy. Dummett wants to stress "the essential role of continuity in even formulating what is to be said".[99] I sympathize entirely. I am just unconvinced that
Dummett himself has taken this point seriously enough in his efforts to make
sense of what the time-slicer – the believer in time as a continuum of dimensionless instants – is up to. Dummett still speaks as if he can make sense of the
notions of the time-slicers. He then 'shows' that the sense these notions make
is nonsense.[100] But, again, *that* is nonsense; Dummett should rather have ques-
tioned whether he – or they – are in the first instance clear at all about what
these alleged notions are.

So: it would of course be a mistake to argue that even in principle, even
idealizing, nothing can hold good only for an instant; in particular, that something cannot be in a given position only for an instant: in the standard,
'Classical' account, if you throw a ball vertically, it is at its greatest height, and
at rest at that point, only for an instant. *But*: it is only with a non-instants-
composed account that one can speak of a ball having *velocity*. Considered
purely as being what it is at an infinitely thin time-slice, everything might as
well be at rest. You don't know anything about *objects* (which persist) which
move, if you know only of infinitely thin instants. This is what it means to take
seriously what Dummett wants to take seriously: "the essential role of continuity in even formulating what is to be said". Attempts to speak 'outside' of that
sense of continuity – of its not *making sense* to speak of instants *alone* – misfire
even more quickly, at an even earlier stage, than Dummett allows. He has
missed the initial move in his opponents' conjuring trick. He has failed to see
the way that the stage has already been set before he even realized he had
arrived on it.

The cash value of my remarks, much earlier, that one could not see the
writing on an infinitely thin slice of the eponymous 'piece of rock' might then
be said to be that no quantity could assume a particular value for an instant if
that value was discontinuous with its values before and after that instant. But
one should beware: for there is a wrong impression here that something is
being expressed. To say anything other than this would not be to say *anything*,
would not be to express or 'formulate' anything. So, symmetrically: to state the
'cash value' is actually not to say anything, but merely to issue a reminder. To
reorient one ('back') towards one's language.

So: one might say that one could see nothing on the surface of the jellyfied
version of the rock, considered much earlier, if what was there was not
changing continuously with what lay further along the jelly. But, again, if we
take Dummett's own remark seriously, it becomes unclear how we could even
describe anything else.[101] And this again shows that there is something that
misfires when we attempt to think the surface of the rock without thinking
everything below it. In the case of time, what is 'below the surface' does not
stand there, quasi-physically: to think that it does *is* already to spatialize time.
So, what the jellyfied version of the rock metaphor can be doing is only to
remind us of something that it misleadingly allows the opposite of to be
represented:[102] roughly, as we might put it, that time is *a continuum*. But *not* a

continuum *of instants*. In ruling out that time is a continuum of instants, one is not ruling out *anything*. Dummett gives the misleading impression that one is ruling out something that at least makes enough sense that we can see what its proponent is trying to say. But to take seriously "the essential role of continuity in even formulating what is to be said" is to see that to concede this is already to concede too much. The 'time-slice conception' is nothing at all. It is *only* a hovering, one systematic (set of) failure(s) to mean.

3.2.8 Against Time-slice Talk?

But is there not some revisionism in all this, even some unfortunate tyrannical policing?[103] Am I not committed to saying that all talk of slicing time is henceforth banned? On the contrary: I have already made clear in my Garfinkelian and Wittgensteinian musings earlier (and in my brief remarks on geology) that, so long as we reject the kind of theoreticist fantasies to be found in the work of Lewis, Jackson, Sider *et al.*, then *slicing time is just fine* – as (ordinary) people do it . . . all the time. Albeit in very different ways. Compare for instance the likely attitudes towards time of a prisoner ('doing time'), a dying person ('running out of time', perhaps), and a keen large-scale drinker (running out of time each night at the bar). What isn't fine is the fantasies of what time-slicing is (or should be), fantasies which are imposed by social scientists upon these (diverse, ordinary) people, and by philosophers upon not only them but also upon natural scientists (i.e. philosophers sometimes appear to want to tell even practising physical scientists how they ought to think about what time is, what it is 'composed' of). And the final reason why such purely theoretic impositional time-slicing isn't fine is that the fantasies of philosophers and social scientists hereabouts are simply not needed. We – drinkers, the dying, prisoners,[104] and (in their particular way) working physicists – can by and large experience and divide up time perfectly well, thank you very much.[105] And in those cases where we cannot experience and divide up time perfectly well (e.g. if we are painfully superstitious about dates; or if we are always *hurrying* through our lives; or if we frequently just miss deadlines – e.g. if we don't deal well with "Last Orders at the bar, please!!", etc. etc.), it is I venture not a philosophical or sociological theory of time that is likely to help us, but rather, counselling, or meditation, or an evening *relaxing* down the pub, or perhaps a kick up the backside, or perhaps social revolution, or . . .

For the boggle at time, the feeling that there is something peculiar about an existence that is not static, an existence that rather '*unfolds*',[106] an existence whose presence is apparently 'only' in the fleetingly evanescent present . . . this boggle is not, I venture to suggest, at root an *intellectual* problem – if, at any rate, we mean by 'intellectual problem' a problem demanding resolution by means of the production of a theory (or even dissolution by means of a merely worded therapy).[107] The boggle at time, the feeling in particular of being 'confined' in the present without 'access' to the past (or future), is not a genuine motivation for a theoretic picture (e.g. of 'time-slices'), but should be honestly admitted to be rather a *mood*, a mood of rebellion against the human condition,[108] or, more broadly, against the condition of actually being, existing, *at all*. For, of course, unless something unfolds, unless one is not literally in (e.g.) the past, then one does not live *at all*. Being-in-time, becoming-over-time . . . this is a privilege reserved for those beings which are not (as God supposedly is) 'timeless'.

So the boggle at time, as manifested for instance in a feeling of 'ungroundedness' in one's past, in one's life . . . this boggle, if it is actually felt, is to be responded to not with words that would silence or force to a conclusion, but with methods, 'therapies' of one kind and another (philosophical, psychological, socio-political, etc.), therapies which re-accustom the anxious or confused bogglee to their *living*, which just means living-in-time, not stuck in a series of static instants; nor statically coexisting in past, present and future; nor reified outside all time. (This is and/or would be *true* application, true *use*, of Wittgenstein.)

And I am not mocking the 'bogglee' here – for I would be mocking myself. I too have felt this boggle, which can be horrible, truly and deeply terrifying.[109] But if and when one finds oneself able, through talk and love and luck, to change one's mood . . . to give up the sense of confinement in a fly-bottle that under continued psychological pressure shrinks to nothing at all (solipsism of the present moment) . . . to feel the 'Now' not (absurdly) as a static moment but as part of a continuity, a life . . . then one can perhaps enjoy even more than before the incredible opportunity of being, of living . . . rather than feeling 'confined' to a static yet evanescent Now or condemned to an imaginary stale, 'Godly' fixedness outside time altogether. (This latter fixedness is I think what many philosophers have in fact envied God – this is philosophy's rebellion against being (human). The desire to see all of history as from outside, the desire to be able to look at it as one looks at the words on a stick of rock, is covertly a desire not to be, not to become and not to change and not to live – at all.)

If the risky question, "What is 'the present'?" still be asked, then, the safest answer is a negative one, such as, "It's *not* a (durationless) instant."[110] But let me take the risk, in closing, of venturing a few more 'positive' words about what it is to experience time in a mood undistorted by any pathology, intellectual or otherwise . . . the risk of employing a few spatial metaphors of my own (but I urge the reader to bear in mind throughout that these are only metaphors, and almost certainly uncashable ones).

The present has to be 'embedded in' and '*intermeshed*' with past and future. The present might be presented as a 'growth' or growing out of the past and into the future. It has no definite duration (compare "When did this plant start growing?"; or, indeed, "When did it start dying?"). As discussed above in reference to Garfinkel, and in relation to the potential usefulness of the notion of time-slices *if* they are taken to have duration and understood to reside in people's lives as lived, *one can give 'the present' as much or as little duration as is contextually apposite.* And in our actual practices, such context is almost invariably presupposed, generated or (more rarely) explicated. This is much of what the Ethnomethodologists work on presenting to their readers – the ways that actual 'language-games' etc. (e.g. those of prisoners, of school-children, even of astrologers, and so on) yield variegated lived senses of past, future and present . . . of *time.*

And once more: 'the present' may be the briefest of moments, or this year, or as long as this mood lasts, or a thousand other things, depending on context.[111]

In its actuality in particular everyday contexts, the present is far less likely to *dissolve* on one than under the mode of presentation which we tend to find in 'mainstream' philosophy of time and of identity. I believe that standard philosophic modes of 'atomizing' and analysing time pose an actual socio-psychological-psychiatrical risk: they risk alienating one from time as lived, and trapping one in a 'private' durationless present . . . in a nothing which leaves one no grounding. I venture to suggest that, unlike the Wittgensteinian (and the best of the phenomenological/ethnomethodological) approach which I have been endeavouring to lay out in this book, standard Metaphysical and 'Analytic' ways of thinking time (as exemplified paradigmatically for instance in the Anglo-American technical concept of '[instantaneous] time-slice') may actually be psychologically dangerous.

If 'being in the moment' or 'living in the present' means something, then, what it means surely must reflect the rich phenomenology of everyday life, not (e.g.) the rarefied fantasies of Anglo-American philosophers. For instance, it must mean things more like "I am now walking down the street through Camden Town to meet my mother," or like "This rose is exquisite," than like (say) "Black spot here now" or "The state of the Universe at time *t* was as follows; molecule *a* was in position [such-and-such], molecule *b* was . . ."

3.2.9 In Closing

My primary target in this section has been the view, if intended as a *view* (as a controversial thesis[112]), that there are temporally infinitely thin, spatially three-dimensional time-slices. In questioning, in interrogating, this would-be view, I took the tack of proposing a temporary 'object of comparison' for our thinking: my stick of Brighton Rock might in this respect be compared with Augustine's 'view' of language. Through inhabiting such a picture, we feel its full attractions and come to comprehend its full likely disasters. Through a moving away from such pictures, towards something that actually works for us, we recover time as it is.

In endeavouring thoroughly to diagnose and dissolve away the time-slice 'view', I have undertaken also to question the debates in which such a view is located, *and* the *underlying* projects of spatializing time, or even of thinking of time as a dimension, at all, in prose. It is just possible for there to be contexts in which spatializing time *can* be harmless; but I have showed some of the harm it usually does; and how it is a permanent hostage to fortune, and without even any good genuinely scientific motivation. I have urged then that, for the sake of clarity, we need to be against time-slices (*if* by that expression we mean anything more than the mundane meanings which it can assume in the lives of geologists and other ordinary human beings). *Time is up*, I think, for the 'instantaneous time-slices' beloved of most philosophers. Influential philosophies of time as apparently diverse as those of Lewis, and (even against his intentions) Dummett, and (even against *his* intentions) Bergson, thus must come to grief. *The very idea* of 'time-slice' upon which in their different ways (for or against) they rest – the very would-be philosophic idea of spatializing time, and of rendering the resulting 'slices' of potentially 'infinitely small' measure – turns out on closer acquaintance simply not to amount to anything that has yet been made sense of, in despite of the vast amount of ink that has been spilled over it. In the previous section, I argued roughly this in detail, via Wittgenstein, in the case of Dummett's recent conception of time; the present section has generalized that case, by means of applying my resolute under-standing of Wittgenstein to most of modern philosophy, thinking of philoso-phy not only, by the way, as what goes on in Philosophy departments, but far more broadly than that.

Farewell, then, to epistemologically or metaphysically consequential time-slices. *Roll on* rather acquiescence in time as a motley, as a multifarious (continuous and divided) organizational phenomenon. As a ubiquitous lived 'tool' for the organization and coordination of human activities,[113] a tool so completely involved in those activities that Anti-Realism about it is as unstat-able as Realism about it is unnecessary.[114]

Conclusion

Philosophical Problems are at Root Problems of Mood

Rupert Read and Laura Cook

> My propositions are elucidatory in this way: he who understands me finally recognizes them as nonsensical, when he has climbed out through them, on them, over them. (He must so to speak *throw away the ladder*, after he has climbed up on it.) // He must *overcome* these propositions . . .
>
> (Wittgenstein, *Tractatus* 6.54)

> The most important point is to establish yourself in a true sense, without establishing yourself on delusion. And yet we cannot live or practice without delusion. Delusion is necessary, but delusion is not something on which you can establish yourself. It is like a stepladder. Without it you can't climb up, but *you don't stay on the stepladder.*
>
> (Shunryu Suzuki, *Not Always So*, p. 41)

In this Conclusion to our book, we wish to flesh out and build on the suggestions made in the previous section concerning the critical role of mood in the generation of (and dissolution of) philosophical problems.

The previous section has thrown into relief two fundamental problems with traditional metaphysics.

Firstly, the attempt to construe a concept such as time 'atomistically' results in a thesis which is ungrounded and unstable. All efforts to escape such lack of compelling grounds and such instability turn out to be self-refuting.

Secondly, and more insidiously, such attempts to define the concept include a tacit admission of scepticism as a genuinely inhabitable position. Wittgenstein urges us to recognize in ourselves the desire for theoretical mastery; the impulse to philosophize which is a result of dissatisfaction with language. The 'time-slice' thesis just examined is just such a response to the perceived inadequacy of our everyday talk about time, seeking to introduce 'precision' to our familiar ways of speaking. This endeavour is motivated by (and we might say *haunted* by) the suspicion that were we able to 'transcend' the 'merely parochial boundaries' of our language or 'localized' form-of-life, then we would be able to achieve precision.

Such sceptical doubts concerning (for instance) language, the existence of other minds and the past are shown to one by Wittgenstein to be empty, *meaningless*. This is *not*, however, because the words we ordinarily use are somehow defective, or are being 'illegitimately used'. Rather, as Witherspoon deftly expresses it, the perceived parochiality of language, and the sense that it must have an 'outside', is in fact "a confusion in the speaker's relation to her words – a confusion that is manifested in the speaker's failure to specify a meaning for them".[1] It is the tacit allowance of scepticism to somehow be offering *meaningful* propositions (if only we could understand them!) that is a problem which has been found in most of the commentaries examined in this book.

In Part 2, we saw how Stevens' poetry directly challenges what we *want* to say of a poem; (e.g.) that it provides us with different ways of 'seeing' a blackbird. Instead we are given a 'Wittgensteinian' reminder of the many *meanings of "meaning"*, since a more careful reading of the poem reveals that it means nor speaks of any blackbird, real *or imaginary*, except insofar as one takes literary/grammatical effects to count as a kind of 'meaning' or signification. For example, one can say that the poem means *itself*. Thus Stevens' poetry undercuts one's attempts to extract a 'meaning' *beneath* the surface of the text, or to offer a final interpretation which would 'unlock' the meaning of the poem. In terms of what one would normally refer to as meaningful utterance, there is 'nothing' there to decode; one is constantly thrown back to the surface of the text as one's attempts to offer a stable depth-interpretation are frustrated. Next in Part 2 we saw a supposedly 'Wittgensteinian' approach to interpretation which attempted to attribute *meaning* to strange utterances of the schizophrenic. Sass attempts to render schizophrenic utterance into common (philosophical) parlance thus enabling one to 'understand' the experience of the sufferer as a kind of lived-scepticism. Sass' work is genuinely novel, at times brilliant, very often insightful. However, again we diagnosed in Sass' work the spectre of a presumed 'outside to language' in which scepticism is considered as meaningful, for solipsism has no *substance* which if one were to know it would analogically enable one to understand what happens in severe instances of schizophrenia. To remind the reader: to suggest that neither Benjy's narrative nor Wallace Stevens' poetry is conventionally meaningful is not to suggest that such narratives can't be revealing or insightful. On the contrary. But one must be cognizant of the many meanings of *meaning*, and not translate these texts into (*our*) everyday language. For, *if* Stevens' poetry, the schizophrenic's utterance, and indeed, the notion of the time-slice can be said to mean, in the way they invite you to think, *this 'meaning' is of a radically different 'kind' than the ordinary, everyday use of the term*. Finally in the previous Part of the book we saw in Dummett's work the spectre of a presumed 'outside' to language, even as he purports to provide a non-metaphysical account of time. For, whilst claiming that there is something unintelligible ('conceptually impossible') about the 'Realist' picture of time, Dummett continues to speak as if he *understands* it perfectly well.

So, it seems that Sass' interpretation of schizophrenic utterance, 'translations' of Benjy's narrative into sense (and indeed, all paraphrases of strong literary works!), and sensicalizations of what the metaphysicians of time tell us all somehow miss the mark, failing to capture or to make comprehensible the strange and disconcerting power that these things exert upon us. That power needs to be brought home and defused. What the analyses in the preceding Parts have shown is that attempts philosophically to master time, to offer a final interpretation of a text, or more broadly, to conceptualize our everyday experience, are prone to collapse. For once we begin to seek a theoretical underpinning on which to base our experiences, we begin to feel a sense of *loss*: it seems that there is something which remains inexpressible, lost to us in theory and language which we are nevertheless attempting to address or approximate. As argued in the first Part of this book, the ineffablist 'position' is not coherent. Indeed, what could it possibly mean to get closer, or approximate to, 'something' which is, in principle, unsayable? Wittgenstein urges us to recognize that scepticism is *not* a 'position' that one can in fact entertain or genuinely inhabit. By extension, it is not one that therefore stands in need of 'refutation'. Put plainly, there is nothing there to 'refute'. However, there seems to be, and this is important. Once one begins to theorize, one becomes trapped as one's words are experienced as increasingly inadequate. One is compelled, as it were, to footnote oneself endlessly, something that is true both of literary works[2] and of philosophical debate.[3]

However, as we saw in the latter sections of Part 2, such attempts at refutation ultimately serve to mire one in nonsense. What is needed is not *argument*, but rather to *be shown* that one can be brought, oneself, to agree that the spectre of scepticism had no substance, and was not meaningful as had originally been thought/feared. In order to bring this realization about, one must be shown that one's original . . . was not *ineffable*, but rather *redundant* and empty (and to see that there is *nothing lost* in this realization!). 'Solutions' to scepticism are actually more likely to exacerbate one's mental 'boggle' at notions of time, other minds, the existence of the external world. More theorizing is unlikely to help since moods are largely simply orthogonal to the methods at solution – intellectual problem-solving – that standard kinds of responses to scepticism, including most alleged Wittgensteinian dissolutions thereof, actually are.[4] Thus recent accounts by people like Hacker, Stroll, Stroud, Marie McGinn and Michael Williams (though the latter two are definitely moving in the right direction), whilst purporting to be Wittgensteinian, are in fact more continuous with traditional philosophy than one might at first suspect, evidencing overtly or covertly an all-too-comfortable assurance of having 'refuted' scepticism. We believe that such readings obscure the importance of philosophers whose work might actually be otherwise considered to be truly therapeutic: particularly Wittgenstein, but also other philosophers such as Nietzsche[5] and (at least parts of) Heidegger, who show that scepticism and the related temptation to mean more than we can say is just that: a temptation, *a desire*. Epistemological and metaphysical questions concerning time, other minds, and the external world are, we submit, not best viewed as intellectual problems, but, at root, as problems of *mood*.

If one wishes to use Cavell's dangerous phrase 'the truth of scepticism' then we urge regarding it in the following terms – the 'truth' in scepticism is that *scepticism is as good as true if and when one gets in the mood for it.* To reiterate: there is no intellectual answer to such moods. This point has been illustrated in the preceding analyses. For example, this is we think the truth in Sass' rendition of the schiz-spectrum disorders. And with regard to Benjy's narrative, Part 2 suggested that attempts to understand this apparently 'logically alien' mode of thinking yield only further nonsense – there is nothing to make sense *of.* Rather, the strength in such a literary presentation is in fact best located in its ability to draw us into a mood of strangeness, in which the ordinary becomes thematized. A mode of representation meanwhile is offered for various alleged experiences; but it is absurd to think that those experiences (if that is the right word) are thereby 'captured'. They remain enigmatic, as do the words offered us by Faulkner (and Stevens).

It is this mood of strangeness, this kind of enigma, that suggests to one a 'lack' of grounding in one's practices and words. To return precisely to the example of time discussed at the close of Part 3, now perhaps in a better position to see just how this can be: the feeling that there is something peculiar about an existence that is not static, an existence whose '*presence*' is apparently 'only' in the fleetingly evanescent present . . . this boggle is not at root an *intellectual* problem, demanding resolution by means of theory. The 'boggle' at time, the feeling in particular of being 'confined' in the present without 'access' to the past (or future), is a *mood*, a mood of rebellion against the condition of actually being, existing, *at all.*

The aim of the remainder of this Conclusion is as follows:

Firstly, to show – more forthrightly than has been possible thus far in the book, drawing together the strands implicit in the various Parts, and following up on the discussion immediately above – that scepticism (and much more besides) is to be considered as a question of mood in which the everyday becomes thematized and uncanny.

Secondly, to recap on the resolute Wittgensteinian understanding of terms such as "everyday" and "ordinary" etc. as not being theoretical terms, and rather being 'self-deconstructing' and transitional.

Thirdly (and in part in order to achieve fully the aim just described under the 'heading' "*Firstly*"), we examine briefly an apparently deeply different 'philosophical' tradition – Zen Buddhist practice – which has arguably put into practice the type of project we have attempted to offer up for the reader's consideration and employment throughout this book. For, what one comes to understand, when one sees one's fears and sees one's experience, in deep meditation, is (among other things) respects in which one's ordinary experience and knowledge of time is sophisticated, inviolable, and deeper than any intellectualization of it, without needing to be a resource for pointless policing of language.[6]

In what follows, we hope then to sketch that and how Wittgenstein and Zen can *mutually* inform: on the methodology of philosophy, on time, on scientism and metaphysics. What Zen Buddhist practice shares with the reading of Wittgenstein offered and implicit in this book is a dissolution of metaphysical difficulty through a return to ordinary language/life. We return thus to where our reading of Wittgenstein differs from the 'canonical' reading offered by Hacker *et al.*, the feature of our reading of Wittgenstein which *allies* it with Zen Buddhism: the rejection of ordinary/everyday language considered as a species of supra-evidence with which to settle such philosophical problems, and the rejection of the methodology of 'category mistakes' as the alleged way in which language can be policed.

Fourthly and finally, following this re-evaluation, we go on to suggest some ways in which this provides space for a re-reading of a number of other philosophers, whose truly therapeutic vision has not yet been fully realized. We sketch out in particular how Heidegger can be thought as a perfect partner to Wittgenstein, particularly as regards the issues of *mood*.

The typical refusal of the philosopher to speak in the first person is symptomatic of the fantasy that one can somehow set oneself above and aside from our everyday practices. Speaking in the first person renders more perspicuous the problem inherent in attempting to conceptualize our everyday experience of the world. If we try to rest everything upon 'truths' about the self and the present, then we incline either to intellectually dishonest denial or to becoming terrified, for there turns out to be nothing solid to rest upon: 'concepts' such as the present, the self, or indeed 'meaning as use' are entirely transient, evanescent.[7] It arguably makes no sense to separate out 'time' or 'language' from 'the self', as if they represented separate philosophical problems or issues.[8] The self – or the present – becomes smaller and smaller the harder one looks for it, to the point of becoming dimensionless/vanishing altogether. However, the tendency of the philosopher to speak in the third person obscures this difficulty. What Nietzsche, Wittgenstein, Cavell and Heidegger have aimed towards, and what has made them so difficult to assimilate into 'the academic world', is that they do not treat the Cartesian impulse as principally to be evaluated by means of further third-person arguments for and against its philosophical position. They take such arguments to be ultimately impotent, and indeed a distraction, a sublimation, an avoidance of real (and scary and harmful, as well as in a way revelatory) experience. The root of the Cartesian impulse, the impulse that eventually results in 'Dualism' as a theory or background assumption in the human sciences, is an attitude, an anxiety, a *mood*, a mood in which the world doesn't feel real. All premises and conclusions are impotent in the face of such a mood. 'The Cartesian mood' can be understood only by entering into what one not in the grip of such a mood will find to be nonsense – but that something 'is' nonsense doesn't always stop one from feeling persistently as though it isn't. And moods can be altered only by processes which are largely orthogonal to 'the space of reasons'. As suggested in Part 2, Sass can help one to understand these moods by giving us entry points into them 'imaginatively' – (but) not by literally making sense of them. Rather, by offering one strategems for understanding their aetiology – not by supposedly reducing them to nothing, or repressing them by rational argument. By offering us quasi-behavioural strategems for taking our attention and our practice into places where these moods are less likely to arise or persist – not by denying that the phenomenon of boggle at body (or, symmetrically, of boggle at consciousness) is a phenomenon which people experience, suffer, and even use. The specifically Cartesian mood, the mood in which the reality of the body is doubted, is particularly uncanny or terrifying, as Sass describes in relation to a number of the schizophrenic patients he has encountered. When such doubt proceeds still further, as it easily does, as Sass shows, by a 'rational' process, to throw doubt, seemingly impossibly, on the existence of the self or of one's own consciousness, the self seems to disintegrate or perhaps actually does so, and/or one's very consciousness becomes a problem and a trial to one. Such experiences take on not a mystical beauty but a terrifying dread or apparent finality. We think that we would all do ourselves and our philosophical (and cultural) inheritance a great service if we were honest about this. If those of us who have experienced such moods wrote honestly about their/our experience, and wrote honestly about (we suspect) the irrelevance to that experience of all the attempted conceptualization in mainstream philosophy etc. of mind and body, structure and agency, self and other, and so on, then it would be clear that what one is instead discussing hereabouts is *mood*, rather than a 'genuine' *philosophical problem*. It is important that those of us (if there are any) who have truly never experienced such moods confess that they are engaging in debate from a position of mere abstract interest in argument, not from a position of comprehending what it is like to be a participant in a lived experience, an experience which motivates, as desperation motivates, a real debate, discussion, confession or oration.

Before turning to examine the confluence with Zen Buddhism, we should recapitulate the self-deconstructing nature of Wittgenstein's own words, and the way in which the sense of 'ungroundedness' in our practices is revealed, through his first-person confessional, as a question of *mood* rather than a philosophical problem to be mastered.

As was made clear in Part 1 and in Cook's Foreword, we are followers of Cora Diamond and James Conant; thus we maintain that their reading of the *Tractatus*, as a resolutely therapeutic work, not a work of metaphysics, can be applied to the spirit of Wittgenstein's work *throughout* his life,[9] including *to his own terms*, terms such as "language-game", "form of life", etc.[10] We are suggesting that there is not something inherently problematic with (the) language (that we use). For to realize that an utterance is nonsensical is not to thereby identify a defect in the words themselves. Instead, as Witherspoon suggests, in a valuable phrase worth requoting, one is made cognizant of "a confusion in the speaker's relation to her words – a confusion that is manifested in the speaker's failure to specify a meaning for them".[11] Words such as "bedrock" or terms like "form of life" are not defective, but if, as the Buddhists would put it, we *attach* to them, we mire ourselves in nonsense. To put the point slightly 'poetically': we *need* to throw away these words, in the same way that Stevens' poetry encouraged us to cease in our attempts to make the poetry *signify* meaningfully (as opposed to meaning-full-y). *We need to overcome these words of Wittgenstein's*, if we are truly to follow Wittgenstein, and apply him. Most of Wittgenstein's 'followers', regrettably, *hold on to* his words, and in effect turn them into technical terms that they are attached to in just the sense we have just criticized.[12]

Our problem – the underlying reason for instance why the jargonization even of Wittgenstein is such a strong trend, even though it was the one thing above all that Wittgenstein feared would happen to his work, and wanted to avoid – is at bottom one of will and lived attitude, not one of carrying out a once-and-for-all intellectual achievement or discovery. Our problem is one of finding a way of responding to good efforts at philosophical therapy which does not turn such efforts, as one always can turn them if one is so minded, into the statement of a position or view or opinion, into a reified philosophical object . . . and yet which does not, in the course of being impressed or persuaded by the attempt at aspect-switching involved in the therapeutic manoeuvre, attach to the manoeuvre itself.

It is here that we suggest that there are deep lessons to learn from mystical spiritualities and philosophies, perhaps especially from Zen and Ch'an Buddhism, on the question of *how in practical terms to do what Wittgenstein urges*. Buddhist traditions such as Zen[13] have a long tradition of conquering the will, of conquering one's desires – not by repressing them, or giving into one's desire to fight against them, but rather by simply letting them be, and observing them until they die back of their own accord.[14] And Zen, perhaps especially among Buddhist traditions, has a venerable tradition too of providing skilful/practical means of attaining insight without becoming attached to the means. A challenge for those impressed with Wittgenstein's philosophizing is to find ways of doing the same, without being committed to the insights attained being ineffable truths. As the Buddhists might put it: if you see a Wittgensteinian on the road to enlightenment, kill him. Our task as Wittgensteinians, let us not forget, is one of leaving everything as it is. The true insight is the 'returning' to the ordinary, where the ordinary is conceived as including, of course, all the strivings for the extraordinary without which life might well be tedious or inhuman.[15] An objector may well ask at this point: what words *can* be absolutely relied on here, unproblematically taken at face value, in philosophy? Our answer is: none. We are always in process, using transitional terms in philosophy. In fact (*sic.*!), we always are in all of life, but we can safely abstract away from our boat-rebuilding-at-sea-ness, usually, and take some frame as given. True philosophy is never taking any frame indefinitely or absolutely for granted. There is no compulsion to accept Wittgenstein's method, a realization that has tended to be sadly absent from Wittgenstein's exegetes, and indeed from his readers more generally. They have looked to be *compelled* by Wittgenstein's 'arguments' (as if by [their fantasy of] a rule . . .), and have been disappointed when they have not been. But (. . . an attempt at saying something helpful; what else can one do?), Wittgenstein's task is to uncover the compulsions we labour under in philosophy, not to impose new ones. If one is shown one's intellectual compulsions, and yet does not want to give them up, there is little or nothing more to say.

When Wittgensteinian philosophy really works, as with Pyrrhonian scepticism, the cure is expelled with the disease. One doesn't keep holding on to – attaching to – "everyday" or "bedrock" or whatever. One overcomes these terms, too. That is, just insofar as these terms risk continuing to mislead one, they need to be 'thrown away'.[16] (Of course, if no-one is misled by some particular use of them, in that sense they are just fine. Just as words like "time-slice" *can* be.) The work of a concept like "form of life" or "the bedrock" in Wittgenstein is probably only done *when* one throws it away.

The search for liberating words – words like "the bedrock" at a certain moment, and then other words, which in turn allow one to liberate oneself from any attachment to 'the bedrock', and so on . . . – is probably endless.[17] For it needs to be continually remade, re-undertaken, as cultural conditions change, as personal life-trajectories and philosophical educations proceed and change, and so on. And in any case, even very well-chosen words will tend to 'ossify' over time; the process of purifying oneself of attachments to particular terms is one which a wise philosopher will continually pursue *vis-à-vis* their own work, as Wittgenstein himself did, as we 'New Wittgensteinians' need to do, as Buddhism has very long experience of doing. The words in this book are no exception. For, even if they are well chosen, and well placed, there can be no such thing as a guarantee against their being misunderstood, against their seeming to state a position, or seeming to be *the* liberating words. As soon as one thinks one has found *the* liberating words, at least for oneself, one is probably again in delusion. The price of applying Wittgenstein is (probably eternal) vigilance.

The Buddhist's main concern is for us to work through delusion, to no longer live in it. Having set out our understanding of Wittgenstein's method, and having already intimated some connections between it and (especially Zen) Buddhism, we wish now to return to the material of the previous Part, concerning sceptical problems in our conception of time. In this instance the Buddhist teaching may reinforce, or render more perspicuous, the Wittgensteinian objections previously offered against the dominance of theoretic pictures such as the 'time-slice'. We will briefly sketch a consideration on and of (a few aspects of) Zen Buddhism on time and time-experience, in order to bring to the foreground a commonality in approach – and, if you like, in 'conclusions' – between Wittgenstein[18] and Zen.

Take this important remark from Wittgenstein, *T-LP* 6.4311: "Death is not an event in life: we do not live to experience death. If we take eternity to mean not infinite temporal duration but timelessness, then eternal life belongs to those who live in the present." If 'living in the present' actually means something, what it means surely must reflect the rich phenomenology of everyday life, not the rarefied fantasies of Anglo-American philosophers. For instance, once more: it must mean things more like "I am now walking down the street through Camden Town to meet my mother," or like "A rose, an exquisite rose", rather than "Red spot here now" . . .

This thought reflects the general tenor of Wittgenstein's thinking; but it also reflects the Zen idea of existence moment to moment, of a life lived in enlightenment as coinciding with a life lived unself-consciously, an everyday life; an idea quite close to Wittgenstein's thinking that time is not a problem to us so long as we do not try to bring pure reason to bear upon it, and that philosophy leaves everything as it is. The fly that has learned to find the way out of the fly-bottle is simply back in the ordinary world. That, we think, is very like true Buddhist enlightenment. *One knows no thing that one did not know before.*

The gain one makes in philosophy then can be described as one of self-knowledge: so long as one doesn't think of self-knowledge as a *kind* of Knowledge. The danger we are after here, in *thus* exploring Buddhism, is that, unless one has truly thought the thoughts which are expressed here, or similar thoughts, one will probably have only the illusion of understanding what we are saying. Psychopathological experience of time, and the insight it can afford through seeming to take one to the place that metaphysics of time yearns for – a place outside ordinary experience of time – offers a quick route; Buddhist practice takes a lot longer. But without either, there is a serious risk[19] that one will never really come to grips with what one wants out of philosophy of time. And that one will think that one will be satisfied by a theory that, in fact, merely imposes on time. The kind of insight into time potentially available through appreciation of or 'expansion' of ordinary time-consciousness, through psychopathology, drugs, meditation, etc., is *much* more likely to leave one able to 'leave time as it is',[20] than is metaphysics of time. In Zen, what is crucial is not reaching intellectual enlightenment, for instance via metaphysics, but *actually feeling the transience of life*, not as only a tragedy, still less as something only uncanny or indeed as a potentially terrifying psychological disaster (as in schizophrenia, following Louis Sass' understanding thereof), but as simply something to *accept*, and perhaps to marvel at – the incredible fact of one's existence, moment to moment. Zen stresses that *none of its formulations matter*, unless one really *feels* them emotionally, and in one's practice.

Compare the following quote, from the founder of the great Soto Zen tradition, Dogen:

> Do not regard time as merely flying away. Do not think flying away is its sole function. For time to fly away there would have to be a separation (between it and things). Because you imagine that time only passes, you do not learn the truth – the truth that time and our being are one and the same. The self does not exist outside time, or *even over time.*

This – both in itself, and in the claim that it must be felt to be of any importance – is something that is just 'incommensurable' with most Western philosophy. So much the worst, we suggest, for most Western philosophy. Only in the likes of Wittgenstein (like Zen, leaving everything as it is (or, as Shunryu Suzuki prefers to put it, in deliberate in-your-face paradox: leaving things as it is)) and Heidegger (like Buddhism on being-in-the-world) do we find a place for it.[21]

Most metaphysics of time seems a desperate effort to escape 'the human condition', the condition of changing and becoming, including all its wonders and beauties (and horrors). These are sacrificed in favour of a sense of time as an endless series of static 'snapshots', or in favour of a perspective upon time such that it appears to be a kind of object, or a kind of space, and such that the universe and all our lives within it can indeed be seen as unchanging, as if from outside or from sideways-on; by a God, roughly.

It is hardly surprising that contemporary philosophy in the English-speaking world looks like this. We are talking about a vision that goes back at least to Plato's forms, and to his founding horror at life. But it is, we think, time that one took more seriously the deep alternative insights available into these matters in (especially) Wittgenstein and Heidegger and Stevens . . . and, still more so, possibly, in Eastern philosophy; especially, again, Buddhism.[22] And when we speak of 'insights' here, part of the point is this: that narrowly intellectual insights are at best only partly to the point. Wittgenstein and Heidegger were about (us) changing our lives, changing our civilization. That is why they have proved so unassimilable to the contemporary academy. Buddhism will be harder still to assimilate. What one comes to understand in Buddhist practice is the way in which our ordinary experience and knowledge of time is subject to change, evaporates and reappears, is not adequate to some of the possibilities of the mindful, embodied self. If the risky question, "What is 'the present'?" is to be asked, then, the safest answer is a negative one, against standard images in recent philosophy (see Part 3) – such as 'it's *not* a (durationless) instant'.[23] But let us take once more the risk of venturing (reworking) a few more 'affirmative' words about what it is to experience time in a mood undistorted by any pathology, intellectual or otherwise. There is a cost-benefit here in and of employing a few spatial metaphors of our own (but we invite the reader to bear in mind throughout that these are only metaphors, and probably uncashable ones). For the Zen Buddhist there really is a lived sense in which all there is *is* the present moment, but it partially 'contains' the moments either side of it. In fact, it partially contains all of the past and future.[24] As such, the present might be presented as a growing or flowing out of the past and into the future. If time-slices are taken to have duration and are understood to reside in people's lives as lived, *one can give 'the present' as much or as little duration as is contextually apposite*. And in our actual practices, such context is almost invariably presupposed, generated or (more rarely) explicated. This is much of what the ethnomethodologists and the greatest of the phenomenologists' work have presented to their readers – the ways that actual 'language-games' etc. (e.g. those of prisoners, of schoolchildren, even in a way of astrologers, and so on) yield variegated lived senses of past, present and future . . . of *time*. So 'the present' may be the briefest of moments, or this year, or as long as this mood lasts, or a thousand other things, depending on context.[25] In its actuality (in particular contexts) the present is far less likely to *dissolve* on one, than under the mode of presentation which one tends to find in 'mainstream' philosophy of time. To reiterate: unlike the Wittgensteinian and Zen 'accounts', the standard Metaphysical and 'Analytic' ways of thinking time (as exemplified for instance in the Anglo-American technical concept of 'instantaneous time-slice') may be psychologically/psychiatrically dangerous. If 'living in the present' actually means something, then, it must be something we can recognize as *describing* our experience as a being-in-time.

Scepticism is, we have argued, in the final analysis a matter not of narrowly intellectual conviction but of mood, albeit often of mood consequent upon a particular mode(s) of intellectual comportment and of a certain 'over-rational' concentration upon (say) the contents of our minds rather than our embodiment and embeddedment in a world of ground, of fellow actors, and of practices (of getting things done). This over-rational examination of the world is deftly described by Sass in his provocative analysis of schizophrenic utterance. A certain fixation upon the world, for a sufficient length of time, brings about a distinct sense of uncanniness in which everyday practices seem at best arbitrary. To use De Chirico's words, the world comes to appear to one "as a vast museum of strangeness"[26] in which our embeddedness is but a contingent situation, which we can somehow transcend. As previously suggested, the tendency for philosophers to avoid speaking in the first person bolsters this sensation of ourselves as somehow separate, as we are then invited to view the world and our practices as a detached (sovereign?) observer, one for whom the very fact of being-in-the-world is problematic. Our discussions in this book can only hope to convince someone whose grip on and placement in practices of intersubjectively comprehensible rule-following etc. etc. is relatively secure. If someone actually is *in the grip of* this sensation of uncanniness, then even our efforts at cure would be most unlikely to be effective. For further 'theorization', which is how our efforts at therapy would then be most likely to be received, will most likely only serve to distance the individual from the world, and to further encourage the reflective attitude of estrangement.

So: for those who are really in the grip of the kind of thoughts proposed by the Cartesian project, weighty and genuine conversational interaction is going to be an extremely tricky and probably counter-productive enterprise. In such instances, even our Wittgensteinian efforts at diagnosis and cure are unlikely to be efficacious.

For our own part, we are probably thankfully subject to such conditions only relatively rarely.

For those – and we suspect that this class includes virtually all philosophers virtually all the time – who do not know scepticism as other than a sophism, our occasionally polemical or short-tempered tone is perhaps appropriate. We have hoped, throughout the course of this book, to coax any readers genuinely tempted by scepticism (but yet far from the terror that is almost inevitably going to attach to really feeling an abyssal absence of meaning) away from this clever trickery and back towards the everyday, as present in and implicated in Wittgenstein's own work. Such philosophers need to understand not only that the conjuring trick does not get off the ground, but that – to those who nevertheless *actually feel as if it does* – the matter is too *weighty* (and too much a matter of mood rather than of purely rational conviction) to play philosophical games with.

We have not offered a refutation of scepticism, but rather a fragment of a cure of the impulse towards scepticism, an impulse *which is a matter less of narrowly philosophical than of existential origination and significance.* (Which has to do, as it were, with signifying, not with ordinary meaning.) And one reason why this is only a fragment is: that a fully effective cure, insofar as there can be any such thing, likely involves changes in one's life and perhaps the life of one's entire society. Insofar as this is correct, we do not have a naïvely optimistic picture of the likely effectiveness of our writing here. Cartesian and 'Kantian' etc. impulses[27] towards scepticism and scientistic ways in which those and other related impulses (including those impulses prompted by 'recoil' from scepticism) are likely in the end to diminish seriously only if the kinds of changes in 'form of life' which Wittgenstein urged parenthetically but powerfully upon his disciples and readers – upon his (and our) culture – were to be realized . . .

We have hoped to show then, that attempts to 'mimic' the person tempted by scepticism is a humane endeavour, which gives us at least some modicum or kind of insight into the phenomenology of the boggle at time, the adequacy of language, the past, and the existence of other mind (see section 2.2.3 'Creative Mimicry' and the Untranslatable Metaphor). However, as suggested elsewhere in the book, this is not to be confused with *making sense* of scepticism, or what it could *be* to experience the self as extraneous to, or a mere observer of the world. It seems, then, that it is time for a re-evaluation of the motivation for philosophy, and broadly speaking, the urge towards conceptual envelopment in general. Our (Cavell-inspired) re-reading and new application of Wittgenstein has gone a significant way towards furthering the appreciation of *mood* (as a sensation of *estrangement* from the world) as the motivation behind the impulse to philosophize. However, this type of re-reading and re-application may also be appropriate for other thinkers in the Western philosophical tradition.[28]

Heidegger, for instance, perhaps offers one of the best analyses of the role of mood or state-of-mind, for his characterization of *anxiety* involves just such a 'boggle' at the possibility of meaning at all. His characterization of anxiety describes the curious 'doubling' which occurs when we are struck by the ungroundedness of our practices, *whilst at the same time we realize that there is no other option open to us.* There have been many different readings of Heidegger, for instance pragmatic, and platonic, but there is certainly room for a re-evaluation of his work which characterizes his thought as at times truly 'therapeutic', along the same lines as those which have been attempted in re-reading and applying Wittgenstein, in the body of this book.[29]

Heidegger suggests that *Dasein* (roughly, human – and suchlike – being) in its 'fallenness' (or immersion in the everyday world of shared social practice) is constantly *fleeing* from itself – that is to say, fleeing from the *idea of itself as contingently embedded in the world.* An anxious fleeing *in the face of,* wherein we shy away from the terrifying 'realization' that our embeddness in the world is a contingent matter (and thus perceive our practices as arbitrary and ungrounded) differs from the sensation of fear, as *Dasein* is not fleeing from a perceptible single object or collectivity of objects in the world. As has been suggested throughout this book, there is *nothing* that it could be to stand above or outside of our practices; thus anxiety (*angst*) cannot be explained in theoretical terms, nor by means of pointing to an entity in the world. Rather, anxiety is the *suspicion* we have of there being a gap between ourselves and the world, the nagging doubt that our actions may prove at base to be *meaningless.* When we experience anxiety, the threat remains only dimly perceptible and inchoate as (a) *mood,* a sense of distrust in the legitimacy of shared practice. When an individual becomes immersed in this mood, the familiar networks of signification recede, and the world appears as being different from the self-separated and thematized.[30] Thus *Dasein* has anxiety in the face of *being-in-the-world* as such, the very possibility of being meaningfully embedded in the shared world. *Dasein,* as *fleeing* from itself, is fleeing from the very *possibility* of its own existence (as that which is necessarily with others, *in* the world) – it is, as we have put it above, a rebellion against the human condition or, more broadly, against the condition of actually being, existing, *at all.* We might then draw a parallel here with Wittgenstein, since we are speaking here about the 'boggle' at the possibility of meaning *in itself* – the sense of uncanniness that the fact of language's working can evoke, and 'despite' the fact that it is without a theoretical 'underpinning' which would be lastingly 'satisfying' as such for us. Heidegger is at pains to suggest that *Dasein is being-in-the-world,* and cannot be described in terms of a self as separable from the world. Indeed, the language of causation is redundant here as anxiety *defies* a determinate conception, remaining in this sense 'resolutely' non-cognitive.[31] Thus the mood of anxiety engenders a curious doubling, wherein we experience the troubling doubt that we are somehow separate from that which surrounds us, that our immersion in the world is a matter of contingency, while yet we continue inevitably to act in *spite* of this realization. There is no possibility of an overview which would allow us to justify (in conceptual terms) the mood of strangeness engendered by the very fact that *meaning exists.* For Heidegger, anxiety is utterly ontically indefinite; it does not impinge on the individual in the way in which we are used to talking about an ontic-impingement, as in cases when one experiences fear as a result of a specifiable entity in the world. There is no definite entity from which one must flee, and neither is there one which *Dasein* can flee to, whether this be theory or further regression into a separately existing 'self', in order to alleviate the feeling.[32] Thus further theorization is highly unlikely to help, and is quite likely to exacerbate further the sensation of estrangement from the world, as we have been at pains to demonstrate elsewhere in this book.

Such moods *can* arise from the attempt to underpin our practices theoretically, but anxiety is most frequently the result of a certain fixation, a certain 'stare' in which the usual structures of use recede, and we are confronted by the brute 'thereness' of objects.[33] To return to an earlier example, let us look again at Renée's words from *Autobiography of a Schizophrenic Girl* which is highly resonant with Heidegger's description of anxiety:

> . . . I [complained] bitterly that things were tricking me and [of] how I suffered because of it. // As a matter of fact, these "things" weren't doing anything special; they didn't speak, nor attack me directly. *It was their very presence that made me complain.* I saw things as metal, so cut off, so detached from one another, so illuminated and tense that they filled me with terror. When, for example, I looked at a chair or a jug, I thought not of their use or function – a jug not as something to hold water and milk, a chair not as something to sit in – *but as having lost their names, their functions and meaning*; they became things and began to take on life, to exist.
>
> This existence accounted for my great fear. In the unreal scene, in the murky quiet of my perception, suddenly "the thing" sprang up. The stone jar, decorated with blue flowers, was there facing me, defying me with its presence, with its existence. To conquer my fear I looked away. My eyes met a chair, then a table; they were alive, too, asserting their presence. I attempted to escape their hold by calling out their names. I said, "chair, jug, table, it is a chair." But *the words echoed hollowly, deprived of all meaning: it had left the object, was divorced from it, so much so that on the one hand it was a living mocking thing, on the other, a name, robbed of sense, an envelope emptied of content.* Nor was I able to bring the two together, but stood there rooted before them, filled with fear and impotence. (Italics ours)

Here, Renée apparently experiences just the type of anxiety described above, in a particularly virulent personally apocalyptic/'psychotic' form. Objects such as chairs and jugs have lost their everyday meaning, i.e. as something to sit on and something to drink from. In other words, they have lost their status as objects ready-to-hand, as things (to) put to use. We venture to suggest that Renée is experiencing the sort of thematization of objects which occurs when one is caught up in the 'wonder' that such intricate systems of meaning (and indeed *any* purposeful action) can exist *at all.* Renée also speaks of the sense of "being tricked" by such objects, protesting that they are "alive". In saying this, as pointed out at the close of Part 2 above, she doesn't mean that they have human qualities, or can 'speak' for instance; rather it is their existence as a brute fact which somehow is 'life', this 'life' filling her not only with wonder, but with incredulous and unresting horror. The sense of being 'tricked' evidences the suspicion of oneself as only contingently in-the-world, as if there could be other meanings (or no meaning!) to be found in the way in which we orientate ourselves towards these objects.

The anxious feeling that our practices are contingent and arbitrary can be the motivation for a theoretical picture. For we desire to *explain* our practices, and to legitimize our seemingly groundless way of speaking/doing. However, the construction of a philosophical system is continually at variance with the 'primordial' way in which *Dasein* orientates itself as *being-in-the-world*. Heidegger uses the term *Dasein* (literally being *there*) rather than 'self' to bring into prominence the absolute indivisibility of self and world.[34] When we try to legitimize our practices, and to break apart this fundamental unity we either mire ourselves in nonsense, or more dangerously, lose a sense of ourselves as agents acting meaningfully in a shared world. What Heidegger shares with Wittgenstein is his insistence that an inhabited solipsistic world is in one fundamental respect in principle impossible, that it is a fantasy through and through – and so such a move could have no form. It is in fact a terrifying loss of significance that one experiences. The world becomes defamiliarized and uncanny. But this is *not* because one is *living* scepticism or solipsism in the sense that one has somehow managed to gain passage to a world of occurrence in a purely cognitive way or fashion. Anxiety does not remove one from the world to a separate vantage point where one looks upon a totality of the present-to-hand (for such a move is not possible; i.e. it does not amount to anything, to seemingly describe one), but one may experience a terrifying loss of attachment to the world, where this absurdity appears as a real possibility. 'The sceptic',[35] or someone *tempted* to say that they have adopted a sceptical position, has not found, as it were, another way of *being-in-the-world*. For *Dasein*, as *being-in-the-world*, is not separable into component parts – as it is through-and-through embedded in the world; it makes no sense to separate time, language, or everyday practices from the self. Worldless occurrence must remain a fantasy, perhaps facilitated in the adoption of an ontical (self-?)description of anxiety. Instead, anxiety throws *Dasein* back upon itself/oneself *as* being-in-the-world, the possibility for meaning as such. The individual is thrown back upon their own being-in-the-world, as the attempts at (quasi-theoretic) conceptualization self-deconstruct. In Wittgensteinian terms: we are returned to the ordinary, perhaps with a new sense of wonder. Moods, as intrinsic potentialities of the human condition, therefore offer possibilities for authenticity – a way or ways of looking at the world which, in a Buddhist sense, allow(s) us to 'let it be'. Leaving everything as they are . . .

We have then begun to suggest some ways in which a re-evaluation of the centrality of mood may inform and modulate our conception of philosophy,[36] our sense of some of the great figures of the Modern philosophical canon, and the way we are wont to conceive the related areas of literature and psychopathology. Rather than theorizing the effects of literature upon us (i.e. when we suggest that literature works by reference and signification) we have been working towards the 'conclusion' that works such as Faulkner's *The Sound and the Fury*, and Steven's "Thirteen Ways of Looking at a Blackbird" or "Anecdote of the Jar" are effective *not* because they describe, explain or *articulate* anxiety (or 'lived scepticism', or speaking 'beyond' language) but because they engender a certain *mood* in which the *ready-to-hand* loses its significance, throwing us back upon *being-in-the-world* with a new receptivity.

The type of therapy then which Wittgenstein advocates, and which is followed and applied in this book, *may* be able to help re-accustom the anxious or confused individual to their *living*, which just means living-in-time, or living-with-others, not stuck in a series of static instants, nor statically coexisting in past, present and future, nor reified outside all time. As was suggested towards the close of 3.2, above: if and when someone who has felt those torments finds themselves able, perhaps through words and talk (such perhaps as these) and love or luck, to change their mood, then they can perhaps enjoy even more than before the incredible opportunity of being, of living . . . rather than feeling condemned to a static yet evanescent Now or condemned to an imaginary stale, 'Godly' fixedness outside time altogether.

We have argued that most of what one is presented with in Anglo-American philosophy is actually an evasion of the uncanny or indeed of terror: the terror of loss of time, loss of self, and the terror of and at change. Most Anglo-American epistemology, we have tried to suggest, is a (pathological, though understandable) defence against losing ordinary human being-in-the-world, *and against that ordinary human-being-in-the-world.* The domestication of inductive scepticism and doubts as to the reality of the past, or other minds, the turning of these into mere excuses for mental gymnastic, mere play-puzzles for 'Analytic' philosophy to bat back and forth – philosophy Sudoku – is we think founded upon a turning away from the horrors actually experienced by those (many) 'unfortunate' individuals who, for a moment, for a night, or for a lifetime, feel themselves to have no 'grounding' in practices, no reliable sense of time, no sense of the reality of others. As we saw in Part 2, the further effort to 'solidify' time, to spatialize it,[37] that one often finds in metaphysics of time, has a more fundamental pathology at its heart: not the terror of losing time, but the horror at being-in-time, the horror of being subject to change, and decay, and death. That is, what we have suggested that most metaphysics of time is a desperate effort to escape the human condition, or, more 'basically', the condition of being and living.

To go further into all this would be the subject of another book. But we hope we have said enough to at least cause our readers to find the (perhaps initially strange) alignment of Wittgenstein with Modernist literature, Zen practice, and *some* high-Continental philosophy more plausible than it originally seemed. Unless the reference of the term "intellectual" is made exceedingly wide, then central 'epistemological' and 'metaphysical' questions are better understood as 'questions' of what mood one is in, of how one comports oneself in the world, of psychopathological experience or of resistance to such experience, of 'altered states' and mystical/religious experience or of one's resistance to such experience. But it/they can potentially lead to transformation of mood, transformation of suffering. And so we hope that philosophy might turn a little, might kink, from being a sublimated terror at loss of humanity or a sublimated horror at humanity, to being a more or less practical investigation of the possibilities for humanity. The possibilities, that is, for how we are to live (in) the world. Possibilities whose exploration can be considerably enhanced, we have argued, *by applying Wittgenstein.*

Afterword

Further Prospects for Applying Wittgenstein

In this book, I have counted the following as criteria for *applying* Wittgenstein: (1) Moving *beyond exegesis*, (2) *extending* Wittgenstein's insights or taking them to domains where he did not particularly *focus*, and (3) taking in a domain of thought or life that is of some moment *beyond the academy*. I have also sought to be true to Wittgenstein's conception of philosophy: meaning, that to take his alleged *doctrines* or *opinions* and simply 'extend' them to new areas is *not* to apply Wittgenstein (and thus many apparent previous 'applications' of Wittgenstein by other philosophers do *not* count, by my lights, as applying Wittgenstein; they are 'pseudo-applications' at best . . .). Rather, one should seek to do 'the same kind of thing' as Wittgenstein, in puncturing (in ways that are actually effective) delusions that we are prone to, and helping us to attain peace with regard to our words: no longer (at least temporarily) being tormented by incompatible desires with regard to our words.

This is *resolute*[1] practice of Wittgensteinian philosophy. Beyond the merely Carnapian idea of violations (of 'logical syntax', of the 'limits' of language-games), beyond the widespread pseudo-Wittgensteinian notion of the alleged restrictions imposed by the rules of language-games,[2] being resolutely Wittgensteinian involves taking seriously the much-abused German of *PI* 116: "[M]uss man sich immer fragen: Wird denn dieses Wort in der Sprache, in der es seine Heimat hat, je tatsachlich so grbraucht? – *Wir* fuhren die Worter von ihren metaphysischen, wieder auf ihre alltagliche Verwendung zuruck."[3] Anscombe translates this as "[O]ne must always ask oneself: is the word ever actually used in this way in the language-game, which is its original home?" But the word "game" is strikingly absent from the German. A better (though, obviously, in *part* a 'freer') translation, in order to *get* the philosophical point – the *reminder* – that Wittgenstein is offering here, would I believe be roughly this: "[I]s the word ever actually used this way in the *language*, i.e. in that which is – as goes without saying – the home of all words?" Rendered thus, one is not being offered a scalpel with which to excise from and via philosophy words or uses that 'violate' the practices of particular language-games; rather, one is simply being gifted a therapeutic tool. One is being thereby returned to the language as it actually is. And what it is is 'something' dynamic, and unclosed. One is being returned to oneself, and to ourselves. Reminded that there can be such a thing as, in fantasy, taking one's words on holiday to 'somewhere' where they will no longer do the work one wanted them to do. One is being reminded of the utter truism, which diseased patterns of thinking can yet somehow alienate one from, that words don't mean except in uses, in contexts. One is not being pointed to some restricted domain of usage and told not to depart from it. That way lies the traditional, standard, hopeless interpretations of Wittgenstein as a language-policeman, as a kind of Ordinary Language philosopher. That is the way in which Wittgenstein has traditionally been (pseudo-)applied, by very many philosophers, *including by most would-be true believers in Wittgenstein* – Malcolm, Phillips, Hacker, Johnston, etc. etc., in the fields of the mind (e.g. dreaming), of religion, of cognitive science, of ethics, etc. etc. But what Wittgenstein licenses in *PI* 116 is none of that. To apply Wittgenstein is not to delineate and quasi-theorize particular restricted 'language-games'. The concept of a language-game was intended by Wittgenstein as an *object of comparison* (see *PI* 130–2), nothing more. It was not intended as a quasi-technical term, as a prolegomenon to would-be 'applications' which – hopelessly – try to police what we say, to rule certain words or terms in and others out, and to license or prohibit certain combinations. The question is whether there is a use in our language as it is in the now that we are always on the cusp of, the now that is unfolding, for the term, whatever it might be (e.g. "time-slice", "(the) now"), that one is investigating. That is always an *open* question, whose investigation requires a genuinely dialogical spirit *vis-à-vis* the person(s) wishing to use the word in question in a certain way. One needs to understand what they are trying to do, and determine, (actually or notionally) with them, whether they can succeed. This is what I have tried to do in looking at some literature, literary criticism, madness and its would-be interpreters, and various people (including philosophers) trying to think adequately about time. One has to try to figure out whether the desires that they (often, we) have in relation to the words that are perhaps causing trouble are compatible. I have suggested some reasons in this book for concluding that in a number of cases such compatibility is not forthcoming: that one's failure to produce a sense in (some of what (some-)one wants to say about) (e.g.) Benjy, or about time-slices, without paraphrasing into submission – distorting – in an unacceptable way the very phenomenon one was wanting to account for, is a sign that one has not succeeded in making sense in the area in question. That one is deluded into taking nonsense (a failure to mean) for sense.

Language-in-action is the home of words. Our language – the language we live, speak, inhabit, use. A device that is 'infinitely' flexible – but which can still in a certain sense be knowingly or unknowingly abused or misused. If one (absurdly) treats it as having limits, and then seeks to speak outside of those. If one takes nonsense – nothing, the relentless failure to mean – as sense, and pretends that one is doing something harmless, or indeed deep and grand.

Applying Wittgenstein is not policing the limits of language-games – for 'language-games' are merely utterly temporary non-theoretic constructs tentatively put forward for purpose-relative therapeutic reasons. It is not helpful to claim that religion and science *are* separate language-games, for instance, as pseudo-appliers of Wittgenstein have done; for all that it is *vital* to teach differences between a scientific approach to things and the possibility of a non-superstitious religious approach to things (though one cannot avoid normative engagement, in claiming that the latter is (or in claiming that it is not) an actuality).

Applying Wittgenstein is not the policing of 'the limits of language' – for there is in philosophy *no such thing as* a well-defined limit to language. There is no outside – outside you cannot breathe . . . These metaphors, and their internal tensions, lead us to understand the profound sense in which there is a *dis*analogy between the limits of language and (say) the limits of the atmosphere (usefully vague though the latter is). A better analogy would be to the Universe, which physicists plausibly tell us is not infinite, but yet which it makes no sense to speak of an outside to.[4] There is nothing outside the Universe, not even a vacuum. Somewhat similarly: there is nothing outside language. There is yet one thing outside language . . .: nonsense. And its delusions – the delusions which it seems naturally to foster, and which certain cultural etc. conditions can worsen, by making much said delusions more natural – of being outside yet a shadow-version of what is inside. Or somehow straddling the frontier, the 'limit'. All 'nonsense' is a failure to mean, an absence of language-at-home, in potential use. The existence of nonsense makes language more mysterious, more liable to vex, even than the Universe.

Applying Wittgenstein is working through all of this, in all its complexity, with regard to all the aspects of our life where we are liable to get confused or deluded, which are many. Applying Wittgenstein is thinking and talking sense, and (transitionally) nonsense too, to attain the tranquility of common sense, to 'regain' language-untroubled.

In this book, I commenced in Part 1 by barely yet applying Wittgenstein at all, but simply looking at (as it were) Wittgenstein at home, in 'the most' everyday of language. In Part 2, I turned to trickier cases: to applying Wittgenstein to Modernist literature, and to madness, to help us understand how they work, and to help us understand them – and to help us understand where our understanding comes to an end, and what (perhaps nothing) is on the other side of that 'limit'. In Part 3, continuing and both focusing and expanding the meditation on time initiated in Part 2, I applied Wittgenstein to the thoughts and talk of philosophers and others about time. The real point was to 'return' one to (diverse modes of) *living* time (e.g. I discussed ethnographies of lived time, physicists' accounts of time, and psychopathological time-experience), and to begin to indicate the critically important role of *mood* in fomenting philosophical and psychological lived problems with time. This theme expanded to be the main concern of the Conclusion of the book: philosophical problems and problems analogous thereto as problems of *mood* and not in the standard sense problems of intellection, nor even of language.

But this book is of course by no means the first effort resolutely to apply Wittgenstein's method in the way sketched here.[5] Furthermore, it is worth pointing out that I am not committed to the claim that the kind of thing Wittgenstein did is *sui generis* in the history of philosophy *up* to his arrival. And, in fact, I do not believe that. I think that many of the great philosophers who preceded Wittgenstein had to a lesser or greater extent a *resolute* conception of philosophy, which they applied or which was ready, after them, to apply – only, I believe that very few scholars and philosophers outside these great ones have understood this. Thus I have argued elsewhere that there is more of the spirit which is most plainly visible in Wittgenstein than one might have expected in Hume,[6] in Frege,[7] in Marx,[8] and in Nietzsche.[9] Others have argued the same of some of these authors, and also of Berkeley,[10] Kant[11] and Kierkegaard;[12] and indeed the same may be argued of the Ancient Sceptics (and Socrates), and perhaps even of Descartes[13] and Montaigne.

. . . But even leaving aside these controversial claims, which I cannot support here, to what I term 'the hidden greatness of the canon', what I have elsewhere called (with a self-consciously anachronistic smile and wink) the influence of Wittgenstein on Nietzsche, on Hume, on Sextus, etc.,[14] what is for sure is that there are more or less resolute appliers of Wittgenstein that have written, before this book. Here are a few of the finest of the others who have gone before me:

James Guetti (with whom I co-wrote the predecessor paper to the 'consequences of meaning' material in Part 1 of this book) is perhaps the ablest expositor of a roughly resolute conception of Wittgensteinianism (arrived at largely independently of Diamond *et al.*) with regard to literature. He uses Wittgenstein both to show what is wrong with most 'literary theory', and to facilitate a better understanding of how (Modernist, but not only Modernist[15]) literary texts actually work (upon one). And he does so with a rich diet of examples: he is an aurally sensitive literary critic. In Parts 1 and 2 of this book, I hope to have followed as much in his footsteps as (sometimes more indirectly) in those of Wittgenstein himself.

Louis Sass applies Wittgenstein very thoughtfully to vexing questions in psychopathology: especially, to how to understand the 'Apollonian' disorders, such as the schiz spectrum. In the process, he too sheds light on some great Modernist literary texts. My criticisms of him as insufficiently resolute are nevertheless to be found in Part 2, above.[16]

Martin Stone has also done some fine Wittgensteinian philosophy of literature, notably in his contribution to *The Literary Wittgenstein*,[17] but he is also, and most notably, a deeply impressive resolute philosopher of *law*[18] (as is Lisa van Alstyne).

Thomas Kuhn drew on a subtle understanding of gestalt psychology, of the law, of politics, and more, and used key Wittgensteinian insights (notably, on paradigms and 'rule-following') in his epochal philosophy of science. My *Kuhn*[19] extends these into a thoroughgoing reading of Kuhn's rendition of science as Wittgensteinian.

Juliet Floyd is the leading resolute philosopher of maths. Along with a handful of others – such as some recent Putnam, and Michael Kremer – she has succeeded in overcoming the baneful influence of earlier 'Wittgensteinian' philosophers of maths who in some cases failed to understand the maths they were philosophizing about, and in most cases produced an unhelpful revisionism about maths, through attempting to police what one was allowed to say, or 'able' to mean, in maths.

Peter Winch famously applied Wittgenstein's philosophy to 'social science' etc. There were some philosophical or at least rhetorical problems with his approach, such as the degree to which he did not (in his famous and brilliant polemical little book) seem to have overcome the temptation to a metaphysics of rules; most of these problems were however fully rectified in his subsequent work, notably his less problematic later essays "Understanding a Primitive Society", "Understanding Ourselves", and "Persuasion" (and in the very valuable new (1990) Preface to *The Idea of a Social Science and its Relation to Philosophy*). Along with Wes Sharrock and Phil Hutchinson, I seek to 'complete' a resolute post-Winchian approach to 'social science' in my *There is No Such Thing as Social Science: In Defence of Peter Winch*, forthcoming (in 2007) with Ashgate.

Phil Hutchinson's forthcoming (Palgrave, 2007) book on the philosophy of the emotions is the first full-length resolute treatment of this highly important 'area', which has been much misunderstood and deformed in recent years by both scientistic and post-modernistic thinkers.

Linda Zerilli is one of the ablest appliers of Wittgenstein in the field of political science/theory. Others very worth mentioning in this connection include Alice Crary, Naomi Scheman and Nigel Pleasants.

So, what are the best *further* prospects for applying Wittgenstein? Here are some of them:

Literature

There remains huge scope for reading more Modern literature after and with Wittgenstein. *Kafka*, for instance: James Conant has made a beautiful start here, with his 'optimistic' philosophical and political re-reading, in "In the Electoral Colony: Kafka in Florida". Some of Kafka's texts (e.g. his extraordinary too-little-known short story, "The Burrow") invite a Sassian reading: Laura Cook intends in the coming years to re-read Kafka (and other Modernists) in a somewhat Sassian fashion, but yet *without* sticking so closely, as arguably Sass does, to reading these authors in a psychopathological context.

Among contemporary authors, *J. M. Coetzee's* novels in many cases (e.g. *Disgrace, In the Heart of the Country, The Lives of Animals*) invite re-reading as 'Wittgensteinian' therapeutic works. (The reading of novels as works of therapy in Wittgenstein's sense (derived from the *Tractatus* and *PI* alike) is more explicitly and decidedly Wittgensteinian than the broader and loosely-influenced-by Wittgenstein tradition of literature as moral philosophy, as in Nussbuam and Diamond etc.) While my late and much-lamented colleague *Max Sebald* is one perhaps-similar author whose at-times-*explicit* influence by and treatment of Wittgenstein's own philosophy, as well as his (roughly 'Apollonian', in Sass' sense) investigation of mental suffering, invites much more discussion than it has as yet received.

Film

Clearly, much resolute Wittgensteinian thinking has already gone into philosophy-and-film in recent years. The work of Cavell (and his interpreters, such as Stephen Mulhall) has of course been of great importance here; and see my co-edited collection, *Film as Philosophy: Essays on Cinema after Wittgenstein and Cavell.* There is room for much more to be done here, in applying broadly Wittgensteinian approaches to film, including to films as works of therapy.[20] Phil Hutchinson and I hope to launch a journal, *Film as Philosophy*, to focus and further such work. Among the films that we think particularly amenable to a Wittgensteinian approach, but that have not yet received such an approach, are *Donnie Darko, 2001: A Space Odyssey,* and the films of Peter Greenaway (up to about 1991).

Maths

There is room too to apply Wittgenstein quite a lot more to thinking about maths. For instance, I am working with Christian Greiffenhagen on the important matter of establishing a resolute approach to infinity, which I think has not yet been achieved, and on trying to extend the interesting application of Wittgensteinian thinking that Floyd and Putnam made to our understanding of Godel's famous Incompleteness Theorem.

The Human Sciences and 'Cognitive Science'

Much 'Wittgensteinian' work on 'cognitive science' and linguistics has I believe misfired, because it has simply and uselessly tried to police the language, rather than looking at what 'cognitive scientists' actually want to do and actually have done.[21] I hope in future to participate in correcting these failures, and in applying Wittgenstein resolutely to the human sciences; primarily, in my planned future monograph, *Wittgenstein among the Human Sciences.* In this work, I hope to reflect usefully on what we want to mean when we call something a 'science', and thus bring more clearly into focus in what respect it is and is not helpful to think of particular enterprises as cognitive, social or human *sciences*. I believe that there is much light potentially to be shed on subject-matters as diverse as Chomskian linguistics, 'transport science' and the status of the increasingly vital discipline of 'environmental science' (e.g. whether environmental science can hope in any meaningful sense to be value-free), by means of such application of Wittgenstein.

There is room and need for Wittgensteinian work to be done in reflecting too on the foundations and achievements of cognitive science, an application of Wittgenstein that looks closely at the actual practices and assumptions of cognitive science, and does not presuppose that 'cognitive (and 'social') neuro-science' is trying to locate (what philosophers think of as) cognition in the brain. That – rather – attempts to see if some cognitive science can be read as attempting to tell us why we all (or most of us) go on in the same way. In other words, of cognitive science as *itself* an endeavour to apply Wittgenstein, trying to fill out a certain Wittgensteinian picture of 'knowing how to go on', etc. (And in re-thinking 'representation' such as to move away from the barren outdated 'cognitivist' philosophical version of this term to a new version, consonant with Aristotle as with the best of recent brain science, that casts representations rather as "sensible forms or species, which can be realized both in the regular stuff in our environment and in sensory systems".[22]) In my view, my former teacher Anne J. Jacobson is the person with her finger most closely on this neglected and intriguing pulse.[23]

Politics

My main research project for the next few years[24] will be to follow not just Mac-Intyre and Sandel but also Wittgenstein in critiquing the political philosophy of liberalism. There is a widespread view, intriguingly propagated by one of the doyens of 'resolutism', Burt Dreben, that John Rawls was or became a Wittgensteinian thinker. In my view this is an understandable but disastrous misunderstanding of one or both thinkers. I seek to uncover the delusions of allegedly 'neutral' (between conceptions of the good) liberalism, and thus lay some groundwork for a sane, green, radical political philosophy suitable for responding to the current challenges to our very survival as a species, and for a philosophy compatible with culture being permanent, and not just a blip.

Spirituality

There is room for a subtler Wittgensteinian philosophy of religion than we have hitherto had, and for connecting Wittgensteinian thought with spiritual and Eastern traditions to a much greater extent than has been realized. I believe that a key object of comparison for and application of Wittgenstein in the twenty-first century will be Buddhism.[25]

In sum: what is to be done? What can philosophy do, that is of *relatively* wide use, and new, in the twenty-first century? How can it best 'apply' itself; how can philosophers best 'apply' themselves?

Wittgenstein conceived his central task as being to find in each and every case and context "the liberating word". I believe that the prospects *for applying Wittgenstein more*, as lightly indicated hereabove, are good. And that the task is one of some considerable cultural importance, far beyond the academy. I have sought in this book to offer applications of Wittgenstein to areas of deep human interest, such as the edges of writing, and of reason. But what if, for instance, Wittgenstein can help us too to understand spiritual traditions which have paradoxical and transitionally invaluable wisdom to offer us; or if applying his methods can suggest ways of leading us beyond suicidal and ecocidal modes of social and political organization . . . ?

Never forgetting that when Wittgenstein wrote that philosophy leaves everything as it is, he had in mind the *explanation vs description* dichotomy, not the normative vs descriptive dichotomy.[26] Wittgenstein urged us to give up the fantasy of philosophical *explanation*. But he certainly hoped (when he wasn't too down) that his descriptions might be of some use in *changing* these times from being 'dark' ones to being 'lighter'.

The task of applying Wittgenstein is among other things the task of philosophy shifting from absurd ambitions of *explaining* the world to being able rather, at last, to participate reflectively in a meaningful and useful sense in *changing* it. *Through*, paradoxically, the paradoxical manoeuvre of "leaving everything as it is". Through, that is, reflecting it back to us – reflecting us back to us – in such a way that we *cannot* any longer remain silent, but rather have to act.

To liberate.[27]

Notes

Foreword

1 See Fish (1980).

2 For an elegant account of the distinction between "doctrinal", "elucidatory" and "resolute" readings of Wittgenstein, see Hutchinson, Phil (forthcoming). See also Read and Hutchinson's various published joint-authored works.

3 On this term, see not only the 'New Wittgensteinian' scholarship on the *Tractatus*, but also Wittgenstein's own precisely parallel use of the term at points in Waismann (2003).

4 For Austin as *not* in this sense an 'Ordinary Language Philosopher', see Eugen Fischer's recent work.

5 For more detail on the nature of resolution, see the dispute between Conant and Diamond on the one hand and Williams and Sullivan on the other, in Weiss and Kobel (2004).

6 For Read's own exegetical account of Wittgenstein's resolution, in his early, later and last stages, see especially his "The *Real* Philosophical Discovery" (Read 1995), "Is There a Legitimate Way to Raise Doubts about the Immediate Future 'from the Perspective of' a *Doubted* Immediate Past?" (Read 2000), "Nothing is Shown" (Read and Deans 2003), "The Career of 'Internal Relations' in Wittgenstein's Work" (Read 1997), "Throwing Away 'the Bedrock'" (Read 2004), 'An Elucidatory Interpretation of Wittgenstein's *Tractatus*: A Critique of Daniel D. Hutto's and Marie McGinn's Reading of Tractatus 6.54', in Read and Hutchinson (2006). See also Read's other joint-authored works with Phil Hutchinson.

7 In these remarks, and in the following paragraphs, I am influenced heavily by Diamond's great essay "Throwing Away the Ladder: How to Read the *Tractatus*", and also by Read's "Throwing Away 'the Bedrock'" (Read 2004) and his "On the New Hume's New Antagonists", the closing essay in his edited volume *The New Hume Debate* (Read and Richman 2000).

8 A useful – allied – comparator here is Thomas Kuhn's practice in the history and philosophy of science, which strikingly did not involve the ongoing use of the terms (such as "paradigm") that he himself made famous. See especially Part I of Read and Sharrock's *Kuhn* (2002).

9 Helpful here is Wittgenstein's insistence, in his discussions with Turing recorded in *Lectures on the Foundations of Mathematics*, that he has *qua* philosopher no opinions at all, and that if Turing catches him putting an opinion forward, he will instantly give it up.

10 For some discussion of how this enterprise can be valuable, and (more basically) possible, see Read's "What Theory of Film do Wittgenstein and Cavell Have?" in Read and Goodenough's *Film as Philosophy* (2005).

11 See *The New Wittgenstein* (2004), a now-famous collection of papers edited by Rupert Read and Alice Crary.

12 Drawing on published and unpublished work of his own, and particularly on material an earlier version of which he co-authored with James Guetti.

13 See *PI*, Part II, section xi; see also section 268 of Part I.
14 Against the accusation that this is an over-intellectualization of the text, Read can offer I think two responses: (1) Faulkner's text is being used *as an object of comparison, not* as (absurdly) a quasi-scientistic model for the schiz spectrum; and/or (2) Benjy, on the standard reading of the text, *is no idiot* (he is far too perceptive for that; his sound and fury signifies a vast amount); just as, on Sass' non-standard reading of schizophrenia, it involves no cognitive deficit. What Read does is to look and see whether there can be any such *thing* as Benjy's non-standard way of seeing the world; Read argues that Benjy's sound and fury signifies nothing, *in terms of meaningful consequences*; and that, similarly, following and applying a resolute understanding of Wittgenstein, schizophrenia, and Sass' model for it (solipsism) involve a failure to signify, *in terms of meaningful consequences*. A rich array of grammatical effects, a cascade of failing attempts to mean that yield words but not (in the ordinary sense of the word) meanings, is another matter entirely.
15 For explication, see e.g. Conant's essay in *The New Wittgenstein*, Crary and Read (2004).
16 My thanks to Rupert Read for his helpful comments on this Foreword.

Introduction

1 See Cook's Foreword, above, for some suitable emphasis on both the 'literary' character of Wittgenstein's work and the literary character of literature. What I am adding together here is the consequence of these, for our understanding of Wittgenstein's own semi-unparaphrasability.
2 For example, Peter Hacker, perhaps the pre-eminent living Wittgenstein scholar, claims precisely to follow and to be faithful to Wittgenstein's method in philosophy, to understand and practise his 'therapeutic' conception of philosophy, to reject root and branch the anti-Wittgensteinian predilections of most English-speaking philosophy. I have argued in a series of papers (cited elsewhere in this book), however, that Hacker, far from achieving these desiderata, is by and large held just as tightly in the grip of the heresy of paraphrase – the idea that it does no harm to paraphrase Wittgenstein into a very different form – as are those he criticises. (And thus he is more dangerous than they – for in him, the intellectual disease that Wittgenstein was combating has gone deep underground. He purveys it, while claiming *par excellence* to resist it. The neurotic symptoms that are visible elsewhere in English-speaking philosophy are profoundly and thus dangerously disguised, in his work and that of his followers.)
3 In this regard, it closely resembles something that present-day academics know all too well: the audit culture, auditing being something else which also must come to an end somewhere . . . Thus Onora O'Neill's quite correct applied philosophical musings on trust. The point was already very clearly established in Foucault's discussions of 'Panopticism', and has been beautifully applied to the interpretation of schizophrenia as lived solipsism in Sass (1994). The failure to find a secure resting-point in which one trusts entails endless hungry motion, the kind of endless pushing back already depicted with great psychological acuteness in the closing chapters of Laing's *The Divided Self* (1990). (For further discussion, see Part 2, below, and also my reading of *The Lord of the Rings* (see www.uea. ac.uk/%7Ej339/LOTR2.htm.)
4 There will inevitably be different good ways to take the returning and circling movements of my text, just as (more obviously) there are in Wittgenstein's *Investigations*, where tracks lead off from some of his remarks in a number of different directions.
5 The contrast between 'meaningful consequences' – the consequences of *meaning*, without which it (the noun or the verb, and the verb active or passive) is not itself – and 'grammatical effects' is in fact pretty much coterminous with the contrast

between the two senses of "signify" under consideration here. 'Grammatical effects' are the consequences of being meaning-*full*, in the way that literature so often is: overflowing with meaning, with significances.

6 Thus it is an important feature of the analysis in Part 3 that I consider in the course of it (at least in passing) fictions of time, physics, sociological and historical scenarios involving the life of time, and so forth.

7 For more of those respects and domains, see the Afterword, below. My thanks, for helpful comments on this Introduction, to Laura Cook, Angus Ross and Phil Hutchinson.

Part 1: Language

1 Distinctively, and – in terms of my interests in this paper – *especially* consequential. (Note that meaning (and its consequences) is not necessarily at all close in meaning or role to 'denotation': Wittgenstein's conception of meaning as related to use is much broader than and indeed orthogonal to the question of whether something is being asserted, or denoted (one 'speech act'). However, the concept of 'connotation' IS pretty close to the concept, that I explore below, of the 'other' to 'meaningful consequences': namely, 'grammatical effects'.)

2 I mean to allude here to Cora Diamond's and James Conant's important and influential picture of the methods of Wittgenstein's philosophizing, and their account of even early Wittgenstein as transcending the philosophical categories in which he has almost invariably been placed. See for example Diamond's "Throwing Away the Ladder: How to Read the *Tractatus*" in her *The Realistic Spirit* (Diamond 1991), wherein she explains how the *Tractatus* can be read as disavowing any notion of 'positive', 'substantial' or 'profound' nonsense; and see Conant's "Elucidation and Nonsense in Frege and Wittgenstein" in Crary and Read (eds) (2000). Diamond and Conant emphasize that what seems to one most essential for a philosophical account to be given of something must actually go without saying (be 'presumed'). But not because it is ineffable – rather, because the philosophical account of it can at best be 'transitional', a means of dealing with confusions, not an assertoric thesis (for example a positive assertion of conditions of possibility of such and such). My account here too is intended to be transitional: I am not laying down timeless philosophical truths, but only working to eliminate certain powerful philosophical illusions and delusions. (This itself is again an 'ultimately' nonsensical – and so at best transitional – remark . . .! A number (a much larger number than might first appear to be the case) of my remarks in this book, like a number of Diamond's and Conant's, after Wittgenstein's 'Sätze', may 'flip' before the reader's eyes roughly from appearing to be quasi-positivistic contributions to a theory of language, to attempts to say the unsayable, to perhaps-helpful ways of giving therapy to the philosophically deluded, to plain nonsense, to simply senseless (and thus unobjectionable – because not saying anything).)

3 Of course, to say that this is perhaps Wittgenstein's most famous remark does not imply either: (1) That people usually give it in its full form, as here. On the contrary, it is usually reduced to the dangerously misleading slogan, "Meaning is use". (For an attack on such sloganizing, see pp. 110f. of M. McGinn (1997). (2) That this remark is rightly read as a claim, a thesis, or even a proposition. It should, rather, be heard as a methodological prophylactic, or at most as a 'grammatical' reminder. And ultimately, as nothing at all.

4 On pp. 51ff. of my "Acting from Rules: 'Internal Relations' *versus* 'Logical Existentialism'" (Read and Guetti 1996), joint-authored with James Guetti. (In relation to the discussion which follows, one way of summing up our approach in that earlier paper would be that, surprisingly enough, Baker and Hacker's approach to Wittgenstein on rules is overly static, theoreticistic and reificatory to

the point of being positivistic. Perhaps just as surprisingly, if one had to choose between an ineffabilistic and a 'positivistic' rendition of (later) Wittgenstein on meaning, one would be better off choosing the former.) See also the Afterword to Guetti's (1993).

5 That my talk of "presumptions" is decidedly not to be equated with the assertion of transcendental conditions of possibility will, I hope, become evident as the reader follows my argument, below.

6 Wittgenstein's proviso, "for a *large* class", should give us pause with regard to either reaction – it could also be cited as a reason for doubting any argument against *PI* 43 in the service of an alternative 'thesis'. For it is an initial indication that no "thesis" is intended here. (See also my: "Perspicuous Presentation: A Perspicuous Presentation", co-authored with Phil Hutchinson, forthcoming in *Philosophical Investigations*, for detail on the 'modal' terms crucial to right interpretation of *PI* 43.)

7 Let me note here that for the 'new' Wittgenstein of Conant and Diamond, nonsense does not consist in strings of words with an 'illicit sense', strings combined such as to generate 'substantial' items of nonsense (see also *PI* 499–502), but rather of words for which we have, as yet, no use. Thus the 'idea' that the meaning of sentences in real contexts is literally compositionally generated by combining together the meanings of individual words is itself nonsense, a non-starter. Individual words have only what I, after Wittgenstein and Frege, call 'senses'; they do not yet have use, and thus they are not yet meaningful. (As further detailed below, I take Wittgenstein to have thoroughly grasped the kind of use-oriented linguistic wholism this involves as early as the *Tractatus*. Support for my thus taking Wittgenstein is extensive in M. Kremer's "Contextualism and Holism in the Early Wittgenstein: From *Prototractatus* to *Tractatus*" (Kremer 1997).

8 Here, I allude to Tony Kenny's useful pioneering paper on Wittgenstein's middle and later misprision of his own early work ("The Ghost of the *Tractatus*", reprinted in his *Wittgenstein's Lasting Significance* (Weiss and Kobel 2004)). I take it that such an *over*-harsh attitude on Wittgenstein's part to the dubious and misleading impressions he thought his early work *could* foster, and to its lack of breadth of view in certain respects, facilitates understanding of how the Conant/Diamond reading of the *Tractatus* can avoid being impaled upon the horns of an apparent dilemma: either Wittgenstein was wrong (in a 'positivist' or an 'ineffabilist' fashion) in his early work, or he was sometimes too hard in his later assessment of his early work. I favour the second horn of the dilemma. The first horn, I suspect, only looks plausible while one doesn't take full account of Wittgenstein's excessive uncharity towards his earlier self.

9 Hallett (1967). I focus somewhat on Hallett, as a commentator who has devoted particularly detailed attention to Wittgenstein on use – though it is implicit in what I have already said that this book title must already give one serious pause. For example, was Wittgenstein really giving us a *definition*? Could a definition solve (dissolve) the problems Wittgenstein was interested in helping people with? Is a definition, in philosophy, not usually the initial movement in a theorization of something?

10 Hallett (1967: 102).

11 The problem with such a version of "context", as will be seen when I bring Diamond on rules into my argument, is in brief that "contexts" often sound or act too much like specific grammars statically conceived, which may constitute or invite local theorization.

12 See some of the essays in his *Thought and Language* (Thornton 1998). Other particularly influential 'use-theorists' of Wittgenstein include Ernest Gellner, Stephen Hilmy and (most famously) Saul Kripke.

13 To put the point rather more bluntly, though of course I cannot establish this in

the compass of the present section: I suspect that most philosophers have no right to see Wittgenstein's later work as an advance on his early work, and that actually what one gets as renditions of his later work is typically a type of 'position' which he had already largely successfully overcome . . . *prior to* the close of the *Tractatus*. I take neither positivistic nor ineffabilistic accounts of Wittgenstein's work and methods to be adequate to the *Tractatus*, nor *(a fortiori)* to *PI*.

14 See my "Acting from Rules" (Read and Guetti 1996). I have argued the same case with regard to conventional readings of Wittgenstein's last phase, in my "'The First shall be Last and the Last shall be First. . .': A New Reading of *On Certainty* 501" (Brenner and Moyal-Sharrock 2005).

15 Wittgenstein (1969: 7)

16 To be completely accurate, I do accept that Wittgenstein did 'backslide' a little up until about 1930; but I think that this backsliding was *thoroughly* reversed during/after the *Philosophical Grammar* stage. The subtlety and (by and large) resolution of Wittgenstein's thought in the early 1930s is particularly beautifully captured in large stretches of *The Voices of Wittgenstein*. (Waissman 2003).

17 This view is in fact taken by Peter Sullivan and Roger White. See the debates over their views in my forthcoming *Tractatus Wars*, co-edited with Matt Lavery.

18 Wittgenstein (1975: 59–60). For argument as to the limitations and inadequacy of conceptions of use which reduce it to static grammatical relations – or to usage – see "Acting from Rules" (Read and Guetti 1996).

19 See my (1997) "The Career of 'Internal Relations' in Wittgenstein's Work", and "Acting from Rules" (Read and Guetti 1996) where Guetti and I look at how one ought to understand the notions of "static" and "dynamic" here. For detail on how other would-be Wittgensteinians (e.g. the 'Oxford Wittgensteinians') fail to take the dynamic character of language seriously, see my "Perspicuous Presentation: A Perspicuous Presentation", forthcoming (jointly with Phil Hutchinson) in *Philosophical Investigations*.

20 For detailed exposition of what exactly is meant here by "idling language", consult Guetti (1993: 179–97), "Idling Rules". Here is his conclusion, on p. 197: "[A] figure or an image "with aspects" is analogous to an isolated and inactive concept – like "reading" or "love" – with its plurality of possible meanings." Such concepts, such language, is, as Guetti puts it, "meaning-full", rather than "meaningful". "Sense" is just such *possible* meaning. Meaning is not actually meaning until it is actual – until it is language applied, until it has "consequences". And though we see very clear intimations of this in Wittgenstein's early writing, one sees it most fully, I suggest, only after the 'Big Typescript'.

21 See *The Blue and Brown Books* (1969: 1–5).

22 For a clear and full view – and a more thorough critique – of the powerful role of these meaning-objects in those thought-systems that we are raising questions for, see Niles (1992: 202–3).

23 P. M. S. Hacker (1990: 127–48). See also my (2001) "What is Chomskyism? Or, 'Chomsky against Chomsky'".

24 Here of course I do *not* mean to imply that meaning something or understanding someone to mean something is an action, in the sense of an 'inner action'. (What exactly I *do* mean unfolds, below.) Nor yet do I mean to neglect expressions like, "Did you really mean that?", which can make meaning look like it is an inner action but which, when viewed aright, is an expression involved in (roughly) a 'secondary' phenomenon, parasitic on the ordinary activities of meaning and understanding, of practical language use. This can be clearly seen if one asks oneself questions like whether it would be logically intelligible for a child to ask whether someone really meant something *prior to* learning vast amounts on the back of the 'presupposition' of actual public language use. I.e. getting things done in various language games – the fundamental phenomenon of meaning – is

logically prior to any questions of sincerity or insincerity. This is a point which, in different ways, Wittgenstein makes over and over again in his later work.

25 See the notes on p. 59, and also on p. 18, of *PI*.

26 See *Remarks on the Philosophy of Psychology, Vol. I* (1980: para 1025).

27 See *Remarks on the Philosophy of Psychology, Vol. I* (1980: para 1027).

28 How this "doing" proceeds, and how it has to do with language itself and "as such", is again examined in detail in my "Acting from Rules" (Read and Guetti 1996).

29 Lee (1982: 57), my emphasis. These are of course not Wittgenstein's own words but Lee's notes upon them; still – except for the word "usage" in the third sentence, which surely, in accord with what precedes it, would be less liable to mislead if rendered as "use" – I think their direction entirely consistent with Wittgenstein's attitudes throughout his later philosophy, even when he is sharply conscious, as he is especially in Part II of *PI*, of the apparent weight and substance of inactive linguistic expressions and of the temptations to regard them as meaningful language (see again, Guetti 1993). Incidentally, my differentiating between "use" and "usage" echoes Vassiliki Kindi's argument against sociological theorizations of Wittgenstein's invocation of "use", in her "Wittgenstein's Resort to Ordinary Language" (Kindi 1998: 298–305). Kindi takes the distinction in the first instance from Ryle's interesting paper on "Ordinary Language", in Caton (1963).

30 One must not lose sight of the difference, crucial to Wittgenstein, between language in use and 'language' in citation, exemplification (see *PI* 16), grammatical description, etc. And one must insist that the transformation of linguistic expressions effected by citation of all varieties continues to be woefully misconceived and under-estimated in language studies. In significant part due to the impact of some of Derrida's writing – and especially to his inflationary conceptions of the flexible play (through "grafting", etc.) of cited (or "decontextualized") expressions – one loses sight not only of what might in actual use separate one mode of discourse from another but also, and more important for my purposes, of what might separate discourse from *non-discourse*, from isolated and exposed linguistic forms that do no communicative work (though this is not to say, of course, that such idling forms have no "effects" – on their manifold and in many cases pleasurable or striking effects, see Guetti (1993)). Here, even if one cannot through Wittgenstein's various admonitions and proposals understand the seductive weight and intractableness of countless expressions "freed" or set loose by all manner of citation, one must at the very least consider that at these points he was very worried about *something*. In this respect – contrary to the current views of some philosophers and 'literary theorists' – his thinking must, as Mulhall and others have correctly emphasized, be strongly distinguished from Derrida's.

31 I am thinking particularly of her "Rules: Looking in the Right Place", in Phillips (1990).

32 Phillips (1990: 12).

33 Phillips (1990: 15).

34 Phillips (1990: 23). Compare also David Cerbone's essay, "How to Do Things with Wood", in Crary and Read (2000).

35 Diamond (1995: 24). Diamond is indicating here the direction – which I explore further shortly – according to which Wittgenstein on "the stream of life" etc. may be read post-positivistically without lapsing into ineffabilism. This direction is also indicated by much of the work of Peter Winch. See for instance Lyas (1999: 192).

36 Diamond (1995: 17).

37 In other words, I want to see how we can succeed in finding a Wittgensteinian (Diamondian) *post*-ineffabilist non-theoretical way of taking use, of understanding meaningful linguistic development.

38 This is roughly the same question that Hallett addresses with his distinction between "operative use" and "formal use" (Hallett 1967: 103) which corresponds

more or less to what I described earlier as the difference between the actual employment of words to do things and their mere "form" or "sense". (Hallett unfortunately does not make sufficiently clear that "formal use" is . . . not really *use*, at all.)

39 To avoid confusion here, it helps to recall that Wittgenstein of course considered the idea of language as something which connects self or mind and world as a nonsense. See for instance *PI* 16, which deflates the whole supposed issue of the 'hook-up' or 'reference' of words to world.

40 I am thinking particularly here of appeals to 'self-reflexivity' in literary studies; but also in philosophy, and even in sociology (around a supposed 'coming to an (infinitely deferred and self-annihilating) self-consciousness' of language and of subjectivity in 'Post-Modern times', and (more 'radically') around the methodology envisaged by Woolgar, Ashmore etc.).

41 For scepticism as to such surveyability, as an alleged Wittgensteinian trope, see my "Perspicuous Presentation: A Perspicuous Presentation" (Read and Hutchinson 2007).

42 Guetti (1993) has employed some of the following examples, in more or less different ways. The Afterword to that book particularly amplifies the case I am arguing here.

43 In this interleaving of speech acts with one another, and with (other) actions, one finds then a dynamicity in language, but one which involves expressions changing roles from active to stably presumptive, and so on. The relations between these expressions, these linguistic moves, are less likely to be misconstrued if they are called "presumptive", rather than "internal", as Baker and Hacker would have it. Baker's and Hacker's over-estimation of the utility of the "internal relations" way of putting things, a way of putting things virtually never used by Wittgenstein himself after his middle period, runs the risk again of obscuring the strong sense in which rules have normally to be *already in action* in order for there to even *be* a "language-game" (see e.g. *PI* 24).

44 Compare Cora Diamond's remark that "the kind of public-ness a term has is part of its grammar", and that this public-ness may be seen in "the commerce with the word" (Diamond 1995: 23). What I am suggesting here is that this "public-ness" is *continually established and re-established* in the "commerce" of ordinary 'syntactic' – linguistic – developments.

Perhaps I need not add here that these "developments" seem reciprocal, or all of a piece. At any rate, it is neither because one makes a subsequent observation that a prior one turns "grammatical" nor vice versa. One might want to say instead that the "causing" goes both ways; but that would just mean that we cannot talk about causing here.

Nor should it be inferred that these adjustments of grammar by discursive sequencing are simply restrictive, as from the leaves of trees more generally to those particularly of maples or oaks, or from all the land to a hill or a valley: as if the work of any descriptive sequence were always to narrow one's "focus", to zoom in on smaller and smaller logical "parts". For this conception may encourage one of the most misleading estimations in language studies: that abstract or general grammar is somehow constant through the development of a discourse even while it is redefined by that development. No; what I am putting forward here *is* precisely a dynamic (dialogical) vision of grammar. Rather than imagining sequential grammatical adjustment as the progressive refinement or restriction of some general concept, one might consider it as a series of choices, each one from the specific set of options immediately preceding. More metaphorically, one might risk saying that each "step" in a descriptive sequence is potentially not so much a narrowing or pointing of the same logical "track" as a sidestep on to another, usually "near", one. As Wittgenstein says in exactly a context such as this: "A multitude of familiar paths lead off from these words in every direction" (*PI* 525). And I think it more helpful to conceive, for example, "The leaves are changing," as an aggregation of such paths – of various, possible, particular expressions with "family-resemblances" to each other – than (as both 'meaning-change' theorists of "use" and Pragmatist theorists of "use" usually do) as some general concept that paradoxically is modified but maintained as the discourse in which it occurs progresses.

45 In "Acting from Rules" (Read and Guetti 1996: 49) I describe this as follows: the 'bridge' between moments in a linguistic interaction is "*footed in grammar on both sides*". Again this will obviously not be sufficient *if* one sticks to thinking of grammar as (say) Chomsky does.

46 Wittgenstein (1975: para 98).

47 Wittgenstein (1975: para 167). Compare also Kuhn's account of the same kind of process occurring over long time-scales, in the course of conceptual change in science.

48 Hilary Putnam may be seen to take a similar view of how grammatical "situations" are constituted by the progress of linguistic sequences: "It is quite true that understanding sentences does involve being able to use the right sentences in the right situations . . . but mostly the 'situations' are defined by what had been *said* previously. . ." (Putnam 1975: 4). Compare also Ian Hacking's "Rules, Scepticism, Proof, Wittgenstein", in Hacking (1985), which looks at an actual example of the application of a rule "constructing" it, and "reconstructing" the game of which it was a part; and at his "The Parody of Conversation", in Le Pore (1989), which rebuts Davidson when the latter goes too far, *abolishing* grammar and language, and leaving in its place a ubiquitous 'interpretivism', much like the Deconstructivists do.

49 Here, as earlier, I am indebted to the great pioneering ideas of J. L. Austin, especially his rich classificatory scheme in *How to Do Things with Words* (Austin 1976). But I think that the distinctions I am making are *both* a little more apposite *and* a little less likely to be misread as an attempt at a theorization of language than were Austin's.

50 *How* such actions might themselves "follow" from linguistic expressions is – especially after Saul Kripke's work – a controversial question. I have given my answer to it in 'Acting from Rules' (Read and Guetti 1996).

51 All too often, students of language are not clear on the difference between effects and meanings, as Guetti (1993) has shown with regard to literary examples. See also Part 2 of this book. The great passage regarding the distinction between communicated meanings and produced effects, in our view, is *PI* 498:

> When I say that the orders 'Bring me sugar' and 'Bring me milk' make sense, but not the combination 'Milk me sugar', that does not mean that the utterance of this combination of words has no effect. And if its effect is that the other person stares at me and gapes, I don't on that account call it the order to stare and gape, even if that was the effect that I wanted to produce.

52 Wittgenstein (1969: 65).

53 Max Black, for example, would probably have said that the kind of adjustment to which the paper crown amounts is more like the laying out the pieces for a game of chess than like any subsequent move in the game. And these sorts of useful gestures in Black's thinking towards Wittgensteinian "stage-setting" considerations are, just because of their "presuppositional" cast, not unreasonably conceived as (in Black's terms) "dummy moves" or "secondary assertions": see Black (1962). But let me add that the logical tension *within* those last two phrases exposes a difficulty that is unavoidable unless one considers how *any* expression's status depends upon how one estimates its position *in a sequence or a set of sequences*, in action. In relation to the first actual move on the chessboard, both the laying out of it and the paper crown might be thought of as preliminary, and perhaps as

"dummy" moves. (Though one should not lose sight of the sense in which they have ceased then to be "moves" at all.) Before any move on the board has been made, however, the game's "preliminaries" might, in their own eventuation from some previous discursive sequence, appear more like "assertions" – actual moves themselves – that followed upon prior presumptions. (Though now one would see no reason to think of them as "secondary".) In this way, even such an expressly or obviously "grammatical" directive as "Now we can play a game of chess" might amount to a particular 'empirical' development from a grammar established by some preceding sequence.

54 On this fundamental question, of what one wants to mean by terms such as "language", see also my "Whose Wittgenstein?" (Read and Hutchinson 2005).

55 See E. Witherspoon's critique of Baker and Hacker (and of Marie McGinn) as in practice positivistic – Carnapian – readers of Wittgenstein: "Conceptions of Nonsense in Carnap and Wittgenstein", in Crary and Read (2000). (It should be noted that *Baker* no longer holds 'Carnapian' views – in fact, his writings over the last decade are very close in practice to the 'therapeutic' vision which I endorse. See my joint papers with Phil Hutchinson for detail.)

56 Except where – as in recent Davidson – it abolishes language altogether.

57 Such 'ineffabilistic' interpretations of Wittgenstein on "use" 'chicken out' (Diamond's phrase), and are 'irresolute' (Goldfarb's phrase), misconceiving Wittgenstein on "use" in a manner here described by Alice Crary (from her "Wittgenstein and Political Philosophy" (in Crary and Read (2000)):

Within the context of such interpretations, [Wittgenstein] appears to be endorsing the view that we recognize certain utterances ([e.g.] those we produce in our futile attempts to apply critical concepts to our form of life) as *unintelligible* because of what they try (unsuccessfully) to say. He appears to be saying that while these utterances are ultimately unintelligible, they are nonetheless to some extent *intelligible* (in so far as we can determine what they are attempts to say). [These] interpretations thus represent Wittgenstein as helping himself to a view of the limits of sense which is philosophically suspicious insofar as it makes room for a notion of *coherent nonsense*. At the same time they also represent him as endorsing a view which is in tension with an important strand of his own thoughts about the relation between nonsensical combinations of words and intelligible bits of language. It is a characteristic gesture of Wittgenstein's, throughout his work, to distance himself from the idea that when we reject a sentence as nonsense, we do so because we grasp what it is an attempt to say and then discern that that cannot be said. (On one occasion [*PI* 500], he puts it this way: calling a sentence senseless is not a matter of identifying a 'senseless sense'.)

58 Once one can understand this in practice, one can *leave behind PI* 218, *PI* 268, and the rest – including this essay, and other essays on Wittgenstein whose intents are genuinely therapeutic and anti-theoretical (e.g. Goldfarb's important paper, "I Want You to Bring Me a Slab" (Goldfarb 1983). See especially p. 279, which is very close to my argument). At least a little like the way one leaves behind earlier parts of a conversational sequence.

59 See also Nigel Pleasants' very thought-provoking attack on the very idea of 'tacit knowledge', as incoherent and un-Wittgensteinian: "Nothing is Concealed: De-centring Tacit Knowledge and Rules from Social Theory" (Pleasants 1996).

60 Though again, against 'ineffabilism', that is not actually a 'depth' *containing* anything, least of all a bunch of 'unfathomable' and 'profound' Truths, the kinds of 'Truths' that some misguided Heideggerians (for example) understandably try to 'excavate' for us. If the term 'form of life', e.g., makes one think of something 'deep' in that sense, one would be better off throwing it away *now*.

61 My thanks go to Alice Crary (and to an anonymous referee) for detailed and

illuminating readings of earlier drafts of this and the preceding sections. Thanks also to Jeff Coulter for useful comments.

62 The case of Derrida is, of course, complex, given that he aims to critique 'the metaphysics of presence', and thus ostensibly opposes psychologism and hopes (sometimes) to deconstruct metaphysics in general. However, he *leaves in place* the kind of picture – or categorization – of language ('signifer' and 'signified') that causes so many of the problems in Saussure and Husserl and their successors. (For a central instance of where 'signification'-talk gets Derrida into trouble, see Derrida (1998: 12).) Derrida's innovation is to bracket or erase the 'signified'. But that is only a reactive response within the categories allowed for by metaphysics (i.e. it is structurally parallel to certain forms of scepticism), and is not yet to move to a genuinely post-metaphysical and '(post-)contextualist' approach of the kind one finds in (e.g.) Wittgenstein. This is one reason why Derrida remains fatally in thrall to metaphysics, and does not see the possibility of a mode of philosophizing that would actually take the ordinary seriously.

   A similar flaw, I shall suggest below, afflicts Lacan. Lacan, like Derrida, makes it sound as though our not 'having' (access to) the 'signified' is a *loss*. Whereas Wittgenstein makes plain that we lack nothing, insofar as our ordinary grasp ('mastery') of the language, of meaning as use, is concerned.

63 See Read's "What does 'Signify' Signify?" (2001: 477–99). The present section of this book is loosely based upon my reply to Gillett's essay, which was published on pp. 499–514 of the same issue, and was followed by Gillett's counter-reply.

64 I shall normally scare quote this phrase, on the grounds that powerful and sensible philosophical voices have often been raised to the effect that to speak of 'the unconscious' using a noun-phrase at all is to risk an unhealthy reification. I cannot explore this further here: but some strong more or less Rylean reasons for thinking this are to be found scattered through the work of the Wittgensteinian ethnomethodologist, Jeff Coulter. For parallel worries about the very idea of "the conscious" as a quasi-thing, worries which *a fortiori* there is no space for here, see my own "What does 'Signify' Signify?" (2001).

65 Guetti makes clear here the issues at stake; whereas at points in Gillett's presentation, Lacan's notoriously difficult writing remains elusive and the point of his 'theses' opaque. It is perhaps surprising that Gillett did not, to counter this difficulty, draw on pre-existing and relatively accessible discussions by others of Lacan and his picture of language: for example, those of his Feminist inheritors and critics, such as Mitchell, Rose, Gallop, and some of the French Feminists; and more recently the intriguing and helpful writings of Slavoj Žižek.

66 See Guetti (1993), also Read and Guetti (1999), which is rewritten as the earlier sections of this Part.

67 My point here is that, whereas ordinary naming is preparatory to making a move in a language-game, the function of 'names' and 'significations' in poems or in the psychopathology of everyday life is not in fact normally that. But as I intimate below, a 'name-theory' of language *is* in fact arguably the lowest common-denominator between post-modernism, Lacan, and Anglo-American psycho-semantics.

68 In *PI* 6, we find the following clear remarks: "Uttering a word [simply as part of a series of sounds] is like striking a note on the keyboard of the imagination. But in the language of *PI* 2 [the builders' language-game'] it is not the purpose of the words to evoke images. (It may, of course, be discovered that that helps to attain the actual purpose.)" Contrast this with the central place accorded in Lacan's 'philosophy of language' to evocation. For Wittgenstein, evocation is a necessary feature of language, when language is considered, is *recovered, in its totality*, which is the ultimate aim of his therapeutic philosophy. But it is *not* 'the primary' or 'the central' feature of language.

69 For explication, and for implicit guidance on how this point is not to be confused

with post-modernist talk of 'free play' etc., consult especially Conant (2000).
70 Lacan (1967: 86).
71 For a detailed treatment of this concept, see Read (2001).

Part 2: Literature

1 Guetti (1993: 55).
2 In her "Ethics, Imagination and the Method of the *Tractatus*", in Crary and Read
   (2000), wherein Diamond argues that much of what interests Wittgenstein philosophically is what in fact we (can) only imagine that we can imagine.
3 Again, let my use of the word "literally" not cause offence here: it is simply a quick
   index of the important – 'grammatical' – distinction between looking with the
   eyes and other things that we call "looking".
4 A very similar process is at work in the process and progress of another of Stevens'
   early poems, "Metaphors of a Magnifico". (It is perhaps worth adding that it seems
   unlikely that any illumination in what is going in stanzas such as these will be
   obtained by means of the kind of considerations adduced by Frank Lentricchia in
   his "Patriarchy against Itself: The Young Manhood of Wallace Stevens" (1987).
   Lentricchia would presumably have us analyse and thus 'comprehend' lines such
   as "A man and a woman and a blackbird are one" through the lens of our knowledge of both Stevens' psyche and gender theory; this seems to me one of the
   points at which the infertility of Lentricchia's method is laid bare.)
5 And such teaching of the poem naturally extends into the following kind of point:
   that the reader has to come to decide for themselves what is well described as one or another
   way of looking, and what isn't, among what is presented here. We shall return to this
   point below, in discussion of Wittgenstein's method in his greatest writing, such as
   in the opening of *Philosophical Investigations.*
6 See for instance the – different – points discussed by Guetti (1993: 169).
7 Crary and Read (2000: 149).
8 Stevens' poems are marvellously replete with such *faux* instructions. Compare for
   instance the two nonsensical commands explicitly encoded into "Fabliau of
   Florida" (emphases added to highlight these commands):

> Barque of Phosphor
> On the palmy beach
>
> *Move outward into heaven,*
> *Into the alabasters*
> *And night blues.*
>
> Foam and cloud are one.
> Sultry moon-monsters
> Are dissolving.
>
> *Fill your black hull*
> *With white moonlight . . .*

9 I have in mind for instance Derrida's infamous – and signally misleading – claim
   in "Signature, Event, Context" that using a bit of language as an example of
   agrammaticality or of error is at all the same kind of thing as using a bit of
   language, such as the same bit of language to undertake a speech act.
10 And even perhaps explained *by* it? See below.
11 I refer here to Wittgenstein throughout his career. One might say that Wittgenstein's early philosophy is an austere and concise therapeutic quasi-poetry of logic,
   his later philosophy an equally austere yet circlingly dialogical and roaming therapeutic quasi-poetry of logic.

An intermediate case, 'between' Stevens and Wittgenstein, of 'weak-grammared' (sometimes somewhat prose-like, sometimes 'explicitly philosophical') poetry, a case that I should like to investigate in depth on a future occasion, is T. S. Eliot, specifically his "Four Quartets". For some indications as to how this investigation might proceed, see my book review of Martin Warner's philosophical reading of the "Four Quartets", in Read (2004).

12 This point is the burden of the closing chapter, 'Saying and Imagining', of Guetti's (1993).

13 See especially Cavell (1979: 115–25) and Crary's and Cerbone's essays in Crary and Read (2000).

14 See also many of Stevens' other poems, such as (famously) "The Idea of Order at Key West".

15 See my "Meaningful Consequences" (joint with James Guetti) (1999) for discussion; or see Part 1 of this book, above.

16 As already intimated, it should not be thought here that I am instituting a crude absolute dualism of nature vs. culture, meaningful consequences vs. grammatical effects. As I will explain more fully below, in comparing my interpretation of Stevens with Simon Critchley's, a crucial ultimate point of Stevens, as of Wittgenstein, is that, handy and vitally ordering as such dualisms are, they must be understood as complementary with a non-dualistic understanding of our place in the Universe, too. It is part of human nature to seek to limn that nature as if from outside. And it is part of human nature to have and inhabit all such riches of culture.

17 Other great artists who I believe do the same include William Faulkner (see my essay in *The Literary Wittgenstein*, Gibson and Huemer (2004) on this) and Peter Greenaway (in his early films, especially the shorts and *The Draughtsman's Contract* and *Drowning by Numbers*; perhaps also in *Prospero's Books*). (The scare quotes used in indexing their achievement are crucial; for if this is violating the limits of language – if this is a use that has at last been found for this term – yet it is not literally the doing of that that Carnap, Hacker and many others have said is impossible.)

18 One fails to understand Wittgenstein, I submit, if one never or only very rarely smiles wryly, giggles or laughs out loud at his text.

19 The proviso here references the great and oft-neglected moments when Frege appears to recognize, albeit reluctantly, that such trafficking in delusion might be necessary. Compare Frege's invocation at some crucial moments in his work of "hints", or of "a pinch of salt", and his audacious reply to Kerry on concepts and objects.

20 Critchley (2005).

21 I argue this in my "On Approaching Schizophrenia via Wittgenstein", in Read (2001: 449–75), and in my "The New Hume's New Antagonists", in my *The New Hume Debate* (Read and Richman 2000).

22 For more on this with particular reference to the (roughly parallel) case of Faulkner, see my "Literature as Philosophy as Psychopathology: William Faulkner as Wittgensteinian" (Read 2003: 115–24), to which the present discussion is a kind of companion piece, and my "On Delusions of Sense: A Response to Coetzee and Sass", on pp. 135–42 of the same issue. These two papers are concisified, updated and expanded upon in 2.2.1 to 2.2.4 of this book.

23 Critchley is broadly right, then, about our being able to encounter 'the things themselves' most especially in Stevens' later work. Though they are also very much present in his early work: not only in poems like "The Snowman" and "The Comedian as the Letter C", but, I would suggest (if I had time), in many more. We might put the point this way: jars, hills, blackbirds, mountains, poems etc. *are things in themselves.*

24 See Critchley (2005: 85, 61).The interlocking complementarity of the two, and the
    way in which the trail of the serpent of the physical is all over the human, and not
    merely (as James held) the reverse, may be seen, I believe, in the motion of
    passages such as section XXII of "The Man with the Blue Guitar" (italics added):

> Poetry is the subject of the poem,
> From this the poem issues and
>
> To this returns. Between the two,
> Between issue and return, there is
>
> An absence in reality,
> Things as they are. Or so we say.
>
> *But are these separate? Is it*
> *An absence for the poem, which acquires*
>
> *Its true appearances there, sun's green,*
> *Cloud's red, earth feeling, sky that thinks?*
>
> *From these it takes.* Perhaps it gives,
> In the universal intercourse.

25 See Critchley (2005: 83, 59). There is indeed a kind of wish to bring poetry to an
    end in Stevens, as there is in Wittgenstein a kind of wish to bring philosophy to an
    end. These are wishes that one can act on or attempt to act on; they are not,
    however (*contra* 'end of philosophy' philosophers, etc.), wishes that one can more
    than temporarily *realize.*
26 Critchley (2005: 86), "On the one hand, literature is an act of idealization
    governed by the desire to assimilate all reality to the ego and to view the latter as
    the former's projection . . . On the other hand . . . literature does not aim to
    reduce reality to the imagination, but rather to let things be in their separateness
    from us." My suggestion is that these two tendencies are happily married in
    Stevens' corpus. In the hands of a magnificently deep and skilled poet, in *Stevens'*
    hands, these two tendencies can be joined, as it were in a *mudra.* (I will explore
    this connection between Stevens and Buddhism in a future paper.)
27 It is also a crucial 'theme' of "The Man with the Blue Guitar":

> A dream (to call it a dream) in which
> I can believe, in face of the object,
>
> A dream no longer a dream, a thing,
> Of things as they are . . .
>   Stevens (1971: 142)

    . . . Dreams too are things. The only 'things' which are truly not anything, which
    are less even than a dream, are the 'contents' of delusions. The nothingnesses that
    are the seeming-substance of nonsenses.
        And compare also Cora Diamond's discussion of 'the truth in solipsism',
    Diamond (1995).
28 See Critchley (2005: 6, 87).
29 And this is one of the points at which I think I part company with Critchley. Critch-
    ley is willing to understand great poetry as involving the submergence of philo-
    sophical "preoccupations into the particular grain of the poems" (p. 32) whereas

I think that we have to let poetry *be*, to let it *stand*. Poetry is *a way we speak;* great poetry is never merely philosophy in another form. If I thought that Stevens merely "submerged" a philosophy "into the particular grain" of certain poems, I would not think him a great poet. I agree with Frank Kermode that later Stevens sometimes does do this, and when he does, his poems fall away from the true greatness of his oeuvre, which is most undoubted, it seems to me, in the early poems of his such as those on which I have focused in this essay. Those are poems which remain strange to us, remain poetical, even 'after' we have worked through them to find their provision for philosophical insight.

30　In this respect, it is akin to my edited collection: Read and Goodenough (2005). (Films such as *Memento* and *Last Year at Marienbad remain* films, even after one has described the philosophical work they accomplish. Or, better: one can only fully understand that philosophical work by seeing how it is inextricably tied to its filmic presentation. Or, better still, riffing on De Man and Harold Bloom: accounts of the philosophical work accomplished are only ever allegories of the work – the film – itself.)

31　While often writing in decidedly odd ways. Taking therapy seriously requires that one (mis-)uses language in ways that *'work'* for oneself and one's audience.

32　I owe a lot in the genesis of these sections to some remarks of Simon Critchley during a talk at UEA on Stevens, though I don't know whether he will see that. My greatest debt in the writing of the paper – and it is a very great debt – is to my colleague Jon Cook, with whom I have worked precisely on these issues for years, in our research and our teaching, including at a joint presentation we made on Stevens to a LitPhil conference at Warwick, on 25 February 2005, a presentation which covered the ground written up here. My thanks also to the audience at that talk for a very stimulating discussion, especially to Christine Battersby and Martin Warner. And finally, I owe a huge debt of thanks to my former colleague James Guetti, who first enabled me to understand Stevens as a deep 'grammatical' poet.

33　See e.g. Faulkner, below.

34　It is critically important to bear in mind the scare quotes around the word "violating", above; that there can *seem* to be such a violation is the phenomenon; but the ('resolute') approach in this monograph is to suggest that no sense has yet been given to the idea of there actually being such a 'violation'.

35　I return to this theme in most detail in the Conclusion to this book, below.

36　There is a close analogue at this point with *Memento;* particularly as explored in the closing pages of my joint paper (with Phil Hutchinson) thereon in Read and Goodenough (2005).

37　Those for instance of Schreber, "Renée", Donna Williams, Artaud, Coetzee's *In the Heart of the Country*, Nabokov's *Invitation to a Beheading*, Kafka's "Description of a Struggle" and "The Burrow", and even (I would add) key parts of *The Lord of the Rings*. Coetzee's too-little-known masterpiece is perhaps particularly salient here: for Magda, its metaphysically unreliable narrator, inhabits a world of pure possibility in which the past and ultimately the present is constitutively 'absent', to a much greater degree arguably than in the case of any of Faulkner's protagonists. I hope to offer a full 'philosophical reading' of *In the Heart of the Country*, and perhaps of some of Coetzee's other, 'therapeutic' novels, in future work.

38　Sass' work may however be of considerable *transitional* value. If read as somewhat akin in method to Wittgenstein's *Tractatus*, it could escape the criticisms I make of it here, and elsewhere.

39　See the Conclusion to this book, below, for further explication of Heidegger beside Wittgenstein.

40　It has been mentioned in a 'review' of an earlier version of some of the material in these sections, at www.thevalve.org, that the structure of my argument there belied my intent *not* to interpret for I *began* with Wittgenstein rather than the